The Use and Abuse of the Spirit in Pentecostalism

This book is a pneumatological reflection on the use and abuse of the Spirit in light of the abuse of religion within South African Pentecostalism. Both emerging and well-established scholars of South African Pentecostalism are brought together to reflect on pneumatology from various approaches, which includes among others: historical, biblical, migration, commercialisation of religion, discernment of spirits and human flourishing.

From a broader understanding of the function of the Holy Spirit in different streams of Pentecostalism, the argument is that this function has changed with the emergence of the new Prophetic churches in South Africa.

This is a fascinating insight into one of the major emerging worldwide religious movements. As such, it will be of great interest to academics in Pentecostal Studies, Christian Studies, Theology, and Religious Studies as well as African Studies and the Sociology of Religion.

Mookgo S. Kgatle is Associate Professor of Missiology at the University of South Africa (UNISA). He completed his PhD (Theology) from the University of Pretoria in 2016. Kgatle is a National Research Foundation (NRF) Y-Rated researcher (2019–2024) in the area of African Pentecostalism. He is the visiting scholar at the Centre for Pentecostal and Charismatic Studies-University of Birmingham (2020–2021). Kgatle has published several peer-reviewed articles in various high impact journals and the book *The Fourth Pentecostal Wave in South Africa: A Critical Engagement* (Routledge, 2019).

Allan H. Anderson is Emeritus Professor of Mission and Pentecostal Studies at the University of Birmingham, an internationally well-known scholar in the study of worldwide Pentecostalism, with particular interest in southern Africa. He is the author of nine books (translated into four languages) and many articles, and has joint-edited four collections on global Pentecostalism. He is a founder-member of the European Research Network on Global Pentecostalism, was editor of *PentecoStudies*, and serves on the international editorial board of five academic journals.

Routledge New Critical Thinking in Religion, Theology and Biblical Studies

The *Routledge New Critical Thinking in Religion, Theology and Biblical Studies* series brings high quality research monograph publishing back into focus for authors, international libraries, and student, academic and research readers. This open-ended monograph series presents cutting-edge research from both established and new authors in the field. With specialist focus yet clear contextual presentation of contemporary research, books in the series take research into important new directions and open the field to new critical debate within the discipline, in areas of related study, and in key areas for contemporary society.

Catholic Social Teaching and Theologies of Peace in Northern Ireland
Cardinal Cahal Daly and the Pursuit of the Peaceable Kingdom
Maria Power

Contextual Theology
Skills and Practices of Liberating Faith
Edited by Sigurd Bergmann and Mika Vähäkangas

Multi-Religious Perspectives on a Global Ethic
In Search of a Common Morality
Edited by Myriam Renaud and William Schweiker

Sustainable Development Goals and the Catholic Church
Catholic Social Teaching and the UN's Agenda 2030
Edited by Katarzyna Cichos, Jarosław A. Sobkowiak, Radosław Zenderowski, Ryszard F. Sadowski, Beata Zbarachewicz and Stanisław Dziekoński

The Use and Abuse of the Spirit in Pentecostalism
A South African Perspective
Edited by Mookgo S. Kgatle and Allan H. Anderson

For more information about this series, please visit: www.routledge.com/religion/series/RCRITREL

The Use and Abuse of the Spirit in Pentecostalism

A South African Perspective

Edited by Mookgo S. Kgatle and
Allan H. Anderson

LONDON AND NEW YORK

First published 2021
by Routledge
2 Park Square, Milton Park, Abingdon, Oxon OX14 4RN

and by Routledge
605 Third Avenue, New York, NY 10017

First issued in paperback 2022

Routledge is an imprint of the Taylor & Francis Group, an informa business

Publisher's Note
The publisher has gone to great lengths to ensure the quality of this reprint but points out that some imperfections in the original copies may be apparent.

British Library Cataloguing-in-Publication Data
A catalogue record for this book is available from the British Library

Library of Congress Cataloging-in-Publication Data
Names: Kgatle, Mookgo S., editor. | Anderson, Allan H. (Allan Heaton), editor.
Title: The use and abuse of spirit in pneumatology in Pentacostal Christianity : a South African perspective / edited by Mookgo S. Kgatle and Allan H. Anderson.
Description: Abingdon, Oxon ; New York : Routledge, 2021. | Series: Routledge new critical thinking in religion, theology and biblical studies | Includes bibliographical references and index.
Identifiers: LCCN 2020034320 (print) | LCCN 2020034321 (ebook) | ISBN 9780367482428 (hbk) | ISBN 9781003038795 (ebk)
Subjects: LCSH: Pentecostalism—South Africa. | Pentecostal churches—South Africa. | Holy Spirit—Miscellanea.
Classification: LCC BR1644.5.S6 U74 2021 (print) | LCC BR1644.5.S6 (ebook) | DDC 269/.40968—dc23
LC record available at https://lccn.loc.gov/2020034320
LC ebook record available at https://lccn.loc.gov/2020034321

ISBN 13: 978-0-367-65106-0 (pbk)
ISBN 13: 978-0-367-48242-8 (hbk)
ISBN 13: 978-1-003-03879-5 (ebk)

DOI: 10.4324/9781003038795

Typeset in Sabon
by Apex CoVantage, LLC

Contents

Acknowledgements

This book is not only the success of the vision and leadership of the editors but of a collective work by all participants who took part in the project. First of all, we want to appreciate all the contributors of the nine chapters in this book for their commitment and diligence in working on their chapters until finalisation. Second, we want to thank the University of South Africa language-editing department for editing all the chapters before we sent the final submission to the publisher. Last, the book followed a double-blind review for all the individual chapters (i.e. the identity of both the authors and the reviewers were not revealed to each other). We therefore want to thank all the reviewers who had the expertise and interest in the chapters they reviewed.

Abbreviations

ABH	African Biblical Hermeneutics
AFM	Apostolic Faith Mission of South Africa
AIC	African Independent Churches
ANA	African News Agency
AOG	Assemblies of God
ASGISA	Accelerated Shared Growth In South Africa
ATR	African Traditional Religions
COVID-19	Corona Virus Disease 2019
CRL	Cultural, Religious and Linguistic Communities
DA	Discourse Analysis
ECG	Enlightened Christian Gathering
FGC	Full Gospel Church
GBC	Grace Bible Church
GEAR	Growth, Employment and Redistribution
KPMI	Kingdom Prayer Ministries International
NPCC	Newer Pentecostal Charismatic Christianity
NAR	New Apostolic Reformation
NDP	National Development Plan
NPC	Neo Pentecostal Churches
NPM	Neo-Prophetic Movement
NRM	New Religious Movements
NT	New Testament
OT	Old Testament
PAIC	Pentecostal-type African Independent Churches
PCC	Pentecostal Charismatic Christianity
PPCC	Prophetic Pentecostal Charismatic Christianity
PHD	Power Healing and Deliverance
PFN	Pentecostal Fellowship of Nigeria
SABC	South African Broadcasting Corporation
SAM	Seven Angels Ministry
SANP	South African neo-Pentecostal
SAPCC	South African Pentecostal Charismatic Christianity
SCOAN	Synagogue Church of All Nations
ZCC	Zion Christian Church

Contributors

Allan H. Anderson is Emeritus Professor of Mission and Pentecostal Studies at the University of Birmingham, an internationally well-known scholar in the study of worldwide Pentecostalism, with particular interest in southern Africa. He is the author of nine books (translated into four languages) and many articles, and has joint-edited four collections on global Pentecostalism. He is a founder-member of the European Research Network on Global Pentecostalism, was editor of *PentecoStudies*, and serves on the international editorial board of five academic journals.

Collium Banda is a Post-doctoral research Fellow in the Faculty of Theology at North-West University, South Africa, and Adjunct Lecturer at Theological College of Zimbabwe. He is an emerging researcher with interests in African Pentecostalism, Christian doctrines in the African public space, African traditional religions, African indigenous knowledge systems and Christianity in African contexts of poverty.

Bekithemba Dube is a Senior Lecturer at the faculty of Education at the University of the Free State (UFS), a guest editor of *ALTERNATION* journal, Managing Editor and Co-ordinator for the International Society for Studies in Rural Contexts. He holds a PhD in Curriculum Studies from UFS. He is a scholar in the field of Education focusing on Sociology, Philosophy of Education and Religion. He has published several peer-reviewed articles in international journals in the same areas.

Maria Frahm-Arp is an Associate Professor in the Department of Religion Studies at the University of Johannesburg, South Africa. She is the author of *Professional Women in South African Pentecostal Charismatic Christianity* (Brill 2010). Her research areas include Pentecostal Charismatic Churches in South Africa with a particular focus on development, politics and gender in these churches.

Mookgo S. Kgatle is Associate Professor of Missiology at the University of South Africa (UNISA). He completed his PhD (Theology) from the University of Pretoria in 2016. Kgatle is a National Research Foundation (NRF) Y Rated researcher (2019–2024) in the area of African Pentecostalism. He is the visiting scholar at the Centre for Pentecostal and

Charismatic Studies-University of Birmingham (2020–2021). Kgatle has published several peer-reviewed articles in various high impact journals and the book, *The fourth Pentecostal wave in South Africa: a critical engagement* with Routledge (2019).

Elise B. Kisungu is a Masters student at University of South Africa. Her interest in urban ministry and migration prompted her to carry out a research on Congolese churches in Gauteng, South Africa. In addition, she has interest for academic contributions that join efforts with the South African voices that rise on the global scale in the commitment of breaking misconceptions about African Pentecostalism and calling on the movement to stand on a biblical ground.

Thabang R. Mofokeng holds an MTh degree in Church History and is currently doing his PhD studies with the University of South Africa. He lectures Ancient, Medieval and Modern Church History at the North-West University. His research interest is the intersection of Pentecostalism with socio-political and cultural dimensions.

Hulisani Ramantswana is Associate Professor of Old Testament in the Department of Biblical and Ancient Studies at the University of South Africa. He obtained his PhD (Hermeneutical and Biblical Interpretation) at the Westminster Theological Seminary Glenside, United States of America in 2010. His research interests are inter alia on African Biblical Hermeneutics, decolonial readings of the Bible, Pentateuch and creation narratives. He is chief editor for *Old Testament Essays* journal.

Kelebogile T. Resane obtained his PhD (Theology) (Dogmatics and Christian Ethics) in 2008. For 31 years (1979–2010), he served in Youth for Christ International. He was a Teaching and Learning Manager for the Faculty of Theology and Religion at the University of the Free State for five years (2014–2018), and continues as a Research Fellow at the same university. His research interests are broadly on the New Apostolic Reformation, Pentecostal theology and public theology in general. Currently serving at Bible League International/South Africa.

Ithapeleng Sebetseli is a Masters student at the University of South Africa (UNISA). His areas of interest are inculturation, biblical hermeneutics, Pentateuch, Prophets, poverty eradication, and slavery in modern and ancient times. He has served as a lecturer, research assistant, and postgraduate assistant at UNISA.

Themba Shingange is a Senior Personnel Practitioner – Employee Health and Wellness and the Limpopo Provincial Power House- Research and Innovation Coordinator at the South African Police Services (SAPS). He obtained PhD in Missiology from the University of South Africa. He is an emerging researcher in the area of African Pentecostalism, Mission and Gender and Post- Heteronormative mission praxis. He has presented papers in local conferences addressing similar topics.

1 Introduction

The abuse of the Spirit in some New Prophetic Churches in South African Pentecostalism

Mookgo S. Kgatle and Allan H. Anderson

1.1 The use and abuse of the Spirit

Since 2014, South Africa has experienced the abuse of religion by some prophets of New Prophetic Churches (NPCs) within South African Pentecostalism. These prophets have promoted such practices as eating grass, drinking petrol, eating snakes, walking on air, resurrecting "dead" bodies and so forth.[1] There have been attempts by scholars to address the issue of the abuse of religion in post-colonial South Africa but they have not related the matter to the "abuse of the Spirit". Therefore, this book on the abuse of the Spirit is an important contribution to South African Pentecostal scholarship. Here, the connection between the abuse of religion and the abuse of the Spirit is clear because all NPC prophets who have engaged in the outrageous acts above have said that "the Spirit" had instructed them to do so. Some prophets were even so bold as to tell a young girl or any woman for that matter that "the Spirit of God" had instructed them to sleep with them.[2] In arguing against the use of the Holy Spirit to perform unusual acts, this book has coined the phrase "the abuse of the Spirit". However, in order to understand the abuse of the Spirit by NPCs, it is first necessary to study the function of the Holy Spirit in the history of South African Pentecostalism.[3] It is equally important to study the hermeneutics of South African Pentecostalism[4] in order to connect its biblical understanding with the abuse of the Spirit as is happening within NPCs. The studies in this book will assist in making proper recommendations on how to deal with the "abuse of the Spirit".

1.2 Research justification

In the wake of the abuse of religion by some NPC prophets within South African Pentecostalism, the Commission for the Promotion and Protection of the Rights of Cultural, Religious and Linguistic Communities (the CRL Rights Commission) in South Africa began two investigations: on the commercialisation of religion[5] and on the abuse of people.[6] The contribution of this book to these two investigations is to provide the link between both the commercialisation of religion and the abuse of people with the abuse of the Spirit within South African Pentecostalism. This book focuses on the abuse of the

Spirit particularly as is happening among NPCs in South Africa. However, while we pay attention to NPCs, we also acknowledge the function of the Spirit in other streams of Pentecostalism like classical Pentecostalism, African Initiated Churches (AICs) and the Charismatics. Most of the chapters will address the abuse of the Spirit from different angles like church history, biblical studies, migration studies, discernment of spirits, commercialisation of religion, and the economics[7] of Pentecostalism. The contributors are experts in South African Pentecostalism as both insiders (i.e. within the Pentecostal tradition) and outsiders (i.e. involved in Pentecostal research).

The abuse of religion is not distinctly South African as there is abuse of religion elsewhere in the continent, with some countries engaging in conflicts that involve the loss of lives in the name of religion.[8] Similarly, the abuse of religion is not new in South Africa as the masters of apartheid used the Bible and the name of God to oppress black people, take their land and isolate them from certain economic activities.[9] What is new in this book is the connection between the abuse of religion and the Holy Spirit in South African Pentecostalism. In addition, this connection is peculiar to the NPCs, which Kgatle calls "the fourth Pentecostal wave in South Africa".[10] The connection is affirmed by the consistent assertions by many NPC prophets that they were led by the Holy Spirit to engage in their outrageous acts. This book seeks to understand this phenomenon of being "led by the Holy Spirit" to engage in the abuse of religion. It is therefore pivotal to discuss the abuse of religion by the NPCs in order to connect it to the abuse of the Spirit.[11]

1.3 The Holy Spirit as the foundation of Pentecostalism

Biblical events like the baptism of the Holy Spirit as recorded in the book of Acts and elsewhere attested to the Holy Spirit as the foundation of Pentecostalism.[12] Pentecostal scholars regard the Holy Spirit as the core of Pentecostal theology, defining Pentecostalism as a movement that exists based on a direct relationship with God through the experiential encounters between the Holy Spirit and a born-again believer.[13] Yong states that the Holy Spirit is the key in understanding the Pentecostal movement as a whole, including among those who do not regard themselves as Pentecostal.[14] Macchia has made us understand the distinctiveness of the Holy Spirit in Pentecostal theology by stating that the Holy Spirit serves as the power that activates the gifts of the Spirit like speaking in tongues and healing.[15] Cartledge regards the personal relationship with the Holy Spirit as the key feature of global Pentecostalism.[16] Stephenson states that the Holy Spirit makes it possible for believers to become active in the world and brings coherence to other fundamental beliefs of Pentecostalism.[17] Thus, the Holy Spirit is the one who makes it possible for a connection between the believer and their God.[18]

The Holy Spirit occupies an important space in African Pentecostalism in all its different streams, whether classical, African Independent Churches or Charismatics, the Holy Spirit is at the centre.[19] In African Pentecostalism, God manifests himself to believers through the power and the work of the Holy Spirit.[20] African Pentecostal scholars have also acknowledged the Holy Spirit as the foundation of African Pentecostalism. One such scholar is Ogbu Kalu who stated that in Africa, healing, miracles and deliverance take place among believers because of the Holy Spirit.[21] Nel adds that the reading and understanding of scriptures in African Pentecostalism happen because of the work of the Holy Spirit.[22] Writing on Nigerian Pentecostalism, Nimi Wariboko states that the power of the Holy Spirit is basically sought to deal with other gods and preserve believers against other spiritual forces.[23] According to Kwabena Asamoah-Gyadu the work of the Holy Spirit is very much connected to Christology because the ministry of Jesus is realised through the power of the Holy Spirit.[24]

Whereas the above aspects of African Pentecostalism have received attention, the abuse of the Holy Spirit among NPCs in post-colonial South Africa has not been addressed. We have to ask an important question: does the Holy Spirit genuinely use NPC prophets or are they extending African magical powers in the name of the Holy Spirit?[25] There have been attempts[26] by scholars to address the issue of the abuse of religion in post-colonial South Africa but they have not related the matter to the "abuse of the Spirit". Therefore, the abuse of the Spirit as outlined in this book makes an important contribution to South African Pentecostal scholarship.

1.4 South African Pentecostalism

In 1908, South Africa was one of the first countries on the continent to receive Pentecostalism. Pentecostals in South Africa include first classical Pentecostals of several denominations, the three largest being the Apostolic Faith Mission, the Assemblies of God, and the Full Gospel Church of God. These were churches founded by European and American Pentecostal missionaries in the early twentieth century. Second, "Pentecostalism" also includes various new Charismatic churches and many non-aligned churches which include the new category presented in this book, the New Prophetic Churches. However, about a third of South African Christianity consists of the third category of almost entirely African "Zionist" and "Apostolic" churches, including the largest denomination in the country, the Zion Christian Church and other large denominations like the St Engenas Zion Christian Church and the St John Apostolic Faith Mission.[27] There are between 4000 and 7000 smaller church organisations of a similar type, many of them house churches which form socially meaningful groups in rural villages but especially in the urban sprawls, where people can find an "extended family" that gives them a sense of belonging and identity.

Almost all of these different kinds of churches, like Pentecostal churches everywhere, emphasise the power of the Spirit in the church, especially manifested through such phenomena as healing, prophecy, exorcism and speaking in tongues.[28] The independent African churches have maintained both historical and theological affinities with Pentecostalism while developing in quite different and distinctive directions. The South African Pentecostal movement, including the many African churches that have emanated from it, is not a North American imposition but collectively one of the most significant African expressions of Christianity today, where at least 15 million people identify with a form of Pentecostalism or Spirit-oriented Christianity.

Returning to the second category above, this rapidly growing new form of African Christianity, that of independent Pentecostal and Charismatic churches and "ministries", plays an increasingly significant role.[29] This movement emerged in the 1970s and has become a significant expression of Christianity on the continent, especially in Africa's cities. We cannot understand African Christianity today without also understanding this movement of revival and renewal. In the South African context, these newer Pentecostal movements are not fundamentally different from the Holy Spirit movements and "Spirit" churches that preceded them in the African Initiated Churches (AICs), but are rather a continuation of them in a quite different situation. Classical Pentecostalism has influenced some of their leaders, and many of them are well educated. However, the older "Spirit" AICs, the classical Pentecostals and the Charismatic churches have all responded to existential needs in the African milieu. Not only do they all represent a response to the inequalities of power and class accentuated during the apartheid system, but they have also all offered a personal encounter with God through the power of the Spirit, healing from sickness and deliverance from evil in all its manifestations, whether spiritual, social or structural – although most of these churches do not really emphasise the social and structural manifestations of evil. This is not to say that there are no tensions or differences between the "new" and the "old" churches – there certainly are, as neither are usually willing to acknowledge any affinity with each other.[30] At an early stage, classical Pentecostals demonised the Zionist and Apostolic churches, mainly because of their distinctive church apparel and symbolic healing practices which these mainly white Pentecostals saw as unscriptural and "heathen". They passed on these prejudices to their African fellow-members, so that today most Pentecostals and Charismatics do not consider members of these African churches to be Pentecostal and in many cases reject them as fellow Christians, for they are not seen as *bazalwane* or "born again".[31] These high walls of separation still need to be broken down.

The classical or denominational Pentecostals still are a very active and growing phenomenon in South Africa, and played a significant role in the emergence of some of the newer groups. Many of the key players in the new Pentecostal churches like Bishop Stephen Zondo were members of Pentecostal denominations. Classical Pentecostals have operated in South Africa for most of the twentieth century. Most of these churches trace their historical origins to the impetus generated by the Azusa Street revival in Los Angeles which sent out missionaries to fifty nations within two years.[32] The connections between the classical Pentecostal movement and AICs throughout Africa have been demonstrated in earlier studies.[33] Some of these classical Pentecostal churches have become vibrant and rapidly expanding African churches, in particular the Assemblies of God, which operates in most countries of Sub-Saharan Africa including South Africa, and has become an African church in its own right, largely through the enormous contribution of Nicholas Bhengu (1909–86).[34] It is generally recognised that throughout the history of AICs there has been a predominance of Pentecostal features and phenomena, but in South Africa it is very difficult to draw lines between different "types" of churches using phenomenological or theological criteria.

1.5 The Holy Spirit in the sub-traditions of South African Pentecostalism

Classical Pentecostal churches see the role of the Holy Spirit especially in Spirit baptism and the initial evidence of speaking in other tongues.[35] Moreover, the Holy Spirit plays a major role in the fellowship of believers, in scripture reading and during prayer meetings.[36] In the Pentecostal African Independent Churches (PAIC), another term for the second category above, the Holy Spirit is central to spiritual experiences like healing, prophecy, deliverance, and other miracles.[37] Furthermore, with few exceptions, some PAICs juxtapose the work of the Holy Spirit with African culture, African traditional religions and African indigenous knowledge.[38] Nonetheless, the PAICs are included in the broader framework of Pentecostalism because of their reference to the work of the Holy Spirit and salvation through the Lord Jesus Christ.[39] In independent Charismatic churches like the Rhema Bible Church in Randburg, the Grace Bible Church in Soweto and numerous others across South Africa, the Holy Spirit is the one who apportions gifts equally among the believers. The main difference among these sub-traditions is that in the PAICs and Charismatic movements Spirit baptism and the doctrine of initial evidence are not emphasised in the same way as in classical Pentecostal churches.

1.6 An introduction to New Prophetic Churches in South Africa

1.6.1 Characterisation of NPCs

NPCs are different from the other three streams or sub-traditions of South African Pentecostalism, but one still classifies them as Pentecostal if the prophetic is considered as one of the characteristics of Pentecostalism. It represents a recent development within Pentecostalism which has seen the rise of churches that are more inclined towards the prophetic tradition. These churches are characterised by four emphases: First, they practice what most of their leaders call forensic prophecy or one-on-one prophecy, where believers receive direct prophecy that involves their daily living, including personal information like cell phone number, car registration number and so forth.[40] Second, their deliverance ministry, unlike other streams, is based on consultations where they charge around R7000 or more per consultation. Thus, members can consult a prophet to receive counselling or direction for their lives but they will need to pay a certain fee depending on the level of their problems.[41] Third, one of the common miracles that these prophets perform while ministering on the podium is "miracle money" that appears in people's accounts without them working for it.[42] Finally, as opposed to the usual titles like Reverend, Pastor and so forth in other traditions, they are known for their love of fashionable prophetic titles. Prophet Shepherd Bushiri is known as "Major One" and others, for example, as "Seer One" or "Mzansi Prophet".[43]

1.6.2 Some prominent figures in the NPCs

There are numerous figures in the NPCs, we are not even able to quantify them here; however, it is important to note that of all the NPC prophets, Prophet Shepherd Bushiri is the most popular in South Africa. Bushiri is a Malawian-born minister of the gospel who operates in Pretoria[44] and lives in one of the most affluent suburbs in South Africa, Sandton, drives several expensive cars, and owns a private jet.[45] Bushiri is not only the founder of Enlightened Christian Gathering (ECG) but also owns and runs a number of companies and has invested in different types of businesses.[46] What actually makes Bushiri so popular is that he has mastered "the art of prophecy" as his followers call him "Major One" signifying that no one can prophesy as he can.[47] Bushiri's popularity only reached such a high level when he came to South Africa; before that he was just an ordinary man following his spiritual father Urbert Angel, a Zimbabwean-born prophet who is currently ministering in the United Kingdom.[48] Angel has since handed over his prophetic baton to Bushiri, calling himself a retired professor of prophecy.

The second figure whom we are highlighting in this chapter is Pastor Lesego Daniel of Rabboni Centre Ministries in the Soshanguve township north of Pretoria. Lesego was born on 15 May 1972 and, unlike Bushiri who grew up outside South Africa in Malawi, Lesego is a South African who grew up in Garankuwa, another township near Pretoria, and did some studies at South African institutions. After completing his studies, Lesego was involved in ministry that included prayer for the sick, prophecy, deliverance and preaching of the gospel of Jesus Christ. Lesego has been involved in ministry for more than twenty years and has served under other senior pastors. However, it was only in 2002 that he felt a calling to start his own ministry where he was fully in charge without supervision.[49] Within Lesego's network are figures like Penuel Mnguni of End Time Disciples Ministries. Mnguni is famous because of his allegiance to Lesego as the latter regards him as his spiritual son.[50] Another figure within Lesego's network is Lethebo Rabalago of Mount Zion General Assembly (MZGA), someone who carries similar spiritual DNA. Lesego has numerous other spiritual sons, scattered throughout South Africa, especially in townships and villages.

Other figures include the Congolese but South African-based Pastor Alph Lukau who together with his wife ministers in Sandton, north of Johannesburg. Lukau, born on 25 October 1975, is the founder and senior pastor of Alleluia Ministries International which, according to their website, is based on the Bible and rooted in the Word of God.[51] Like Bushiri, Lukau owns several luxury cars that he often posts photos of on Facebook, Instagram and other social media platforms.[52] He lives in a big mansion and has a net worth of millions. Lukau is so connected that even the former president of South Africa, Jacob Zuma, once visited his church and asked for prayers.[53]

Another prominent pastor is Paseka Motsoeneng, also known as Pastor Mboro, born on 8 April 1968 and the founder and senior pastor of Incredible Happenings, situated in Katlehong near Germiston, east of Johannesburg.[54] The last pastor to mention here is the Nigerian-born Pastor Tim Omotoso, senior pastor of Jesus Dominion International, based in Durban, South Africa.[55] Other than teaching the Word and praying for people, Omotoso is also known for his singing and instrumental performances. He formed a musical group in his church that has won music awards.[56] At the time of writing he was being prosecuted for alleged sexual harassment.

1.6.3 Impact of the NPCs in South Africa

The NPCs are having a great impact in South African Pentecostalism in terms of membership. For example, Bushiri's ECG has a massive following which is in the millions according to their official website.[57] The NPCs attract different kinds of members in their daily services attended by all ages.[58] What seems to be the major driver behind the NPC's popularity is the practice of prophecy, because many South Africans prefer to receive a prophetic word rather than to listen to a formal sermon.[59] Therefore, in the NPCs the poor come with the hope that they will receive a prophecy that can make them rich, and the rich with the hope that they can protect their wealth.[60] In South Africa, people will even drive from other provinces to come to these churches in order to receive a prophecy for their lives.[61] In addition, the NPCs have great followings in other African countries where members flock to their services. What is interesting is the growing number of international visitors from the global north, from countries like the United Kingdom, United States of America and others.[62] For those who do not personally come to South Africa, they can follow these prophets on their TV channels.

1.7 The abuse of religion in the NPCs

Since 2014, South African society has been taken by storm by abusive religious practices as practiced by the NPC prophets in South African Pentecostalism. For example, Pastor Daniel Lesego fed his congregants with grass and made some drink petrol, arguing that when prayed for, both grass and petrol become bread and wine used for Holy Communion. His spiritual son Penuel Mnguni fed his congregants with live snakes and made others lie down while he drove his car over them. Another outrageous example happened when Lethebo Rabalao sprayed a brand of insecticide called Doom on the congregants in the name of healing them.[63] Other examples showing the abuse of religion is the allegation that Bushiri illegally transports R50 million to his home country, Malawi, on a weekly basis.[64] Most recently, Pastor Alph Lukau hit news headlines after he claimed to have raised a dead person in what came to be called "#resurrection challenge".[65]

There is also a tendency among male prophets of touching the private parts of their female followers whenever they say prayers for them. One of the well-known NPC prophets, Paseka Motseoneng, exhibits this tendency. When praying for his female members, he touches their private parts and calls them "biscuits".[66] Most of the time, the prophets do these things to illustrate that through a sexual encounter, God will deliver female members from barrenness and other challenges.[67] Another example of the abuse of women by the NPC prophets can be seen in the ongoing trial of Tim Omotoso,[68] whom Cheryl Zondi and other young girls have accused of rape and sexual harassment.[69] The Omotoso trial has touched many people in society and has painted a grim picture of the NPC prophets, especially since the trial has been broadcast live on television.

1.8 The abuse of the Spirit in the NPCs

There is a link between the abuse of religion as stated above and the abuse of the Spirit. Most of the NPC prophets who did these acts connect their actions with the Holy Spirit.[70] They refer to the Holy Spirit so that the audience cannot connect their practices to other sources like divination in African Traditional Religion (ATR). They manipulate congregants to believe that these abuses emanate from the spiritual and prophetic revelation they have received for a particular service.[71] Lesego claimed to have heard from God through the Holy Spirit when he fed his congregants grass, stating that the grass would have harmed them if God had not instructed him to do that. Lesego was quoted as saying, "When the Holy Spirit comes you will be able to see. Do not worry when people criticise you because they cannot see the Spirit of truth, they could not welcome or understand."[72] In a similar way, Lethebo Rabalao claimed to have heard a voice from the Holy Spirit when he sprayed insecticide upon a congregation whose members were looking for healing. When asked why he sprayed insect repellent on his congregants, Lethebo said,

> Doom is just a name, but when you speak to it, it becomes a healing product. People get healed and delivered through Doom. It is not by might nor by power, but by the Holy Spirit. Through spraying the Doom, I anoint them.[73]

Therefore, the prophets see and interpret everything around them as spiritual and related to the work of the Holy Spirit. This aspect of the NPCs has left many unsuspecting followers very vulnerable, as they do not want to fight against the work of the Holy Spirit.[74] Therefore, whenever they deliver a message, the NPC prophets will always refer to the Holy Spirit in order to make their message very believable to the people.

There is also a link between the abuse of women among the NPCs and the abuse of the Spirit, as perpetrators often claim that the Holy Spirit told them to sleep with their congregants. Concepts like healing and deliverance are used as ways to manipulate the followers in order to abuse and harass them in a sexual manner.[75] What is also common among some of these pastors is to tell their members that an evil spirit has possessed their bodies and in order to receive their deliverance, they have to sleep with the pastor.[76] One of the pastors claimed to be "obeying prophetic/spiritual injunction to do the will of God, which is to impregnate any one chosen and revealed by the Holy Spirit, irrespective of whether the woman is married or not".[77] The connection to the Holy Spirit makes any word spoken by the pastor to any of their followers believable, and therefore women fall prey to sexual abuse. In this instance, it is difficult to go against the word of the prophet because it will be like going against the word of God because the prophet hears from God through the Holy Spirit.

1.9 Approaches in dealing with abuse of the Spirit in the NPCs

This book uses different approaches to study the abuse of the Spirit in Pentecostalism. The first is the historical approach that looks at the history of South African Pentecostalism from its beginning. This is not an easy task given the complexities of South African Pentecostalism.[78] It means that a historian has to look at various streams of Pentecostalism in the South African context, including classical Pentecostal churches, AICs, Charismatics, with an ability to connect them with current developments like the NPCs. Classical Pentecostalism is connected to the nineteenth- and twentieth-century American Pentecostalism and a historian should be able to make such a connection.[79] We should also understand South African Pentecostal history within the context of broader Protestant movements and also within the broader history of Christianity in South Africa.[80] This will help us to distinguish some Pentecostal churches from (for example) mainline missional churches in South Africa, as the latter (like some classical Pentecostal denominations) are imported forms of Christianity from the west.[81]

The second approach is that of African Biblical Hermeneutics (ABH), the rereading of the Christian scriptures from a premeditatedly Afrocentric perspective. It is contextual, since interpretation is always done in a particular context. Specifically, it means that the analysis of the biblical text is done from the perspective of an African worldview and culture.[82] It is called ABH because the interpreters of the Bible should be able to borrow from African culture, African indigenous knowledge and an African religious context.[83] Masenya and Ramantswana add that ABH should be a decolonial reading of the Bible that is able to use African heritage, African wisdom[84] and be rooted in an African context.[85] The African context in this instance is not only defined by location but by a determination to address African issues from a biblical perspective; thus ABH should guard against interpretations of westernised African eyes.[86] An ABH approach must explore the concept of the abuse of the Spirit from biblical perspectives and be able to apply it to an African context. An ABH should be a contextual reading that addresses current issues within Pentecostalism by remaining true to biblical teachings and faith in God.[87] An African Pentecostal biblical scholar should be able to connect without prejudice the issues concerning Pentecostalism with what is written in the Bible about those issues.

The third approach is the migration approach, given the fact that South Africa is an attractive destination for many African migrants, including pastors who are planning to start churches outside their home countries. Therefore, this approach has to look at how the African continent is affecting the landscape of the practice of pneumatology in South African Pentecostalism, compared to the influence of other continents. The migration approach should also be able to look at the migrant Pentecostal churches in South Africa and how such churches treat the issue of pneumatology. For example, the problems identified in this book of the abuse of the Spirit probably started elsewhere on the continent and have been reproduced in South Africa.[88] A scholar looking at the issues of migration and diaspora should be able to address other dynamics like xenophobia, Afrophobia and other challenges related to the abuse of the Spirit in South African Pentecostalism.[89] In addition, such a scholar should be able to explore issues of intercultural encounters, transnationalism and decolonisation within South African Pentecostalism, where pneumatology responds to the interaction between various people of different cultural backgrounds.[90]

The fourth approach is what the New Testament (1 Corinthians 12) describes as the "discernment of spirits", which is an approach that should try to assess the type of spirit or Spirit that operates upon NPC prophets. Scholars in this approach explore the role of the Holy Spirit in discernment with the aim of distinguishing between various spirits. In addition, the approach is used to discern between a real prophet and a false one.

Moreover, this approach is also used to discover true Christians from those who are not, and to assist followers of NPCs to identify the motives behind their prophets. This approach should look at the development of the theology of discernment, especially the works of Ignatius of Loyola and others on discernment. The approach will also look at the practice of discernment in other churches like the Roman Catholic Church in order to apply it to NPCs. This approach is related to ABH discussed above, because scholars here can look at scriptures that speak about discernment, interpret them and apply them to NPCs. Discernment is important not only for scholarship but also to assist church members on the ground to know the spirit behind the words of the NPC prophets.

The fifth approach is one that considers the commercialisation of religion; this means that services provided to members by a church body have a price tag, overtly or covertly.[91] For members of the NPCs to buy such services, there is an attachment of spiritual benefits attached to the price tag in order to encourage the members to buy those services.[92] Since some NPC pastors began the abuse of the Spirit, the CRL Rights Commission was given a government mandate to investigate the commercialisation and commodification of religion, whereby many pastors are involved in the selling of various products in the church like oil, water, and clothes.[93] These materials are used for the healing and deliverance of the congregants, but they have to pay a certain fee to access them. In addition, some NPC pastors charge members a certain amount to consult them in a prophetic session, where their problems are diagnosed and given a spiritual prescription. Scholars in this approach must study how the abuse of the Spirit is related to the commercialisation and commodification of religion within the NPCs.

The sixth approach is the economic strength of Pentecostalism according to Benyah, who writes:

> Despite the criticisms that are mounted to some of the practices relating to religious commercialization and commodification, there is no doubt that religion, in some instances, has produced the very kind of results or solutions people want to their problems.[94]

What are the reasons behind the success of Pentecostal churches even in the midst of neoliberalism for example? How can Pentecostal churches be used to solve problems like inequality, poverty and unemployment in South Africa? What is the relationship between the abuse of the Spirit and the economic role played by the NPC in South Africa?

1.10 Outline of chapters

In this first chapter, Mookgo S. Kgatle and Allan H. Anderson have introduced the subject of the abuse of the Spirit as practiced by some NPCs within South African Pentecostalism. In order to understand the abuse of the Spirit it is important to look at the Holy Spirit as the foundation of Pentecostalism by engaging leading scholars on the subject. The chapter explains the role of the Holy Spirit in various streams of Pentecostalism like classical Pentecostalism, African Initiated Churches and Charismatics. It outlines the approaches on how to study the abuse of the Spirit used in this book.

In Chapter 2, Thabang Mofokeng uses a historical perspective on the abuse of the Spirit. The author profiles the neo-prophetic movement that has attracted much attention from the South African public and government because of the abuses and even criminality by some of its leading figures. Using the "causes and consequences" approach of historical research, Mofokeng seeks to understand the causes of what he categorises as dangerous, criminal and deceptive acts of some actors within neo-prophetism. He finds the causes in different kinds of deprivation, inadequate theological preparedness, Pentecostal contextuality, pragmatism, postcolonial socio-political failures, and attempts at Africanisation. This combination of multiple causes prevents one from identifying any single person or cause for these problems that undermine its Christian witness. The challenge lies in rallying the whole church to challenge and assist neo-prophetism to maintain a credible witness.

In Chapter 3, Elise Kisungu uses a migration approach and looks at how migrants, particularly Africans, arrive in South Africa from various parts of the world leading to an increase in churches planted by migrants. This chapter highlights South Africa nationals' disapprobation of foreign church leaders due to the growing abuse of pneumatology and the commercialisation of religion. Kisungu traces the roots of Pentecostalism in South Africa within the context of global and African Pentecostalism. She discusses factors that contribute to the abuse of the Spirit and the gullibility of people in the face of those who practice these controversial acts. The chapter demonstrates the necessity of addressing these concerns within a general African context, as these predicaments are not merely local. The paper concludes by making proposals to stop African Pentecostalism from allowing these abusive practices and to develop a biblical pneumatology relevant to the African context.

In Chapter 4, Ithapeleng Sebetseli and Hulisani Ramantswana probe the question "Where have all the prophets come from?" through the approach of ABH. In the South African context, many have lamented the silence of the prophets – especially those who used to be vocal during the apartheid period. However, over the years, many prophets in the South African context emerged from the neo-prophetic movement. The chapter focuses on the prophetic/oracular types who usually deliver their messages in a way similar to the Old Testament prophets as *ruach*-filled agents of YHWH, This chapter assesses the "neo-prophets" from this perspective.

In Chapter 5, Kelebogile T. Resane contributes towards the knowledge and understanding of the "commercialisation of religion" approach commonly found among some Pentecostal preachers today. The chapter compares the commercialist preachers with Simon the Sorcerer found in Acts 8. Through analytical and textual examination of this text, the conclusion is drawn that the commercialisation of the gospel is not something new but has existed since the early church. The chapter shows that the modern commercialist preachers who pursue wealth accumulation at the expense of the purity of the gospel of salvation and holiness of life apply Simon the Sorcerer's tactics and methodologies. There is an appeal for these preachers to return to the Pentecostal fundamentals of holiness, hope, and humility. These three doctrinal values are the marks of the ministry of the early Pentecostal forbears who championed this movement with integrity and outstanding character. Nicholas Bhengu is one particular example of a minister who expressed the dignity of the Pentecostal movement. Unfortunately, today commercialist preachers ignore Bhengu because they use the gospel for financial gain.

In Chapter 6, Themba Shingange looks critically at how African Pentecostal and Charismatic Christians read and interpret the signs of the times in the advent of the abuse of the Spirit in South Africa, by using the "discernment of spirits" approach. Whereas controversial practices are common within the new mushrooming Pentecostal and Charismatic churches, the older and more established African Pentecostal and Charismatic Churches have the responsibility of correcting these errors. However, since they too seem to have lost direction, there is a need for them to go back and stand at the crossroads of their history. As a result, they will be in a position to redefine their mission in this regard as discernment and that will be a step in the right direction.

Chapter 7 by Bekithemba Dube uses decoloniality motifs such as the coloniality of being, knowledge and power. The chapter seeks to problematise the praxis of pneumatology by some emerging ministries. It focuses mainly on the Seven Angels Ministry in relation to the use of the Spirit, and answers two questions: First, what is the ambivalence of pneuma (the Spirit) in the context of religious delinquency and "mafia" tendencies? Second, how can the praxis of pneumatology be constructed as a counter hegemony strategy to address these mafia tendencies? The main argument of the chapter is that there is a need to rethink the use of pneuma in South Africa and that religious ministries prone to decoloniality should begin to take a revolutionary approach against the abuse of pneuma in the context of social injustice, criminality and the "mafia" hiding under the banner, "thus says the Spirit of the Lord".

In Chapter 8, Maria Frahm-Arp examines the lived, oral pneumatology being created and re-created by prophets in three prophetic Pentecostal and Charismatic churches in South Africa during the first weeks of the COVID-19 crisis. The chapter uses discourse analysis to analyse six television programmes that the leaders of Enlightened Christian Gathering, Rabboni Ministries and Kingdom Prayer Ministries International aired via their Facebook pages. These "men of God" proclaimed that they understood the will of God through the filling of the Holy Spirit, and this crisis was God's plan for the end times. God was giving everyone a chance to turn back to Him and begin worshipping Him.

In Chapter 9 Collium Banda uses an economic lens to analyse the continued growth of neo-Pentecostalism in South Africa despite several big scandals reported in the media with resultant harsh criticism from some state organs. The chapter attempts to answer the question: what is the essence of neo-Pentecostalism in South Africa that makes it continue to thrive in spite of scandalous acts by some of its leaders and subsequent severe criticism by the authorities? Since these churches function as places of hope for many poor South Africans, what should these churches do to play a meaningful role among poor people? The answers to these questions emanate from a theoretical framework of religion as a means to human flourishing. After describing the theoretical framework, there is a discussion of controversial religious activities. Banda analyses socio-economic inequality in South Africa and shows how it makes the poor reliant on controversial religious practices. Neo-Pentecostalism can play a meaningful role in empowering the poor to confront inequality in South Africa. However, there are deeply disturbing and controversial aspects of neo-Pentecostalism that need radical improvement in order to enable this meaningful role. Banda then proposes what neo-Pentecostalism must do in order to empower poor South African congregants to address their lack of human flourishing meaningfully.

The epilogue by the editors brings all these contributions together with a summary of the significance of the collection as a whole in identifying a new form of Pentecostalism, avoiding generalisations, illustrating how these churches "abuse the Spirit", and presenting the more positive aspect of the role of the Spirit in meeting people's existential needs. It ends with some recommendations for the churches, religious leaders, and government agencies.

Notes

1 Mookgo Kgatle, "The Unusual Practices Within Some Neo-Pentecostal Churches in South Africa: Reflections and Recommendations," *HTS Theological Studies* 73, no. 3 (2017): 1–8.
2 Chima Agazue, "He Told Me That My Waist and Private Parts Have Been Ravaged by Demons: 'Sexual Exploitation of Female Church Members by Prophets' in Nigeria," *Dignity: A Journal on Sexual Exploitation and Violence* 1, no. 1 (2016): 10.
3 Allan Anderson, *Moya: The Holy Spirit in an African Context* (Pretoria: University of South Africa, 1991).
4 Mookgo Kgatle and Thabang Mofokeng, "Towards a Decolonial Hermeneutic of Experience in African Pentecostal Christianity: A South African Perspective," *HTS Teologiese Studies / Theological Studies* 75, no. 4 (2019): 9.
5 Paul Kibuuka, Carel Kiyingi, Van Aardt, and Deon Herold, *Tustin, an Investigative Study of the Commercialisation of Religion in the Republic of South Africa 2016 Gauteng Pilot Study* (Pretoria: CRL Rights Commission/UNISA, 2016).
6 CRL Rights Commission, *Report on the Hearings on the Commercialisation of Religion and Abuse of People's Beliefs Systems* (Pretoria: CRL Rights Commission, 2017).

7 Mookgo Kgatle, "The Relationship Between the Economic Strand of Contemporary Pentecostalism and Neo-Liberalism in Post-1994 South Africa," *Religions* 11, no. 4 (2020): 156.

8 Jacob Olupona, *African Religions: A Very Short Introduction*. Vol. 377 (Oxford: Oxford University Press, 2014).

9 Allan Boesak, *Children of the Waters of Meribah: Black Liberation Theology, the Miriamic Tradition, and the Challenges of Twenty-First-Century Empire* (Eugene, OR: Wipf & Stock, 2019), 5.

10 Solomon Kgatle, *The Fourth Pentecostal Wave in South Africa: A Critical Engagement* (Abingdon: Routledge, 2019). The reason these churches are studied in the broader scope of South African Pentecostalism is that although they seem outrageous, some of them have maintained the fundamental teachings of Pentecostalism like baptism in the Holy Spirit with the evidence of speaking in tongues. Besides, other characteristics of NPCs like prophetism and miracles are characteristics of Pentecostalism.

11 By "Spirit" in this chapter and the book, we refer to the Holy Spirit. Therefore, the "abuse of the Spirit" specifically refers to the abuse of the Holy Spirit. Reference shall be made in this chapter and other chapters to other spirits in order to differentiate them with the Holy Spirit.

12 Acts 2:1–4 records that as the believers where gathered together in one accord the Holy Spirit came upon all of them and they began to speak in other tongues. It is from this account that most Pentecostals have drawn the doctrine of initial evidence, which means that every believer who claims to be baptised with the Holy Spirit should speak in tongues.

13 Allan Anderson, *Zion and Pentecost: The Spirituality and Experience of Pentecostal and Zionist/Apostolic Churches in South Africa*, vol. 6 (Pretoria: Unisa Press, 2000).

14 Amos Yong, *The Spirit Poured Out on All Flesh: Pentecostalism and the Possibility of Global Theology* (Grand Rapids, MI: Baker Book House, 2005), 18.

15 Frank Macchia, *Baptized in the Spirit: A Global Pentecostal Theology* (Grand Rapids, MI: Zondervan Publishing House, 2006), 21.

16 Mark Cartledge, *Testimony in the Spirit: Rescripting Ordinary Pentecostal Theology* (London: Routledge, 2016), 2.

17 Christopher Stephenson, *Types of Pentecostal Theology: Method, System, Spirit* (Oxford: Oxford University Press, 2013), 36.

18 Veli-Matti Kärkkäinen, *The Holy Spirit: A Guide to Christian Theology* (Louisville, KY: Westminster John Knox Press, 2012), 2.

19 Allan Anderson, *Spirit-Filled World: Religious Dis/Continuity in African Pentecostalism* (Cham: Palgrave Macmillan, 2018), 7.

20 Allan Anderson and Samuel Otwang, *Tumelo: The Faith of African Pentecostals in South Africa* (Pretoria: University of South Africa, 1993).

21 Ogbu Kalu, *African Pentecostalism: An Introduction* (Oxford: Oxford University Press, 2008), 9.

22 Marius Nel, *An African Pentecostal Hermeneutics: A Distinctive Contribution to Hermeneutics* (Eugene, OR: Wipf & Stock, 2018), 156.

23 Nimi Wariboko, *Nigerian Pentecostalism*, vol. 62 (Suffolk, NY: Boydell & Brewer, 2014), 24.

24 Kwabena Asamoah-Gyadu, *Sighs and Signs of the Spirit: Ghanaian Perspectives on Pentecostalism and Renewal in Africa* (Eugene, OR: Wipf & Stock, 2015), 149.

25 Anderson, *Moya*.

26 The article by Kgatle, "The Unusual Practices" is an important attempt as it outlined the abuses of religion, the gullibility of society and reasons for their gullibility. Similarly, the other that Kgatle wrote with Mofokeng, "Towards a Decolonial Hermeneutic" is also important as it highlights the experiential

hermeneutic in South African Pentecostalism that is related to the works of the Spirit. Last, Kgatle's book "The Fourth Pentecostal Wave" is pivotal as it arguably categorises the New Prophetic Churches within the broader South African Pentecostalism cf his latest "New paradigms of pneumatological ecclesiology brought about by new prophetic churches within South Africa Pentecostalism."

27 Another 30% of the population belonged to Protestant churches and 12% were Catholics. Percentages given are very approximate estimates, based on available statistics, and do not include the numbers of people in Protestant and Catholic churches who were 'Charismatic'. See Anderson and Otwang, *Tumelo*, 3–9, 14–15.

28 Allan Anderson, "The Lekganyanes and Prophecy in the Zion Christian Church," *Journal of Religion in Africa* 29, no. 3 (1999): 285–312; idem., *Zion and Pentecost*, 56–63; Bengt G. M. Sundkler, *Zulu Zion and Some Swazi Zionists* (London: Oxford University Press, 1976); James P. Kiernan, "Salt Water and Ashes: Instruments of Curing Among Zulu Zionists," *JRA* 9, no. 1 (1978): 27–32; idem., "Zionist Communion," *JRA* 11, no. 2 (1980): 124–36; idem., *The Production and Management of Therapeutic Power in Zionist Churches* (Lampeter: Edwin Mellen Press,1991); idem., "Variations on a Christian Theme: The Healing Synthesis of Zulu Zionism," in *Syncretism/ Anti-Syncretism: The Politics of Religious Syncretism,* eds. Charles Stewart and Rosalind Shaw (London and New York: Routledge, 1994), 69–84.

29 For more details on new Pentecostals throughout Africa, see Allan Anderson, *African Reformation: African Initiated Christianity in the Twentieth Century* (Trenton, NJ: Africa World Press, 2001), 167–86. See also David Maxwell, "Witches, Prophets and Avenging Spirits: The Second Christian Movement in North-East Zimbabwe," *JRA* 25, no. 3 (1995): 313; Gifford Paul, *African Christianity: Its Public Role* (Bloomington: Indiana University Press, 1998), 31; Anderson, *Zion & Pentecost*, 237–55.

30 See Marthinus L. Daneel's discussion in "African Initiated Churches in Southern Africa: Protest Movements or Mission Churches?" in *Christianity Reborn: The Global Expansion of Evangelicalism in the Twentieth Century*, ed. Donald M. Lewis (Grand Rapids, MI: Eerdmans, 2004), 185–87.

31 These are common terms used in South Africa to refer to evangelical Christians.

32 Walter J. Hollenweger, *The Pentecostals: The Charismatic Movement in the Churches* (Minneapolis: Augsburg Publishing House, 1972), 22–24; Vinson Synan, *The Holiness-Pentecostal Tradition: Charismatic Movements in the Twentieth Century* (Grand Rapids, MI and Cambridge: Eerdmans, 1997), 84–106.

33 Anderson, *African Reformation*, 69–163; Allan H. Anderson and Gerald J. Pillay, "The Segregated Spirit: The Pentecostals," in *Christianity in South Africa: A Political, Social and Cultural History*, eds. Richard Elphick and Rodney Davenport (Oxford: James Currey & Cape Town: David Philip, 1997), 228–29; Allan Anderson, "Dangerous Memories for South African Pentecostals," in *Pentecostals After a Century: Global Perspectives on a Movement in Transition*, eds. Allan Anderson and Walter J. Hollenweger (Sheffield: Sheffield Academic Press, 1999), 88–92; idem., *Bazalwane*, 22–24; idem., *Zion & Pentecost*, 56–74; David Maxwell, "Historicizing Christian Independency: The Southern African Pentecostal Movement 1908–1950," *Journal of African History* 40 (1999): 234–64.

34 See Anthony Balcomb, "From Apartheid to the New Dispensation: Evangelicals and the Democratization of South Africa1," *Journal of Religion in Africa* 34, no. 1–2 (2004): 23–27; Anderson, *Bazalwane*, 45–48; C. Peter Watt, *From Africa's Soil: The Story of the Assemblies of God in Southern Africa* (Cape Town: Struik

Christian Books, 1992); Allie A. Dubb, *Community of the Saved: An African Revivalist Church in the East Cape* (Johannesburg: Witwatersrand University Press, 1976); Philip Mayer, *Townsmen or Tribesmen: Conservatism and the Process of Urbanisation in a South African City* (Cape Town: Oxford University Press, 1961).

35 Mookgo Kgatle, "Spirit Baptism and the Doctrine of Initial Evidence in African Pentecostal Christianity: A Critical Analysis," *HTS Theological Studies* 76, no. 1 (2020): 1–7.

36 Peter Gräbe, "A Perspective from Regent University's Ph. D. Program in Renewal Studies: Theology in the Light of the Renewing Work of the Holy Spirit," *Pneuma* 27, no. 1 (2005): 124–29.

37 Allan Anderson, "New African Initiated Pentecostalism and Charismatics in South Africa," *Journal of Religion in Africa* 35, no. 1 (2005): 66–92.

38 Sibusiso Masondo, "The African Indigenous Churches' Spiritual Resources for Democracy and Social Cohesion," *Verbum et Ecclesia* 35, no. 3 (2014): 1–8.

39 Anderson, "New African Initiated Pentecostalism," 69.

40 Revelator, *The Prophetic Dimension: A Divine Revelation of How to Accurately Prophesy and Operate in the Prophetic Realm of God* (Sandton: Global Destiny House 2017).

41 Christian Tsekpoe, "Contemporary Prophetic and Deliverance Ministry Challenges in Africa," *Transformation* 36, no. 4 (2019): 280–91.

42 Obvious Vengeyi, "Zimbabwean Pentecostal Prophets," *Prophets, Profits and the Bible in Zimbabwe* (2014): 29.

43 These titles depend on the function of the prophet. For example by calling himself, 'major 1', which derives from a military rank 'major general', Bushiri, is assuming that he is above other prophets. Other titles like seer 1 are taken from the Old Testament (1 Sam 9:9). Mzansi prophet means the 'prophet of South Africa'. Other information on the subject can be found in the article "Prophets praying for, or preying on people's faith: A reflection on prophetic ministry in the South African context" by Ramantswana.

44 Douglas Bafford, "The Prosperity Gospel and an Unprosperous Reality in Post-Apartheid South Africa: Conservative Evangelical Responses to Charismatic Christianity," paper presented at the Wits Interdisciplinary Seminar in the Humanities, Wits Institute for Social and Economic Research, University of the Witwatersrand, Johannesburg, March 4, 2019.

45 "Shepherd Bushiri: Meeting the Man Who 'Walks on Air' – BBC," accessed March 5, 2018, www.bbc.com/news/world-africa-43245126/.

46 Bekithemba Dube, "'Go and Prophesy in Your Own Land': Foreign Prophets and Popularism in South Africa. Evoking the Need of Jonathanic Theology for Peaceful Resolution of Difference," *Religions* 11, no. 1 (2020): 42.

47 Ramantswana, "Prophets Praying for," 4.

48 Edward Mitole, "Demystifying the Prosperity Gospel: The South African Case Study," *SABC News Documentary Production*, March 4, 2019, www.moderng hana.com/news/927817/demystifying-the-prosperity-gospel-the-south-afri.html.

49 Rabboni Centre Ministries, "Rabboni Centre Ministries/home/Facebook," accessed May 15, 2017, www.facebook.com/rabboniministries/.

50 Tinyiko Maluleke, "Between Pretoria and George Goch Hostel-God in South Africa in 2015," *New Agenda* (2015): 35–39.

51 The information, visit the alleluia ministries international official website https://alleluiaministries.com/.

52 Mookgo Kgatle, "Social Media and Religion: Missiological Perspective on the Link Between Facebook and the Emergence of Prophetic Churches in southern Africa," *Verbum et Ecclesia* 39, no. 1 (2018): 1–6.

53 The information was retrieved online via www.timeslive.co.za under the topic "There Are Prophets and Then There Are Profits – Just Ask Pastor Alph Lukau VIP Escort, Fast Cars and Yes, Even a Zuma Connection," accessed February 26, 2019.

54 More information can be found on https://sacd.christians.co.za/.

55 "House of Jacob Coming to Lagos State, Nigeria on 9 November 2012," accessed March 11, 2015, www.thenigerianvoice.com/news/101102/house-of-jacob-coming-to-lagos-state-nigeria-on-9-november.html.

56 "Grace Galaxy'S Biography," Modernghana.com, September 2, 2012, accessed March 11, 2015, www.thenigerianvoice.com/news/97445/grace-galaxys-biography.html.

57 The information was retrieved from the official website of the Enlightened Christian Gathering, www.ecgministries.org/.

58 Ramantswana, "Prophets Praying for," 5.

59 The spiritual services of NPC are centred on prophecy and followers are always willing to stay for many hours to hear the word by the prophet. This phenomenon has caused people to move from classical Pentecostal churches to more prophetic ones.

60 Tinyiko Maluleke, "The Prophet Syndrome: Let Them Eat Grass," *Mail and Guardian*, 24 October, https://mg.co.za/article/2014-10-23-the-prophet-syndrome-let-them-eat-grass/.

61 It is based on fact that most South Africans love prophecy.

62 Most NPCs have international services to host international visitors.

63 Kgatle, "The Unusual Practices," 3–4.

64 Ramantswana, "Prophets Praying for," 8.

65 Dube, " 'Go and Prophesy," 42.

66 Maluleke, "Between Pretoria and George Goch Hostel," 39.

67 Agazue, "He Told Me," 10.

68 Omotoso is head of the Jesus Dominion International Church and was arrested at the Port Elizabeth International Airport for allegedly having molested and raped at least 30 young women who attended his church.

69 Hulisani Ramantswana, "Wathint'Umfazi, Wathint'Imbokodo, Uzakufa [You Strike a Woman, You Strike a Rock, You Will Die]: Dinah and Tamar as rape protestors," *HTS Theological Studies* 75, no. 1 (2019): 1–8.

70 Kelebogile T. Resane, " 'And They Shall Make You Eat Grass Like Oxen' (Daniel 4: 24): Reflections on Recent Practices in Some New Charismatic Churches," *Pharos Journal of Theology* 98, no. 1 (2017): 2.

71 Collium Banda, "Redefining Religion? A Critical Christian Reflection on CRL Rights Commission's Proposal to Regulate Religion in South Africa," *Verbum et Ecclesia* 40, no. 1 (2019): 3.

72 The quotation was retrieved from sowetan under the title "Pretoria Pastor Convinces Congregation to Eat Grass," accessed January 10, 2014, www.sowetanlive.co.za/news/2014-01-10-pretoria-pastor-convinces-congregation-to-eat-grass/.

73 The quotation was retrieved from sowetan under the title "Doom Prophet Says He Was Chosen Before Birth," accessed November 21, 2016, https://rekordcenturion.co.za/.

74 Resane, "They Shall Make You Eat Grass," 6.

75 Sarojini Nadar and Adriaan van Klinken, " 'Queering the Curriculum': Pedagogical Explorations of Gender and Sexuality in Religion and Theological Studies," *Journal of Feminist Studies in Religion* 34, no. 1 (2018): 101–9.

76 Agazue, "He Told Me," 10.

77 The quotation can be followed on the article titled, "Pastor Impregnates 20 Members of His Congregation and Claims the Holy Spirit Told Him to Do It," accessed July 9, 2014, www.christianpost.com/news/pastor-impregnates-20-members-of-his-congregation-and-claims-the-holy-spirit-told-him-to-do-it.html.

78 Derrick Mashau, "Ministering Effectively in the Context of Pentecostalism in Africa: A Reformed Missional Reflection," *In die Skriflig* 47, no. 1 (2013): 10–17.
79 Ibid., 2.
80 Ibid., 3.
81 Allan Anderson, "Structures and Patterns in Pentecostal Mission," *Missionalia* 32, no. 2 (2004): 233–49.
82 David Adamo, "What Is African Biblical Hermeneutics?" *Black Theology* 13, no. 1 (2015): 59–72.
83 Kelebogile Resane, "Biblical Exegesis and Hermeneutics of Biblical Texts: African Approaches," Teaching and Learning Manager: Centre for Teaching and Learning University of the Free State South Africa, 2018.
84 Madipoane Masenya and Hulisani Ramantswana, "Anything New Under the Sun of African Biblical Hermeneutics in South African Old Testament Scholarship? Incarnation, Death and Resurrection of the Word in Africa," *Verbum et Ecclesia* 36, no. 1 (2015): 1–12.
85 Hulisani Ramantswana, " 'I shavha i sia muinga i ya fhi?': Decolonial Reflection on African Biblical Hermeneutics," *Stellenbosch Theological Journal* 2, no. 2 (2016): 401–29.
86 Hulisani Ramantswana, "Beware of the (Westernised) African Eyes: Rereading Psalm 82 Through the Vhufa Approach," *Scriptura* 116 (2017): 1–18.
87 McGlory Speckman, "African Biblical Hermeneutics on the Threshold? Appraisal and Wayforward," *Acta Theologica* 36 (2016): 204–24.
88 Ogbu Kalu, "African Pentecostalism in Diaspora," *PentecoStudies* 9, no. 1 (2010): 9–34.
89 Rafael Cazarin, "The Social Architecture of Belonging in the African Pentecostal Diaspora," *Religions* 10, no. 7 (2019): 440.
90 Victor Counted, "African Christian Diaspora Religion and/or Spirituality: A Concept Analysis and Reinterpretation," *Critical Research on Religion* 7, no. 1 (2019): 58–79.
91 Madipoane Masenya, "Church Breakaways as a Prototype of Commercialisation and Commodification of Religion in the Pentecostal Church Movement in South Africa: Considering Curricula Offerings for Pastors," *Stellenbosch Theological Journal* 4, no. 2 (2018): 633–54 cf Thinandavha Mashau and Mookgo S. Kgatle, "Prosperity Gospel and the Culture of Greed in Post-Colonial Africa: Constructing an Alternative African Christian Theology of Ubuntu," *Verbum et Ecclesia* 40, no. 1 (2019): 1–8.
92 Ibid., 635.
93 Ibid.
94 Francis Benyah, "Commodification of the Gospel and the Socio-Economics of Neo-Pentecostal/Charismatic Christianity in Ghana," *Legon Journal of the Humanities* 29, no. 2 (2018): 116–45.

References

Adamo, David T. "What Is African Biblical Hermeneutics?" *Black Theology* 13, no. 1 (2015): 59–72.
Agazue, Chima. "He Told Me That My Waist and Private Parts Have Been Ravaged by Demons: 'Sexual Exploitation of Female Church Members by Prophets' in Nigeria." *A Journal on Sexual Exploitation and Violence* 1, no. 1 (2016): 10.
Anderson, Allan H. *Moya: The Holy Spirit in an African Context*. Pretoria: University of South Africa, 1991.

Anderson, Allan H., and Samuel Otwang. *Tumelo: The Faith of African Pentecostals in South Africa*. Pretoria: University of South Africa, 1993.

Anderson, Allan H., and Gerald J. Pillay. "The Segregated Spirit: The Pentecostals." *Perspectives on Southern Africa* 55 (1997): 227–41.

———. "Dangerous Memories for South African Pentecostals." In *Pentecostals After a Century: Global Perspectives on a Movement in Transition*, edited by Allan Anderson and Walter J. Hollenweger, 88–92. Sheffield: Sheffield Academic Press, 1999.

———. "The Lekganyanes and Prophecy in the Zion Christian Church." *Journal of Religion in Africa* 29, no. 3 (1999): 285–312.

———. *Zion and Pentecost: The Spirituality and Experience of Pentecostal and Zionist/Apostolic Churches in South Africa*. Vol. 6. Pretoria: Unisa Press, 2000.

———. *African Reformation: African Initiated Christianity in the Twentieth Century*. Trenton, NJ: Africa World Press, 2001.

———. "Structures and Patterns in Pentecostal Mission." *Missionalia* 32, no. 2 (2004): 233–49.

———. "New African Initiated Pentecostalism and Charismatics in South Africa." *Journal of Religion in Africa* 35, no. 1 (2005): 66–92.

———. *Spirit-Filled World: Religious Dis/Continuity in African Pentecostalism*. Cham: Palgrave Macmillan, 2018.

Asamoah-Gyadu, J. Kwabena. *Sighs and Signs of the Spirit: Ghanaian Perspectives on Pentecostalism and Renewal in Africa*. Eugene, OR: Wipf & Stock, 2015.

Bafford, Douglas. "The Prosperity Gospel and an Unprosperous Reality in Post-Apartheid South Africa: Conservative Evangelical Responses to Charismatic Christianity." Paper Presented at the Wits Interdisciplinary Seminar in the Humanities, Wits Institute for Social and Economic Research, University of the Witwatersrand, Johannesburg, March 4, 2019.

Balcomb, Anthony. "From Apartheid to the New Dispensation: Evangelicals and the Democratization of South Africa1." *Journal of Religion in Africa* 34, no. 1–2 (2004): 5–38.

Banda, Collium. "Redefining Religion? A critical Christian Reflection on CRL Rights Commission's Proposal to Regulate Religion in South Africa." *Verbum et Ecclesia* 40, no. 1 (2019): 1–11.

Benyah, Francis. "Commodification of the Gospel and the Socio-Economics of Neo-Pentecostal/Charismatic Christianity in Ghana." *Legon Journal of the Humanities* 29, no. 2 (2018): 116–45.

Boesak, Allan A. *Children of the Waters of Meribah: Black Liberation Theology, the Miriamic Tradition, and the Challenges of Twenty-First-Century Empire*. Eugene: Wipf & Stock, 2019.

Cartledge, Mark J. *Testimony in the Spirit: Rescripting Ordinary Pentecostal Theology*. London: Routledge, 2016.

Cazarin, Rafael. "The Social Architecture of Belonging in the African Pentecostal Diaspora." *Religions* 10, no. 7 (2019): 440.

Counted, Victor. "African Christian Diaspora Religion and/or Spirituality: A Concept Analysis and Reinterpretation." *Critical Research on Religion* 7, no. 1 (2019): 58–79.

CRL Rights Commission. *Report on the Hearings on the Commercialisation of Religion and Abuse of People's Beliefs Systems*. Pretoria: CRL Rights Commission, 2017.

Daneel, Marthinus L. "African Initiated Churches in Southern Africa: Protest Movements or Mission Churches?" *Christianity Reborn: The Global Expansion of Evangelicalism in the Twentieth Century* (2004): 118–19.

Drogus, Carol A. "Private Power or Public Power: Pentecostalism, Base Communities, and Gender." In *Power, Politics, and Pentecostals in Latin America*, 55–75. Boulder, CO: Routledge, 2018.

Dubb, Allie A. *Community of the Saved: An African Revivalist Church in the East Cape*. London: University of the Witwatersrand, African Studies Institute, 1976.

Dube, Bekithemba. "'Go and Prophesy in Your Own Land': Foreign Prophets and Popularism in South Africa. Evoking the Need of Jonathanic Theology for Peaceful Resolution of Difference." *Religions* 11, no. 1 (2020): 42.

Elphick, Richard, Rodney Davenport, and T. Davenport, eds. *Christianity in South Africa: A Political, Social, and Cultural History*. Vol. 55. Berkeley: University of California Press, 1997.

Gifford, Paul. *African Christianity: Its Public Role*. Bloomington: Indiana University Press, 1998.

Gräbe, Peter. "A Perspective from Regent University's Ph.D. Program in Renewal Studies: Theology in the Light of the Renewing Work of the Holy Spirit." *Pneuma* 27, no. 1 (2005): 124–29.

Hollenweger, Walter J. *The Pentecostals: The Charismatic Movement in the Churches*. Minneapolis: Augsburg Publishing House, 1972.

Kalu, Ogbu. *African Pentecostalism: An Introduction*. Oxford: Oxford University Press, 2008.

———. "African Pentecostalism in Diaspora." *PentecoStudies* 9, no. 1 (2010): 9–34.

Kärkkäinen, Veli-Matti. *The Holy Spirit: A Guide to Christian Theology*. Louisville, KY: Westminster John Knox Press, 2012.

Kgatle, Mookgo S. "The Unusual Practices Within Some Neo-Pentecostal Churches in South Africa: Reflections and Recommendations." *HTS Theological Studies* 73, no. 3 (2017): 1–8.

———. "Social Media and Religion: Missiological Perspective on the Link Between Facebook and the Emergence of Prophetic Churches in Southern Africa." *Verbum et Ecclesia* 39, no. 1 (2018): 1–6.

———. *The Fourth Pentecostal Wave in South Africa: A Critical Engagement*. Abingdon: Routledge, 2019.

———. "Reimagining the Practice of Pentecostal Prophecy in Southern Africa: A Critical Engagement." *HTS Teologiese Studies / Theological Studies* 75, no. 4 (2019): 8.

———. "New Paradigms of Pneumatological Ecclesiology Brought About by New Prophetic Churches Within South African Pentecostalism." *Verbum et Ecclesia* 41, no. 1 (2020): 6. a2053. https://doi.org/10.4102/ve.v41i1.2053.

———. "The Relationship Between the Economic Strand of Contemporary Pentecostalism and Neo-Liberalism in Post-1994 South Africa." *Religions* 11, no. 4 (2020): 156.

———. "Spirit Baptism and the Doctrine of Initial Evidence in African Pentecostal Christianity: A Critical Analysis." *HTS Theological Studies* 76, no. 1 (2020): 1–7.

Kgatle, Mookgo S., and Thabang R. Mofokeng. "Towards a Decolonial Hermeneutic of Experience in African Pentecostal Christianity: A South African Perspective." *HTS Teologiese Studies / Theological Studies* 75, no. 4 (2019): 9.

Kibuuka, Paul Kiyingi, Carel. J. Van Aardt, and Deon Herold, *Tustin, an Investigative Study of the Commercialisation of Religion in the Republic of South Africa 2016 Gauteng Pilot Study*. Pretoria: CRL Rights Commission/UNISA, 2016.

Kiernan, James. "Salt Water and Ashes: Instruments of Curing Among Zulu Zionists." *JRA* 9, no. 1 (1978): 27–32.

Lewis, Donald M., ed. *Christianity Reborn: The Global Expansion of Evangelicalism in the Twentieth Century*. Grand Rapids, MI: Eerdmans, 2004.

Macchia, Frank D. *Baptized in the Spirit: A Global Pentecostal Theology*. Grand Rapids, MI: Zondervan Publishing House, 2006.

Maluleke, Tinyiko S. "The Prophet Syndrome: Let Them Eat Grass." *Mail and Guardian*. Accessed October 24, 2014. https://mg/co.za.

———. "Between Pretoria and George Goch Hostel: God in South Africa in 2015." *New Agenda* 59 (2015): 35–39.

Masenya, Madipoane. "Church Breakaways as a Prototype of Commercialisation and Commodification of Religion in the Pentecostal Church Movement in South Africa: Considering Curricula Offerings for Pastors." *Stellenbosch Theological Journal* 4, no. 2 (2018): 633–54.

Masenya, Madipoane, and Hulisani Ramantswana. "Anything New Under the Sun of African Biblical Hermeneutics in South African Old Testament Scholarship? Incarnation, Death and Resurrection of the Word in Africa." *Verbum et Ecclesia* 36, no. 1 (2015): 1–12.

Mashau, Derrick T. "Ministering Effectively in the Context of Pentecostalism in Africa: A Reformed Missional Reflection." *In die Skriflig* 47, no. 1 (2013), 10–17.

Mashau, Thinandhava D., and Mookgo S. Kgatle. "Prosperity Gospel and the Culture of Greed in Post-Colonial Africa: Constructing an Alternative African Christian Theology of Ubuntu." *Verbum et Ecclesia* 40, no. 1 (2019): 1–8.

Masondo, Sibusiso T. "The African Indigenous Churches' Spiritual Resources for Democracy and Social Cohesion." *Verbum et Ecclesia* 35, no. 3 (2014): 1–8.

Maxwell, David. "Witches, Prophets and Avenging Spirits: The Second Christian Movement in North-East Zimbabwe." *JRA* 25, no. 3 (1995): 313.

———. "Historicizing Christian Independency: The Southern African Pentecostal Movement c. 1908–60." *The Journal of African History* 40, no. 2 (1999): 243–64.

Mayer, Philip. *Townsmen or Tribesmen: Conservatism and the Process of Urbanization in a South African City*. Oxford: Oxford University Press, 1971.

Mitole, Edward. "Demystifying the Prosperity Gospel: The South African Case Study." *SABC News Documentary Production*, March 4, 2019.

Nadar, Sarojini, and Adriaan van Klinken. "'Queering the Curriculum': Pedagogical Explorations of Gender and Sexuality in Religion and Theological Studies." *Journal of Feminist Studies in Religion* 34, no. 1 (2018): 101–9.

Nel, Marius. *An African Pentecostal Hermeneutics: A Distinctive Contribution to Hermeneutics*. Eugene, OR: Wipf & Stock, 2018.

Olupona, Jacob K. *African Religions: A Very Short Introduction*. Vol. 377. Oxford: Oxford University Press, 2014.

Ramantswana, Hulisani. "'I shavha i sia muinga i ya fhi?': Decolonial Reflection on African Biblical Hermeneutics." *Stellenbosch Theological Journal* 2, no. 2 (2016): 401–29.

———. "Beware of the (Westernised) African Eyes: Rereading Psalm 82 Through the Vhufa Approach." *Scriptura* 116 (2017): 1–18.

———. "Prophets Praying for, or Preying on People's Faith: A Reflection on Prophetic Ministry in the South African Context." *In die Skriflig* 53, no. 4 (2019): 8.

———. "Wathint'Umfazi, Wathint'Imbokodo, Uzakufa [You Strike a Woman, You Strike a Rock, You Will Die]: Dinah and Tamar as rape protestors." *HTS Theological Studies* 75, no. 1 (2019): 1–8.

Resane, Kelebogile T. " 'And They Shall Make You Eat Grass Like Oxen' (Daniel 4: 24): Reflections on Recent Practices in some New Charismatic Churches." *Pharos Journal of Theology* 98, no. 1 (2017): 1–17.

———. "Biblical Exegesis and Hermeneutics of Biblical Texts: African Approaches." Teaching and Learning Manager: Centre for Teaching and Learning University of the Free State South Africa, 2018.

Revelator. *The Prophetic Dimension: A Divine Revelation of How to Accurately Prophesy and Operate in the Prophetic Realm of God.* Sandton: Global Destiny House, 2017.

Speckman, McGlory. "African Biblical Hermeneutics on the Threshold? Appraisal and Way Forward." *Acta Theologica* 36 (2016): 204–24.

Stephenson, Christopher A. *Types of Pentecostal Theology: Method, System, Spirit.* Oxford: Oxford University Press, 2013.

Stewart, Charles, and Rosalind Shaw, eds. *Syncretism/ Anti-Syncretism: The Politics of Religious Syncretism.* London and New York: Routledge, 1994.

Sundkler, Bengt. *Zulu Zion and Some Swazi Zionists.* London: Oxford University Press, 1976.

Synan, Vinson. *The Holiness-Pentecostal Tradition: Charismatic Movements in the Twentieth Century.* Grand Rapids, MI: Eerdmans, 1997.

Tsekpoe, Christian. "Contemporary Prophetic and Deliverance Ministry Challenges in Africa." *Transformation* 36, no. 4 (2019): 280–91.

Vengeyi, Obvious. "Zimbabwean Pentecostal Prophets." *Prophets, Profits and the Bible in Zimbabwe* (2014): 29.

Wariboko, Nimi. *Nigerian Pentecostalism.* Vol. 62. Suffolk, NY: Boydell & Brewer, 2014, 24.

Watt, Peter. *From Africa's Soil: The Story of the Assemblies of God in Southern Africa.* Cape Town: Struik Christian Books, 1992.

Yong, Amos. *The Spirit Poured Out on All Flesh: Pentecostalism and the Possibility of Global Theology.* Grand Rapids, MI: Baker Book House, 2005.

2 "The weird you shall always have"

A historical look into the causative factors behind neo-prophetic scandals in South Africa

Thabang R. Mofokeng

2.1 Introduction

In his article titled "Desperation in an attempt to curb modern-day prophets," Elijah Dube writes:

> On the news in South Africa and Zimbabwe, often one hears a lot about the weird things the modern-day flamboyant 'Prophets' are doing or have been doing. Stories of 'Prophets' spraying 'Doom' insecticide on their followers in church services – asking congregants to eat rats, grass, drink petrol – touching female congregants inappropriately in deliverance sessions – abusing and raping congregants – profiteering, among others, abound. These have become commonplace. In a sense, the 'Prophets' have become 'untouchables'.[1]

The above quotation paints a dire picture of the African-initiated Pentecostalism of the last ten years. Previously Khanyile, Kgatle and Resane had noted the proneness to moral scandal, controversy in doctrine and practice as well as acts bordering on criminality within the recent wave of neo-Pentecostalism.[2] These writers further noted the uproar these aberrations caused within South Africa, prompting the Commission for the Promotion and Protection of the Rights of Cultural, Religious and Linguistic Communities (the CRL Rights Commission) to summon some churches and other religious organisations to hearings.[3] Although in the 2017 final report of these hearings, the CRL Rights Commission includes actors from traditional religion, Christianity and others, its chairperson at the time, Ms Thoko Nonhle Mkhwanazi-Xaluva, made it clear that their main focus and concern was specifically Charismatic churches led by individual apostolic and prophetic figures.[4]

In this chapter, I approach the subject of the scandals in neo-Pentecostalism through the lens of causes and consequences, which is one of the five categories used in framing historical research (the other four categories are continuity and discontinuity; seeing through the eyes of the contemporaries of the events of interest; turning points; and lessons).[5] If the current African Pentecostal pathologies are consequences, what are the causes and the reasons thereof? The eventual conclusion of this historical investigation is that deprivation, deficient theological training, the nature of Pentecostalism and hermeneutic peculiarities, pragmatism, postcolonial socio-economic and political failures as well as Africanisation are significant causative factors behind the dangerous healing practices, criminal acts and deception of this movement.

The chapter has four main sections: the profile of this movement, its place and relation to the broader pneumatic tradition, the different pathologies and the causes thereof.

2.2 Profile of the movement

This section profiles the movement by locating it within a specific period, identifying its specific characteristics, identifying some well-known personalities associated with it, and discussing the problems around conceptualising its identity.

2.2.1 Periodisation

In historical studies, to make analysis easier, it is necessary to delineate a phenomenon or event of interest within a certain time framework. The conceptual tool used for this is called "periodisation". Church history is periodised according to the ancient church era, the medieval and modern eras,[6] covering broadly the apostolic period to AD 590, 590 to 1517 and 1517 to date, respectively. This periodisation is however not very relevant for our study except to say that the subject falls within the modern church era. For our purposes it would be more relevant to use periodisation linked to the socio-political developments that took place in South Africa. In this respect one can say that the movement can be viewed as a post-apartheid phenomenon.

The post-apartheid democratic era was ushered in by the 1994 elections. South Africa, which had been shunned by the world until then because of its racist apartheid policy, began to experience an avalanche of migration, both internally and people coming in from other countries. The migration across our borders was mainly due to post-apartheid South Africa's relaxed attitude towards the cross-border movement of people. This immigrant population brought with it two different forms of neo-Pentecostalism: one from Brazil and another from north of South Africa, bearing a West-African stamp. The characteristics of post-apartheid neo-Pentecostalism in South Africa are discussed next.

2.2.2 Characteristics

The discussion below specifically focuses on the common practices and the use of titles.

2.2.2.1 Practices

The post-apartheid neo-Pentecostal churches in South Africa seem to have a common battery of practices and ministry tools: (1) Apostolic and prophetic individuals lead these churches. Such individuals are generally considered apostolic by virtue of their calling and their ability to work miracles; and prophetic by manifesting diagnostic and predictive abilities. (2) These churches employ a sacramental approach to healing and deliverance, hence the use of blessed water, blessed candles, holy oil, and so forth.[7] Moreover, the person of the apostle/prophet is also viewed as a sacramental "object" imbued with power, which they can impart to people and objects through prophetic decrees, declarations and prayers.[8]

(3) The movement generally has anointing nights and, annually on New Year's eve, "cross-over nights" where the apostle/prophet spends the night ministering to the attendees. In addition, there are usually mid-week deliverance sessions in groups and individually (i.e., one-on-one consultations). (4) The exchange of money between the apostle/prophet and prospective beneficiary of the grace of the man or woman of God is critical. Fees are charged for "one-on-one" consultations as well as water, oil and candles, which the apostle/prophet prescribes as remedies for various conditions. There has been an outcry regarding the exorbitant amounts involved.

(5) This sector is very media savvy and uses various media extensively to spread its message. If one tunes into any of the various community television stations at the designated time, or any of the private prophetic channels on DSTV, there is a great likelihood that one will witness these leaders exercising their prophetic and apostolic abilities.[9] Besides radio and television media outlets, social media, in the form of Facebook and YouTube, play an important role in documenting the practices of this sector and providing access to media consumers near and far.[10]

2.2.2.2 Titles

There is a growing trend in the whole neo-Pentecostal movement in South Africa to adopt other titles besides pastor and evangelist. These titles used to be in vogue during the classical Pentecostal and neo-Pentecostal era until the close of the twentieth century.[11] Today, some well-known figures associated with 1980s and 1990s neo-Pentecostalism have adopted episcopal titles – mainly because of adopting episcopal ecclesiastical structures. Examples of this tendency include Bishop Mosa Sono of Grace Bible Church, Archbishop Gladston Botwana of Zoe Bible Church, Archbishop Abram Sibiya of Christ Centred Church Episcopal, and Archbishop Stephen Zondo of Rivers of Living Waters. The leaders of most churches founded after 1994 predominantly identify themselves as apostles and/or prophets.[12] There is also a growing tendency of using honorific titles such as "doctor" and "professor" awarded by questionable international Christian universities.[13]

2.2.3 Personalities

Profiling post-apartheid neo-Pentecostalism in South Africa would be incomplete without indicating the main personalities and/or church organisations involved. However, the task is made difficult by the absence of a database or study one can access for such information. This difficulty notwithstanding, it is still possible to indicate who might be part of this movement by applying the characteristics discussed above to ministers shown in action on certain DSTV channels. One will also find the main personalities mentioned in the scholarly literature related with abusive and criminal activities among neo-Pentecostal clergy. The following leaders have been associated with controversies: Mancoba brothers of the Seven Angels Ministry, Penuel Mnguni of End-time Discipleship Ministry, Light Monyeki, Pastor Paseka Motsoeneng (Mboro) of Incredible Happenings, Prophet Shepherd Bushiri of Enlightened Christian Gathering, Pastor Alph Lukau of Alleluia Ministry International, Prophet Hadebe, Pastor Timothy Omotoso of Jesus Dominion Ministry;[14] Prophet Lethebo Rabalago of Mount Zion General Assembly, Prophet Lesego Daniel of Rabboni Centre Ministries,[15] "King" Dr HQ Nala of the Church of Plentianity and Bishop Tefo Pitso of the Jehova Shammah International Ministries.[16]

2.2.4 Conceptual clarification

The religious phenomenon that arose from the activities of evangelical and Pentecostal parachurch ministries in the 1970s has attracted various labels,[17] for example "modern Pentecostal", "Pentecostal-Charismatic", "evangelical-Charismatic", "evangelical-Pentecostal", "new Pentecostal" or "new Pentecostal-Charismatic".[18] Even the discussions of the scandalous and criminal activities that proliferated over the last ten years tend to generally trace these problematic activities back to the churches born from the Pentecostal revival of the 1970s. This tends to happen especially when approaching neo-Pentecostal independency through the lens of the prosperity gospel. However, Kgatle differentiates the Charismatic environment underlying the recent scandals from all twentieth-century pneumatic Christian movements and labels it "the fourth wave of Pentecostalism".[19] Ansah, Beki Dube, Omenyo and Ramantswana acknowledge the distinctiveness of the recent charismatic phenomenon within the neo Pentecostalism by using the terms "Charismatic and neo-prophetic churches", "prophetic churches" and "neo-prophetic movements".[20] Kgatle also joins in calling the emerging subculture within neo-Pentecostal independency in South Africa the neo-prophetic movement.[21] Ansah's explanation for the use of the term "neo-prophetic" as acknowledging the earlier prophetic Aladura/Zionist churches is important in proposing the adoption of this term for this emerging trend within African church independency.[22] This emerging movement's characteristic practices and use of specific titles peculiar to itself serve as an argument for a clearer conceptualisation. Following in the footsteps of the trio, the term "neo-prophetic" or "neo-prophetism" will be used in the rest of the chapter.

To summarise the above discussion, it is important to profile the movement in which the recent scandals relating to healing and deliverance as well as criminal acts related to sexual assault and fraud took place. Although several researchers have seen the movement as a continuation of the neo-Pentecostal independency that started in the late 1970s and early 1980s (and rightly so because of the way it subscribes to the prosperity gospel), the scandals plaguing the movement suggest that something has changed. Indeed, there are certain characteristic practices and usage of titles that seem to support the view that this is an emergent subculture within the broader neo-Pentecostal independency. Delineating the boundaries of this subculture may better focus research on this emerging movement. Conceptual clarification is part of delineating the contours of what has become increasingly different to the churches of the 1970s revival. Ansah, Beki Dube, Omenyo and Kgatle have tried to do just that by labelling the movement "prophetic" and "neo-prophetic".

2.3 Place within and relation with the broader pneumatic Christianity

In his article on what he considers to be bizarre neo-Pentecostal practices, Kgatle asserts that to understand the neo-Pentecostal movement one needs an understanding of classical Pentecostalism.[23] Although he uses the term "neo-Pentecostal", reading through his article shows that his focus is on the faction within African neo-Pentecostal independency that shares certain traits which do not typify neo-Pentecostalism as known from the 1970s. His quotations of Khanyile (2016) and the Study Committee Report on Neo-Pentecostalism (1975), make it clear that neo-Pentecostalism differs from classical Pentecostalism in its ecclesiastical experience as a movement, firstly within "traditional mainline churches", and later organised as independent African-founded congregations – thus joining the ranks of African Independent Churches (AICs).[24] Anderson acknowledges the antagonistic relationship between African neo-Pentecostalism and older AICs while teaming up with classical Pentecostalism with which it shared an evangelical ideology.[25] Despite the antagonism, Anderson also argues that African neo-Pentecostalism is an upgraded version of AICs answering to the needs and challenges of a modern, youthful, educated base.[26] Interestingly, however, the emerging neo-prophetic movement appears to gravitate towards older AICs by adopting a sacramental and prophetic approach to healing.[27]

In this section, the neo-prophetic movement is discussed in the context of its chronological, religio-cultural and theological place within as well as relation with the rest of pneumatic African Christianity.

2.3.1 Chronological placement

Besides periodisation, arranging historical phenomena chronologically is another important requirement in the study of history. My aim in this sub-section is to arrange the African pneumatic Christian movements chrono-logically to show their lineage and *inherited* family traits. Starting from the present going backwards, neo-prophetism, which has been shown to pos-sess a set of characteristics that sets it apart, is chronologically the most recent. It corresponds to Kgatle's "fourth wave of Pentecostalism".[28] Behind it stands neo-Pentecostal independency, born of the late 1970s and early 1980s revival, which in South Africa, according to Kgatle, experienced growth in the 1990s.[29] Anderson, Larbi, Mathole, Maxwell, and Van Dijk refer to this revival and the churches born from it as evangelical or born-again Pentecostalism – an ideology it shares with classical Pentecostalism.[30] Other labels applied to this specific movement include: New Pentecostal churches, prosperity gospel movement, Pentecostal-Charismatic Churches and African Pentecostal Churches. The progenitor of neo-Pentecostal inde-pendency, contrary to expectation, is not the Pentecostal movement but the Charismatic renewal within the mainline churches and in secondary and tertiary educational institutions – of course with continuing influence of the Pentecostal movement.[31] Predating the Charismatic renewal in main-line churches is the Pentecostal movement born of the revival of the early twentieth-century. The above is the lineage of neo-prophetism. However, the discussion leaves out the early prophetic movement with which neo-prophetism is increasingly becoming aligned.

Writing from the West African context, Larbi provides a chronology of African pneumatic movements in which the prophetic movement of fig-ures like Wade Harris predates the Pentecostals whom he argues came as invitees from the 1930s.[32] Both prophetic churches (better known as Ala-dura in West Africa, Roho churches in East Africa and Zionist churches in Southern Africa) and Pentecostals grew side by side until the emergence of neo-Pentecostalism in the 1980s.[33] According to Mofokeng and Madise, the Southern African chronology of African-led pneumatic AICs starts with the Zionist Pentecostal movement which separated from the Apostolic Faith Mission in 1910.[34]

2.3.2 Religio-cultural orientation

Kgatle and Mofokeng argue that the neo-prophetic movement has adopted an African traditional religio-cultural orientation, something which the Zionist Pentecostals have been long renowned for.[35] Bishop Mashitisho of the Ark of Noah Church is an example of this African traditional ori-entation in Zionism.[36] In his conversation with Molobi, he reported using both herbs and prayer in his healing repertoire.[37] Chimuka, Landman and Molobi refer to other individual Zionist leaders who also function as or are recognised as traditional healers.[38] However, Daneel and Togarasei quell fears that in being traditionally orientated, Zionism has compromised the gospel.[39] They argue that Zionists have adopted African traditional forms as vehicles to communicate the gospel sensibly to Africans, especially those within the traditional milieu.[40] For those interested in the contextualisation of the Christian faith, Zionism has been at the cutting edge. However, there are concerns with the place and role of the ancestral cult and the powers associated with it. Therefore, the claimed neo-prophetic turn towards African traditional culture has come with suspicion and accusations of using traditional spiritual powers in the church.[41]

The transformation of neo-prophetism into a mirror of AICs and traditional healing movements happened in the course of intense confrontation with the spirits inhabiting the African cosmological landscape, according to Degbe.[42] The suspicion resulting from this transformation has received a boost from claims by some traditionalists that they have granted some prophets powers to prophesy and work miracles. Chimuka alludes to one such claim in the context of Zimbabwean neo-prophetism.[43] Another example comes from a Nigerian national, Andrew Ejimadu, who operated as a neo-Pentecostal prophet in Zambia until his deportation in 2017. He believes in the power that predates the introduction of Christianity to sub-Saharan Africa and claims to have given other prophets access to such power.[44] A Ghanaian traditionalist, Nana Kwaku Abonsam, in a YouTube video filmed at a church of one such Pentecostal pastor he had given traditional spiritual powers to, claims to have availed his powers to many pastors across the continent.[45] Similar claims of pastors appropriating traditional sources of spiritual power in South Africa have been made by a *sangoma* in a local daily newspaper, *Daily Sun*, and by self-confessed former "fake prophet", Apostle Makhado Ramabulana.[46] In his book titled *Church Mafia*, Ramabulana claims to have undergone several initiations into the occult through societies and/or individuals in West Africa, Congo, Mozambique and Zimbabwe.[47] He wanted powers that would enable him to prophesy and perform miracles – which he did – in the quest for a large church following and prosperity. He further claims to have had clients who were pastors and traditional healers. The descriptions of operations at Ramabulana's church during his days as a "false prophet" appear comparable to any of several other apostles or prophets seen on many DSTV channels. Thus, religio-culturally, neo-prophetism exhibits a shift away from evangelical born-again ideology and practice in the direction of Zionism and African traditionalism.[48]

2.3.3 Theological orientation

The preceding discussions speak of the theological differentiation of neo-prophetism from its immediate neo-Pentecostal parentage and even more so from classical Pentecostalism. However, the expression that the fruit does not fall far from the tree applies here. The theological gap between classical Pentecostalism and neo-prophetism is easier to discern than between the latter and 1980s neo-Pentecostal churches.[49] In the same way, the theological gap between classical Pentecostalism and the 1980s neo-Pentecostal churches is negligible – save for the difference in eschatological orientation and the ethics arising therefrom. In the traditional authentic Pentecostal message of Jesus Christ, the Saviour, Sanctifier, Baptiser (in the Holy Spirit), Healer and soon coming King, which Kgatle calls the "Pentecostal full gospel", neo-Pentecostalism shifted the eschatological expectation of the kingdom away from imminence to immanence.[50] The shift was enabled by marrying Norman Vincent Peale, E.W. Kenyon and Robert Schuller's positive thinking to Pentecostal thought, which gave birth to hyped confidence in the power of one's word – hence, the "name-it-claim-it gospel".[51] According to Adedibu and Igboin, the eschatological expectation of the imminence of Christ and his kingdom kept each Pentecostal believer's future assessment in full view and made ethical demands on their daily lives – hence, Pentecostal ethical rigorism.[52] The implication of the above is that the shift in eschatological orientation also rendered useless the ethical demands belief in sanctification made on Pentecostals.

The tension that existed between Pentecostal spirituality and popular culture dissolved – allowing the new Pentecostals to habituate themselves to their new-found culture as they sought to master and harness its goods for themselves – thus, the prosperity gospel was born as a version of, and the means to reach the American dream.[53] Its designers, Kenneth Hagin and Kenneth Copeland among others, trained the pioneers of neo-Pentecostalism on the African continent and availed video and written material as further training tools.[54] With the prosperity gospel, neo-Pentecostalism was better acculturated to what Anderson, Mashau and Kgatle as well as Kgatle and Mofokeng refer to as a "consumerist global capitalist culture" than its ascetic denominational counterpart.[55] Despite Mathole's argument that from the 1970s and 1980s, both classical and neo-Pentecostalism drew from the same youthful, urban and educated demographic, leading to moral laxity in both, the former continues to be characterised by a certain degree of conservatism.[56] On the other hand, the materialism of the neo-Pentecostal movement as evident in its adherence to the prosperity gospel, has been inherited and radicalised in neo-prophetism where a sacramental approach has been adopted and the purported means of blessing, healing and deliverance then commercialised.[57] Kgatle describes neo-prophetic clergy as "entrepreneurs who are dissatisfied with the current religious marketplace" and "typically lacking . . . formal theological education".[58]

2.3.4 Socio-economic context

Kgatle and Mofokeng describe the context within which the "bizarre practices" occurred as one of "ascendant neo-liberalism, increasing economic disparity between the haves and the have-nots, corruption, abuse and religious duplicity".[59] From 2005, South Africa began to experience an increase in community protests linked to dissatisfaction with the quality of service delivery and jobless economic growth.[60] The 2008 financial crisis that hit most of the western world affected South Africa to the extent that for the whole of the second decade, the country's economy struggled to meet growth forecasts of three percent. Reports of rampant corruption and looting of the public purse were regularly reported in the media. The story of the emergence of neo-prophetic figures into the public consciousness, which coincided with the news of criminal acts and unorthodox healing practices, belongs to this second decade too. Kgatle links the state of governance and the resulting socio-economic dysfunction with the increasing strength of neo-prophetism as people search for hope.[61] Considering this socio-economic context, many writers have decried the impact of the prosperity gospel on followers of neo-Pentecostal prophets and apostles whom they accuse of defrauding and as a consequence, impoverishing their hapless followers.[62]

In summary, this section discussed neo-prophetism's chronological, religio-cultural, theological and socio-economic place within and relation to the broader pneumatic African Christianity. Although part of African neo-Pentecostal independency, the neo-prophetic movement is the most recent manifestation of the former, radicalised in its application of the prosperity gospel by a sacramental approach which transforms objects of blessing into commercial products. Besides the whole neo-Pentecostal independency being part of the AICs, in its post-apartheid manifestation as neo-prophetism, it is increasingly closing the gap between itself and Zionist churches.

2.4 Pathologies associated with the movement

With the neo-prophetic movement profiled and located within the historical framework of pneumatic African Christianity, the aim of this section is to focus on what Elijah Dube calls Pentecostal "extreme/s", which he fears is becoming the norm due to the pervasiveness of Pentecostalisation.[63] The discussion starts by first categorising these practices and activities and then discussing their implications for the agents and victims respectively.

2.4.1 Three different categories

The neo-prophetic activities and practices that caused such widespread alarm have been recorded in the CRL Rights Commission Report and given scholarly attention by Dube, Khanyile, Kgatle, Resane and others.[64] I don't list these practices but instead divide them in the following three categories, which I then discuss: dangerous healing practices, criminal acts and deceptive acts.

2.4.1.1 Dangerous healing practices

Beki Dube, Elijah Dube, Kgatle, Kgatle and Mofokeng, as well as Khanyile have written about various outrageous acts perpetrated by some prophets in the name of healing and deliverance.[65] The reports of these acts, which Kgatle, Khanyile and Dube label as "bizarre and extreme", have been derived from photographs on the social media pages (Facebook and YouTube) of the pastors or ministries concerned before they were further circulated in print, on radio and television as well as online news portals.[66] Considering the original source, a possible inference is that the pastors, both in their capacity as content creators and publishers, were intentional in wanting to be identified with these practices, which they viewed in a positive light. The South African public has been shocked by the unapologetic attitude of these ministers once news circulated, and the government, traditional church fraternity and the public expressed their outrage with what they considered the abuse of Scripture and people.

2.4.1.2 Criminal acts

Accusations of financial maladministration and outright fraud have been made against several pastors. Some of them have already appeared in court in this regard. Accusations of sexual predatory behaviour have also led to the arrest and prosecution of some, for example Pastor Timothy Omotoso, Bishop Tefo Pitso and Prophet Bazooka (the latter went into hiding after being bailed out).[67] The above acts all fall within the ambit of the law. Hence, some pastors opposed to the desire of the CRL Rights Commission to enact new laws to govern religious practitioners simply argued for the application of relevant laws.

2.4.1.3 Deception

There is suspicion that some pastors use trickery in their healing and prophetic repertoire. These suspicions are not unwarranted as one can see in the YouTube video documentary, *Miracles for sale*, made by the British mentalist Derren Brown, which shows what goes into the making of a believable healing or miracle.[68] Besides this, a one-time child American evangelist, Hugh Marjoe Gortner, who began preaching at the age of four in the late 1940s and continued until the 1970s, made a documentary of his life as a child preacher which went on to win an Oscar in 1973.[69] In this documentary, he exposes himself as a trickster evangelist, and confesses that greed and tricks drove several ministers including his parents. The documentary is a tragic depiction of the trust and sincerity of ordinary believers versus the hypocrisy and treachery of some of their clergy. Another example is that of Apostle Makhado Ramabulana who has been interviewed on South African television, radio and online media. His book, *Church Mafia*, documents his descent into the occult and his later repentance.[70] Besides the claims of occult powers available to him and others who have been initiated into the occult, he reveals the trickery employed to deceive those seeking spiritual solutions to their problems.[71]

2.4.2 The implications

2.4.2.1 Regarding the perpetrators

It is deeply perturbing that ministers of religion can participate in the kind of practices mentioned above. Elijah Dube calls these infamous prophets and apostles "opportunists"[72] – an apt description in that it points to a trait in them that identifies and seizes opportunities presented by the misery of people and the desire they have to better their lives. The sometimes outrageous wealth of some neo-prophetic pastors has attracted the ire of observers who decry the deprivation of many of their followers. When being described as "opportunists" the genuineness of these leaders' experience of the Holy Spirit is implicitly called into question. Similarly, their commitment to Christianity, with all its concomitant ethical requirements, can be called into question. However, a counter argument regarding these pastors ostensibly amassing wealth at the expense of their followers, is that some, as entrepreneurs, have multiple streams of income – an argument put forward by Prophet Shepherd Bushiri in April 2018.[73] Bushiri's argument does not rule out the possibility of some pastors approaching ministry with an entrepreneurial frame of mind in which identifying a niche market, competitively edging out competing role-players, manipulative advertising and so on, come into play.

2.4.2.2 Regarding the victims

How should we view those caught in this web?[74] In the relevant literature, the alleged victims are often described as lacking spiritual discernment and being mostly ignorant of the Bible and the nature of disease, desperate, poor and gullible.[75] They are thus viewed sympathetically as victims. Doing so raises the question of who would advocate on their behalf against those that take advantage of them.

A dissenting view, however, attributes some agency to the alleged victims while not denying the harm being perpetrated against them. Some vehicles in the parking lots of meeting venues of these ministries suggest significant numbers of relatively well-off patrons. Kgatle corroborates this view of patrons of neo-prophetic churches as often better off in his description of the language used in these churches as "that [which] sits well with high-market people and the elite".[76] Some of the alleged victims play a range of roles in society such as being musicians, and active as well as retired church leaders within the Pentecostal, neo-Pentecostal and Zionist circles. These notable people have received honorary doctorates from institutions listed as fake on the South African Qualifications Authority register.[77] For these people, the term "poor" is clearly an unsuitable description. They may have shown ignorance of how treacherous people can be, and are oblivious that they would be used as advertisement for and endorsement of these ministries to ensnare many others.

In summary, the actions and practices that have earned the post-apartheid neo-Pentecostal movement bad press fall into three categories: dangerous practices, criminal acts and deceptive practices. It is outrageous for a religious movement to be plagued with such unethical, unorthodox and even criminal behaviour. The implications of these misdemeanours are sad and complicated. The scandals associated with this movement have indeed opened up a new terrain of activism against "spiritual abuse".

2.5 Possible causes and reasons for the pathologies

The works of Clark, Degbe, Dube, Frahm-Arp, Kgatle and Mofokeng, Khanyile, Resane and Pondani, point to several potential causes of the aberrations that the neo-prophetic movement has become notorious for during the last ten years.[78] In these works, I marked statements with causative attribution and grouped them to come up with the following themes of causative factors in the genesis of African neo-prophetic pathologies: deprivation, deficient theological training, the nature of Pentecostalism and hermeneutic peculiarities, pragmatism, as well as postcolonial socio-economic and political failures as well as Africanisation. Hereafter, I discuss each theme separately and summarise it all at the end of the section.

2.5.1 Deprivation

One of the categories emerging from the data regarding the causes of these scandals within neo-prophetism is deprivation. This category includes spiritual hunger, dissatisfaction, alienation, desperation, ignorance, gullibility and poverty. Although most of these concepts appeared in relation to neo-prophetic abuses, some apply to the beginnings of neo-Pentecostalism in the late 1970s and early 1980s. For example, Khanyile attributes the genesis of neo-Pentecostal independency to spiritual hunger and dissatisfaction among the rank and file of the membership of mainline churches.[79] Added to this, Van Dijk raises up the youth's dissatisfaction with "gerontocracy" within the denominations, including those of classical Pentecostalism and in social relations.[80] The picture often drawn of the beginnings of the new AICs across the African continent has been one of masses of young, educated, urban Africans launching out on their own, armed with confidence in their new-found, born-again faith, preaching in open-air meetings, buses, trains, store-fronts, halls and homes. As they clashed with church leaders over liturgical practices, they established fellowships that would express their deep-seated hunger and desperation for God to bless them – in a context where their religious concepts were influenced by their expectations within a popular globalised urban culture.

From the first generation of the 1970s, which was better educated, Van Dijk notices the decline in the quality of education in the next generation (at least in Malawi).[81] This observation is probably true, also from a ministerial training perspective. The African pioneers of the 1970s received training in America, but many of those who established ministries later were not trained. This had an effect on the quality of Christian formation already compromised by the prosperity gospel. According to Degbe, this second generation leaders chose to orientate themselves more towards African traditional culture while retaining the prosperity message; they were very media savvy and so forth.[82] Instead of emulating American role models, they turned to their traditional environment and were greatly rewarded with masses of followers willing to bring the traditional parent-child kind of reverence to their relationship with their church leaders. The worsening economic conditions and the anxieties this induced in society created a need for saviour figures whose word promised to turn the tide. Mashau and Kgatle's description of believers whose senses have been twisted into thinking that "instructing a cheque book or bank account" can yield prosperity captures the situation well.[83] That which others could well view as gullibility, these believers might have seen as unreserved trust in a spiritual parent who possessed power to turn the situation of their spiritual child and/or client around. The slogan, "I receive Papa", originated within neo-prophetism and reflects this trusting parent-child relationship.[84] Ansah rightly diagnoses ignorance of the Bible and of the nature of disease to be problematic.[85] He observes an inordinate reliance on the word of prophets and their prescriptions, which, in the words of Frahm-Arp, amounts to cultism.[86]

2.5.2 Theological training deficiency

One of the factors contributing to the rise of abuses within neo-prophetism is the uncertain place and quality of theological preparation of would-be ministers. Theological training within this sector seems to be an ambivalent affair in that on one hand, most apostles and prophets wear with pride their unearned honorific titles of "doctor" and "professor" from a chain of unknown and unaccredited, supposedly Christian universities.[87] On the other hand, they show a preference for personal apprenticeship under a senior apostle, prophet or bishop. Unfortunately, this apprenticeship system proves inadequate to prepare would-be ministers to be professional and theologically grounded. Prophet Lesego Daniel's protégés – prophets Penuel Mnguni and Lethebo Rabalago – serve as examples of the faithful reproduction of a questionable minister/father. From the beginning, the broader Pentecostal movement was an anti-intellectual enterprise. In South Africa, the oldest Pentecostal denomination and one of the largest, the Apostolic Faith

Mission, exhibited this tendency in the first half of the twentieth century by ordaining pastors on the basis of proven ministry track record and not (theological) education.[88] Even though this denomination now boasts the largest number of ministers with post-graduate theological qualifications within the Pentecostal fraternity, Nel still asserts the continued existence of anti-intellectualism due to the Pentecostal grounding in the affective domain than the intellectual one.[89] This background somewhat explains the issue of theological training and neo-Pentecostalism.

The neo-Pentecostal revival of the late 1970s has been described as mostly attracting educated, urban youth.[90] According to Pondani, many of these youths were catapulted into ministry without proper theological training.[91] Their ministerial activities within the mainline denominations proved divisive, resulting in the establishment of independent non-denominational fellowships. While Togarasei points out that some of the pioneers of the movement had some ministry training in the United States of America, while Ray McCauley's Rhema Bible Church trained some here in South Africa, the lack of adequate training was and still remains a problem.[92] The irony, especially among the neo-prophetic clergy – which is a narrower stream within neo-Pentecostalism – is the establishment of many church-affiliated Bible and/or ministry training institutes, deemed to be offering inadequate training, yet the same schools have been awarding doctoral degrees and professorships to an increasing number of these clergy.[93] Even musicians like Hlengiwe Mhlaba and Winnie Mashaba have been honoured with doctoral degrees by Immanuel University of Theology International and Trinity International Bible University.[94] There is also a reaching out to the Zionist sector as can be seen in the Interdenominational Theological Centre_RSA's award of honorary doctorates to Archbishop David M. Mureri of United African Apostolic Church, Archbishop TS Ngcana of St Eli Apostolic Mission Church and Bishop P Makhatseane, who is based in Lesotho.[95]

The deficiency in theological training is based on a belief in the adequacy of one's call to the ministry and the enablement the Spirit gives. Contrary to classical Pentecostals, neo-Pentecostals believe in the spiritual "father-son" relationship which is basically a vehicle of mentorship for ministry novices. The same mechanism is used in pneumatic AICs to orientate young ministers to the history, theology and practices of various churches. Many apostles and prophets have several understudies who are not all their converts, but, sometimes may have requested to fall under the "spiritual covering" of the former. Often, social media play a role in mediating the influence of the apostle/prophet on the understudy including attending certain gatherings called by the former.

2.5.3 The nature of Pentecostalism and its hermeneutic peculiarities

Under this theme, I discuss two important characteristics of Pentecostalism which Clark, Kgatle and Mofokeng, Mofokeng and Madise as well as Pondani link to neo-Pentecostal excesses.[96] The first is the adaptable nature of Pentecostal spirituality which, according to Dube, Mofokeng and Madise as well as Pondani, is responsible for this movement assuming traits of whatever cultures it exists in.[97] The second is the belief in the ongoing revelation by the Spirit, which Kgatle and Mofokeng assert that Prophet Lethebo Rabalago, for example, used to explain his dangerous healing activity.[98]

The history of Pentecostalism is a chronicle of crossing boundaries and reconfiguring cultures as it also gets reconfigured. Born in the context of the American Holiness movement, Pentecostalism exhibited the Holiness reserve and generally remained a working class movement.[99] In the post-World War II era, Pentecostalism first adjusted itself towards the middle class and then by the 1970s further adjusted itself towards a globalist, consumerist culture.[100] A similar trajectory is discernible in African Pentecostalism with Zionist/prophetic AICs being a Pentecostal adaptation to African traditional culture on one side and missionary Pentecostalism being an accommodation of more hybridised African-Western conservative culture on the other.[101] The African prosperity gospel movement came as a Pentecostal adjustment to the postcolonial environment taking advantage of the sense of economic hope and freedom from colonial missionary shackles.[102] In the same way, there are observations that suggest that neo-prophetism may be an adjustment to the resurgent African traditional cosmology and the sense of powerlessness felt by many on the continent.[103]

Besides its adaptability, Pentecostalism has certain hermeneutic peculiarities that make it easier for the kind of abuses noted within neo-prophetism to arise. One such peculiarity is reader-centred inductive hermeneutics.[104] With the history of European socio-political, religio-cultural and economic dominance of African societies in mind, Cezula considers reader-centred hermeneutics African as they highlight the context of the African reader. Therefore, it is not surprising that Pentecostalism addresses the life situations of its adherents.[105] Reader-centredness has always gone together with the assumption of the Bible as a canonical document, which is approached in a literalist fashion.[106] For Dube, the literalist approach to the Bible, which Niemandt confirms, still exists within neo-Pentecostalism and leads to a faith that re-enacts certain Scriptural phenomena.[107] All these form the background to understanding Penuel Mnguni, Lethebo Rabalago and Lesego Daniel in their insistence that the word spoken by a prophet creates a new reality. Hence, Mnguni insisted before the CRL Rights Commission that he never fed anyone snakes; that notwithstanding the snake in the photos, his followers ate chocolate. Resane's view is that the above prophets and others engage in self-serving and cultic hermeneutics that benefit themselves at the expense of their audiences.[108] These people are able to parade themselves as exemplars of the efficacy of their doctrine – which may work to convince some followers to continue exerting themselves whilst hoping for their "breakthrough". This is what concerns the CRL Rights Commission about some clergy: that they live extraordinary lives financed by people desperate for a better life.

Musa Dube, Gabaitse, Garrard, Kgatle and Mofokeng as well as Nel decry the negative impact literalist hermeneutics have had on the Pentecostal movement.[109] From its beginning at the beginning of the twentieth century, Pentecostals have considered themselves participants in the restoration of apostolic Christianity with attendant manifestations. Their interest in the narrative sections of the New Testament arose because of the descriptions of the healings and miracles recounted there. This interest was born out of a cultural self-understanding and self-embrace as Pentecostalism draws from the orality of African (American) religio-cultural experience and supernaturalist orientation. But, as Garrard indicates, the marriage of a literalist reading of the Bible and the supernatural orientation concerned the missionaries and authorities of colonial Africa who feared "extravagance" and political instability[110] – the latter due to the popularity of Pentecostalism. Classical Pentecostalism in South Africa produced early in its history a refusal to use medicine regardless of whether it was western or African traditional. In West Africa, according to Kalu, serious conflict and a separation arose when the locals discovered that missionaries were using anti-malaria medication, because the former held a strong belief in the efficacy of prayer.[111] In recent times neo-prophetism confers efficacy on any object the prophets declare to be effective to bring desired results.

2.5.4 Pragmatism

One other category of causes of neo-prophetic pathologies is pragmatism, which denotes an attitude or approach to life that opts for what works and is attainable in a situation instead of the ideal that, although right and desirable, may be unattainable or seen as impractical. In this context the term comes from Clark's description of the Pentecostalism that has been influenced by the Faith Movement of Kenneth Hagin.[112] The descriptors that constitute pragmatism as a category are: a preoccupation with church growth or numbers; an ardent desire to appear successful; a desire to stand out from the rest and to attract fame; celebrity worship; confrontation with African primal religio-spiritual realities; an openness to African traditional practices in healing and an innovative use of modern media technologies.[113]

The emergence of neo-Pentecostalism in Africa in the late 1970s took place simultaneously with the proclamation of the gospel of prosperity. Elijah Dube, looking at the relationship of the two, concludes that it is difficult to separate one from the other.[114] The prosperity gospel represented a radical departure from the ascetic classical Pentecostals as the adherents of this gospel embraced the possibilities of growing wealth and in fact considered it a designated blessing from God. Those who argue that African neo-Pentecostalism received its prosperity gospel influence from the USA, invoke its rootedness in post-World War II economic boom, the social elevation of Pentecostals and increasing political clout of the born-again movement associated with the Ronald Reagan presidency.[115] Indeed, American neo-Pentecostal personalities visited the continent, trained some of the first African neo-Pentecostals, and availed their written, audio and video materials.

The predilection of the prosperity gospel for material blessing in the form of wealth and good health helped orient its adherents to expectations of exhibiting their success in securing the blessing.[116] In the forefront of this exhibitionism stood the clergy whose blessedness was derived from having a large following, which, in most cases, invariably translated into increased offerings with positive implications for the ministers' financial status. According to Clark, Kgatle and Mofokeng, most neo-Pentecostal congregations have adopted a business-like concern for ever-increasing numbers of patrons and income.[117] Hence, Degbe describes them as "preoccupied with church growth or numbers" because they have "an ardent desire to appear successful".[118] For Pondani, there is a desire to stand out from the rest and "to attract fame" and Resane concurs by describing today's culture as caught up in "celebrity worship" which the clergy seem unable to extricate themselves from.[119] The neo-Pentecostal apostle/prophet appears to be a brand intentionally created for maximum outreach. In this sense, the phenomenon of social media influencers also finds expression in these circles. It comes as no surprise that neo-prophetism, which is the heir of neo-Pentecostalism, excels in the use of social media, community radio and TV stations to saturate society with its version of the faith.[120] In the words of Mashau and Kgatle, neo-prophetism appears as an unstoppable force that pays no attention to anyone's concerns about the destruction it brings to those unfortunate to be its victims.[121] In this regard Dube laments the absence of engagement by theological staff and students.[122]

2.5.5 Postcolonial socio-economic and political failures

With Pentecostalism being a contextually responsive movement, Dube, Khanyile, Frahm-Arp and Ramantswana point at the insecurity and instability of the socio-economic and political environment as an important contributor to the neo-Pentecostal pathologies already mentioned.[123] Khanyile blames the failed promise of "a better life for all" the African National Congress made since assuming power in 1994.[124] Dube concurs and blames this failed socio-economic and political environment for exposing many to a crisis and religious charlatans.[125] Khanyile considers poverty-stricken places as particularly prone to "bizarre forms of spirituality and religious practices" and Africa is littered with such places.[126] This is the context in which she places Penuel Mnguni, dubbed "the snake Pastor", whose ministry, the Endtime Disciples Ministries, she considers "typical of neo-Pentecostalism".[127]

However, postcolonial states' socio-economic and political failures alone do not sufficiently explain the rise of notorious neo-Pentecostal charlatans. It merely points at the pervasive sense of despair that engulfs the populace in such environments. Elijah Dube's designation of these infamous prophets and apostles as "opportunists" is apt in that it points to a trait in them that identifies and seizes opportunities presenting in socio-economically dysfunctional situations.[128]

2.5.6 Africanisation

The concept "Africanisation" belongs together with other concepts such as "enculturation", "contextualisation" and recently, "decolonisation". All these concepts share to a varying degree the necessity of not only engaging people's situation, but also allowing people and their situation to shape the ideas, actions and structures of institutions that originate outside Africa. The call to decolonise ironically takes place in a postcolonial Africa as an indictment of the failure of postcolonial regimes to deliver on the fundamental expectations of the African people. Contextualisation was associated with political theologies such as Black Theology and later the Theology of Reconstruction. Bosch attempted to infuse into the concept a cultural meaning with the argument that "culture is an all-embracing reality" in which "social, economic, political, religious, educational" and other factors play a role.[129]

The issue of Africanisation comes up in Khanyile's analysis of comments on Penuel Mnguni's social media page regarding Mnguni's powers, and also in Kgatle and Mofokeng.[130] One comment Khanyile mentions is particularly interesting as its author seems to marvel at the incredulity of Africans towards ancestral powers and healing in a traditional setup yet fall for the same powers in church.[131] This specific commentator accused Mnguni and pastors like him of misappropriating traditional powers and attributing them to God. The positionality of this commentator is that of a traditionalist as he claims to have seen what Mnguni considered a miracle done by "native healers". His use of "we as Africans", "our ancestors and native healers" puts him outside the ambit of most Pentecostals, both classical and neo-Pentecostal, who reject ancestors and anything to do with them.[132]

While the commentator in Khanyile seems to come from a traditionalist angle, his sentiments are similar to Prophet Dr BS Xaba who invokes the God of African kings and ancestors in his healing ministry while mocking reliance on the use of Jesus' name.[133] Although their ministry setup may be easily mistaken for a (neo-) Pentecostal one, both Xaba and Prophet Dr Samuel Radebe seem to focus more on revitalising African traditional religion. Interestingly, Radebe's influence among the pneumatic AICs may be growing considering his hosting of the Appreciation Ceremony for African prophets such as lady prophets Christinah Nku, Alice Lenshina of the Zambian Lumpa Church, Mantsopa Makhetha and the little known prophetess Nontetha Nkwenkwe.[134] In Xaba's services, some patrons can be seen wearing blue and white Zion-Apostolic uniforms while others the reddish Nguni cloth generally associated with traditional healing practitioners.[135] He uses oil and water in his healing repertoire.[136] According to Matsepe, Zionists in Botswana have begun to use divining objects and Chimuka records an allegation by one traditional healing practitioner to have given traditional powers to some ministers.[137] Ramabulana also claimed to have had pastors and traditional healing practitioners as beneficiaries of his occult powers while serving as neo-Pentecostal prophets and apostles.[138]

The above discussion points to several important considerations:

(1) The claimed entanglement of some neo-Apostolic prophets and apostles in traditional African spirituality.
(2) The apparent need for these neo-prophetic leaders to disentangle themselves from traditional African spirituality by (re)adopting a decidely biblical and evangelical posture. The claims of Christian prophets receiving occultic powers damage the cause of Christ.
(3) The Africanisation of Christianity may be better achieved through the adoption of the ubuntu ethic, which Mashau and Kgatle argue has potential to correct the damage resulting from commercialisation of the gospel in neo-prophetism.[139]

The intention is not to elaborate on the above points, save to say that the adaptable nature of Pentecostalism has assured its adaptation to different religio-cultural, socio-economic and political contexts. The postcolonial era coincided with a new, consumerist globalised culture which also affected the church. This era began with optimism, which, unfortunately, was later shattered by the corruption in and general failure of the postcolonial states. The sense of hope for a better life also characterised South Africa's post-apartheid era. However, the promise began to ring hollow to the populace a decade into the new era, leading to a rise in community protests. The most Pentecostal response to change is to adapt. The increasingly dysfunctional socio-economic conditions exacerbated the increase in extreme healing practices and general religious conmanship. The increasing reliance on African and Pentecostal mysticism while ignoring the kind of hermeneutics that promote spiritual formation and human dignity has unfortunately not helped.

2.6 Conclusion

In this chapter we approached neo-prophetism through the historical prism of "causes and consequences", according to which the controversial beliefs and practices are assumed to be consequences of something. Thus, the question here is: what are the causes of and reasons for these controversial beliefs and practices? The movement within which these unethical, unorthodox and even downright criminal activities occurred, involving several leading figures, was profiled by discussing periodisation, characteristics, personalities involved and conceptual clarification. Such profiling can bring about clearer delineation of the movement. Furthermore, the movement's place within and relation with the broader pneumatic African Christianity was discussed chronologically, religio-culturally, theologically and socio-economically – further contributing to the movement's delineation. The unethical, unorthodox and criminal activities, which in this chapter are dubbed neo-Pentecostal pathologies, were revisited and categorised into dangerous healing practices, criminal acts and deceptive acts – leading to a brief discussion of implications regarding the perpetrators and victims of such acts and practices. Further analysis of the works of several scholars who have written on the topic of these bizarre practices, suggested the following possible causes thereof: deprivation; theological training deficiencies; the specific nature of Pentecostalism and its hermeneutic peculiarities; pragmatism, postcolonial socio-economic failure and Africanisation.

It is important to have clear contours of neo-prophetism as an emerging subculture within the broader neo-Pentecostal movement as that may better focus further research. This subculture interacts differently with what classical and neo-Pentecostalism may have bequeathed to it. As a prophetic movement, its propensity towards Old Testament prophetism and sacramental practice increasingly and radically interpreted from within an African traditionalist cosmology is its most outstanding feature. Neither classical nor neo-Pentecostalism attempted to move into this territory despite the adulation they would have received if they had done so and thus responded to African predilections. That a religious movement can be so plagued with unethical, unorthodox and even criminal behaviour may be unprecedented and does call for increased activism against "spiritual abuse" to stem an increase in extreme healing practices and general religious conmanship.

On the other hand, recognition that the probable causes that were discussed are more than personal, but that they highlight fractures within the socio-economic and religio-cultural environment, may yet arouse the whole Christian church transforming action.

Notes

1 Elijah Dube, "Desperation in an Attempt to Curb Modern-Day Prophets: Pentecostalisation and the Church in South Africa and Zimbabwe," *Conspectus: The Journal of the South African Theological Seminary* 27, no. 1 (May 23, 2019): 29.
2 Sphesihle Khanyile, "The Virtualization of the Church: New Media Representations of Neo-Pentecostal Performance(s) in South Africa" (MA -., University of Witwatersrand, Johannesburg, 2016); Mookgo Kgatle, "The Unusual Practices Within Some Neo-Pentecostal Churches in South Africa: Reflections and Recommendations," *HTS Teologiese Studies / Theological Studies* 73, no. 3 (February 8, 2017); Kelebogile Resane, "'And They Shall Make You Eat Grass like Oxen' (Daniel 4:24): Reflections on Recent Practices in Some New Charismatic Churches," *Pharos Journal of Theology* 98 (2017).
3 Khanyile, "Virtualization," 115; Kgatle, "The Unusual Practices," 4; Mookgo Kgatle and Thabang Mofokeng, "Towards a Decolonial Hermeneutic of Experience in African Pentecostal Christianity: A South African Perspective," *HTS*

Teologiese Studies / Theological Studies 75, no. 4 (2019): 5; Thinandavha Mashau and Mookgo Kgatle, "Prosperity Gospel and the Culture of Greed in Post-Colonial Africa: Constructing an Alternative African Christian Theology of Ubuntu," *Verbum et Ecclesia* 40, no. 1 (2019): 3–4.

4 CRL Rights Commission, "Report of the Hearings of Commercialisation of Religion and Abuse of People's Belief Systems," 2017: 11–12; Xaluva Mkhwanazi, "Money First, God Next: Commercialisation of Religion Report," Facebook, Department of Christian Spirituality, Church History and Missiology, UNISA, August 27, 2018.

5 Nikki Mandell and Bobbie Malone, *Thinking Like a Historian: Rethinking Historical Instruction* (Madison, WI: Wisconsin Historical Society Press, 2007).

6 Gangatharan, "The Problem of Periodization in History," *Proceedings of the Indian History Congress* 69 (2008): 862.

7 Roland O. Ansah, "The Usage of Anointing Oil in in Some Charismatic and Neo-Pentecostal Churches in Kumasi in the Context of Leviticus 8:1–12, and James 5:14–15" (MPhil dissertation, Kwame Nkrumah University of Science and Technology, Kumasi, 2011), 3–6, 42; Kgatle and Mofokeng, "Decolonial Hermeneutic," 6; Hulisani Ramantswana, "Prophets Praying for, or Preying on People's Faith: A Reflection on Prophetic Ministry in the South African Context," *Die Skriflig/In Luce Verbi* 53, no. 4 (November 18, 2019): 6.

8 Ansah, "Anointing Oil," 17.

9 Community television stations where African neo-prophetic preachers broadcast their programmes include Bay TV, Dumisa TV, GAU TV, KZN1 TV, One Gospel, Soweto TV and Tshwane TV. There are also private channels like Prophet Shepherd Bushiri's prophetic channel. See: Mookgo Kgatle, *The Fourth Pentecostal Wave in South Africa: A Critical Engagement* (Abingdon: Routledge, 2019), 66.

10 Kgatle, *The Fourth Pentecostal Wave*, 67–71.

11 Ibid., 34.

12 Ibid.

13 Resane, "Eat Grass," 3.

14 Dube, "Desperation," 2, 5–6; Kgatle, "The Unusual Practices," 3.

15 Khanyile, "Virtualization," 22.

16 Ibid., 26–27; Thandi Ndabeni, "Rape, Sex Assault Claims Pile Up Against Klerksdorp Pastor," *SowetanLive*, February 20, 2018.

17 Allana Anderson, "The Newer Pentecostal and Charismatic Churches: The Shape of Future Christianity in Africa?" *Pneuma* 24, no. 2 (September 1, 2002): 170.

18 Ibid., 167; Ezekiel Mathole, "The Christian Witness in the Context of Poverty: With Special Reference to South African Charismatic Evangelicals" (Doctoral thesis, University of Pretoria, Pretoria, 2005), 184; Lovemore Togarasei, "Modern Pentecostalism as an Urban Phenomenon: The Case of the Family of God Church in Zimbabwe," *Exchange* 34, no. 4 (2005): 111.

19 Kgatle, *The Fourth Pentecostal Wave*, 12.

20 Ansah, "Anointing Oil"; Bekithemba Dube, "'Go and Prophesy in Your Own Land': Foreign Prophets and Popularism in South Africa. Evoking the Need of Jonathanic Theology for Peaceful Resolution of Difference," *Religions* 11, no. 1 (January 2020): 3; C. N. Omenyo, "African Pentecostalism," in *The Cambridge Companion to Pentecostalism*, ed. C. M. (Jr) Robeck and A. Yong (New York: Cambridge University Press, 2014), 134, 132–51; Ramantswana, "Prophetic Ministry," 4.

21 Kgatle, *The Fourth Pentecostal Wave*, 34.

22 Ansah, "Anointing Oil," 4.

23 Kgatle, "The Unusual Practices," 2.
24 Anderson, "Newer Pentecostal," 167.
25 Allan Anderson, "New African Initiated Pentecostalism and Charismatics in South Africa," *Journal of Religion in Africa* 35, no. 1 (2005): 69.
26 Anderson, "Newer Pentecostal," 170.
27 Kgatle and Mofokeng, "Decolonial Hermeneutic," 5.
28 Kgatle, *The Fourth Pentecostal Wave*, 12, 30.
29 Ibid., 11.
30 Anderson, "African Initiated," 69; Kingsely Larbi, "African Pentecostalism in the Context of Global Pentecostal Ecumenical Fraternity: Challenges and Opportunities," *Pneuma* 24, no. 2 (September 1, 2002): 147–48; Mathole, "Christian Witness," 196–97; David Maxwell, *African Gifts of the Spirit: Pentecostalism & the Rise of a Zimbabwean Transnational Religious Movement* (Oxford: James Curry, 2006), 10; Rijk Van Dijk *Christian Fundamentalism in Sub-Saharan Africa: The Case of Pentecostalism* (Leiden, The Netherlands: Africa Studies Centre, 2000), 12.
31 Ogbu Kalu, *African Pentecostalism: An Introduction* (Oxford: Oxford University Press, 2008), 64; Kgatle, *The Fourth Pentecostal Wave*, 10.
32 Kalu, *African Pentecostalism*, 41; Larbi, "African Pentecostalism," 141.
33 Kalu, *African Pentecostalism*, 66, 69.
34 Ibid., 55–56; Kgatle, *The Fourth Pentecostal Wave*, 29; Thabang Mofokeng and Mokhele Madise, "The Evangelicalisation of Black Pentecostalism in the AFM of SA (1940–1975): A Turning Point," *Studia Historiae Ecclesiasticae* 45, no. 1 (March 13, 2019): 12.
35 Kgatle and Mofokeng, "Decolonial Hermeneutic," 7.
36 Victor Molobi, "Vanguard of African Culture: An Analysis of the Oral History of Selected AICs in Tshwane (Pretoria)," *Studia Historiae Ecclesiasticae* 35, no. 1 (2009): 3.
37 Ibid.
38 Tarisayi Andrea Chimuka, "Afro-Pentecostalism and Contested Holiness in Southern Africa," *Studia Historiae Ecclesiasticae* 42, no. 1 (September 28, 2016): 128; Christina Landman, "Faces of Religious Healing in Nkhoma, Malawi: An Exercise in Oral History," *Studia Historiae Ecclesiasticae* 44, no. 3 (2018): 7; Victor Molobi, "Power Struggles, Poverty and Breakaways in the African Independent Churches in South Africa," *Studia Historiae Ecclesiasticae* 37, no. 2 (2011): 10–11.
39 Marthinus Daneel, *Zionism and Faith-Healing in Rhodesia: Aspects of African Independent Churches* (The Hague: Mouton, 1970), 44; Lovemore Togarasei, "Cursed Be the Past! Tradition and Modernity Among (Modern) Pentecostal(s) Charismatics," *Boleswa Occasional Papers in Theology and Religion* 2006, no. 1 (January 1, 2006): 372.
40 Ibid.
41 Simon Degbe, "'Generational Curses' and the 'Four Horns': Illustrating the Shape of the Primal Worldview in Contemporary African Pentecostal-Charismatic Spirituality," *Journal of Pentecostal Theology* 23, no. 2 (2014): 264.
42 Ibid; Ramantswana, "Prophetic Ministry," 6.
43 Chimuka, "Contested Holiness," 130.
44 "Seer 1 Exposed?" YouTube, accessed April 28, 2020, https://youtu.be/K_idrzB-Q6Q.
45 "Nana Kwaku Bonsam Reclaims God from Church," YouTube, accessed April 28, 2020, https://youtu.be/aj1-yFzUhbM.
46 Mgidi, Emily, "Gobela: I Give Pastors Powers!" *DailySun*, December 19, 2019.

47 Makhado Ramabulana, *Church Mafia – Captured by Secret Powers: An Untold African Narrative*, 1st ed. (Pretoria: Makhado Freedom Ramabulana, 2018); Ramantswana, "Prophetic Ministry," 6.
48 See Kgatle, "The Unusual Practices," 3; Khanyile, "Virtualization," 22–23, 102.
49 Khanyile, "Virtualization," 22; Kgatle, *The Fourth Pentecostal Wave*, 30.
50 Kgatle, "The Unusual Practices," 2; The idea of immanence mentioned in the context of a discussion on eschatological expectation carries the meaning that the kingdom has arrived and only awaits realisation.
51 Khanyile, "Virtualization," 44; Mashau and Kgatle, "Culture of Greed," 2.
52 Adedibu, Babatunde A., and Benson O. Igboin, "Eschato-Praxis and Accountability: A Study of Neo-African Pentecostal Movement in the Light of Prosperity Gospel," *Verbum et Ecclesia* 40, no. 1 (January 2019): 3.
53 Nelus Niemandt, "The Prosperity Gospel, the Decolonisation of Theology, and the Abduction of Missionary Imagination," *Missionalia* 45, no. 3 (2017): 205.
54 Mashau and Kgatle, "Culture of Greed," 2.
55 Anderson, "Newer Pentecostal," 170; Kgatle and Mofokeng, "Decolonial Hermeneutic," 3; Mashau and Kgatle, "Culture of Greed," 2.
56 Mathole, "Christian Witness," 189.
57 Kgatle and Mofokeng, "Decolonial Hermeneutic," 5.
58 Kgatle, *The Fourth Pentecostal Wave*, 31.
59 Ibid., 7.
60 Lucius Botes, "South Africa's Landscape of Social Protests: A Way Forward for Developmental Local Government?" *Africa Journal of Public Affairs* 10, no. 4 (2018): 243.
61 Kgatle, *The Fourth Pentecostal Wave*, 26.
62 Mashau and Kgatle, "Culture of Greed," 1; Dube, "Desperation," 28.
63 Dube, "Desperation," 26.
64 CRL Rights Commission, "Commercialisation of Religion," 31–33; Dube, "Desperation"; Kgatle, "The Unusual Practices"; Khanyile, "Virtualization"; Resane, "Eat Grass."
65 Dube, "Go and Prophesy," 2; Dube, "Desperation," 29; Kgatle, "The Unusual Practices," 3–5; Khanyile, "Virtualization," 25–26.
66 Dube, "Desperation," 26; Kgatle, "The Unusual Practices," 1; Khanyile, "Virtualization," 22.
67 Vicky Abraham, "Bailed Ghanaian Pastor on the Run After Alleged Rape of 15-Year-Old," *City Press*, November 20, 2018; Ndabeni, "Rape, Sex Assault Claims Pile Up Against Klerksdorp Pastor"; Ramantswana, "Prophetic Ministry," 6.
68 Derren Brown, "Miracles for Sale," *Sceptica TV*, 2011.
69 Smith and Kernochan, "Marjoe," (DVD. Docudrama, 1972); "Documentary Winners: 1973 Oscars," YouTube, 2014.
70 Ramabulana, *Church Mafia*.
71 See: Ramantswana, "Prophetic Ministry," 6.
72 Dube, "Desperation," 27.
73 *Prophet Shepherd Bushiri Answers on Alleged Money Laundering Claims 1* (Auckland Park: SABC News, 2018).
74 The focus is on the dangerous healing activities including the activities designed to facilitate financial transactions between neo-prophetic clergy and their followers.
75 Ansah, "Anointing Oil," 137; Mashau and Kgatle, "Culture of Greed," 2.
76 Kgatle, *The Fourth Pentecostal Wave*, 29.
77 Department of Higher Education and Training, "Register of Private Higher Education Institutions: Last Update 17 March 2020."

78 Mathew Clark, *Pentecostals Doing Church: An Eclectic and Global Approach* (Newcastle: Cambridge Scholars Publishing, 2019); Degbe, "Generational Curses"; Maria Frahm-Arp, "Why at the Start of the Fourth Industrial Revolution Do We See a Rise in Cult-Type Pentecostal Churches in South Africa?" *The Thinker: A Pan-African Quarterly for Thought Leaders* 82 (2019); Kgatle and Mofokeng, "Decolonial Hermeneutic"; Khanyile, "Virtualization"; Resane, "Eat Grass"; Simbarashe Pondani, "'Prophets of Doom': The Phenomenon of Healing and Power Dynamics in Neo-Pentecostal African Churches" (MTh dissertation, University of Stellenbosch, Stellenbosch, 2019).

79 Khanyile, "Virtualization," 14.

80 Van Dijk, *Fundamentalism*, 13, 17.

81 Ibid., 13.

82 Degbe, "Generational Curses," 264.

83 Mashau and Kgatle, "Culture of Greed," 1.

84 Kgatle, *The Fourth Pentecostal Wave*, 44; Ramantswana, "Prophetic Ministry," 7.

85 Ansah, "Anointing Oil," 137.

86 Ansah, "Anointing Oil," 141; Frahm-Arp, "Fourth Industrial Revolution," 5, 8; Resane, "Eat Grass," 3.

87 Resane, "Eat Grass," 3.

88 Marius Nel, "Rather Spirit-Filled than Learned! Pentecostalism's Tradition of Anti-Intellectualism and Pentecostal Theological Scholarship," *Verbum et Ecclesia* 37, no. 1 (2016): 2.

89 Ibid., 4.

90 Anderson, "Newer Pentecostal," 171; Kgatle and Mofokeng, "Decolonial Hermeneutic," 6; Khanyile, "Virtualization," 15–16; Togarasei, "Cursed Be the Past!" 111; Van Dijk, *Fundamentalism*, 11, 13; Omenyo, "African Pentecostalism," 138.

91 Pondani, "Prophets of Doom," 31.

92 Togarasei, "Cursed Be the Past!" 111.

93 Kgatle, *The Fourth Pentecostal Wave*, 110; Kelebogile Resane, "Commercialisation of Theological Education as a Challenge in the Neo-Pentecostal Charismatic Churches," *HTS Teologiese Studies / Theological Studies* 73, no. 3 (September 29, 2017): 3.

94 Phakamani Mvelashe, "This Is Why Winnie Mashaba Believes She Received Her Honorary Doctorate," *Channel24*, December 2, 2019; Phakamani Mvelashe, "Hlengiwe Mhlaba Awarded an Honorary Doctorate," *Channel24*, February 19, 2020.

95 The Interdenominational Theological Centre-RSA. Facebook, August 2, 2013, https://web.facebook.com/itcrsa/posts/520991824656984; The Interdenominational Theological Centre-RSA. Facebook, October 10, 2014, https://web.facebook.com/itcrsa/posts/718921338197364; The Interdenominational Theological Centre-RSA. Facebook, March 16, 2018, https://web.facebook.com/itcrsa/posts/1696971553725666.

96 Clark, *Pentecostals Doing Church*; Kgatle and Mofokeng, "Decolonial Hermeneutic"; Mofokeng and Madise, "Evangelicalisation"; Pondani, "Prophets of Doom."

97 Dube, "Desperation," 27; Mofokeng and Madise, "Evangelicalisation," 7; Pondani, "Prophets of Doom," 37.

98 Kgatle and Mofokeng, "Decolonial Hermeneutic," 1.

99 Roger G. Robins, *Pentecostalism in America* (Santa Barbara, CA: Praeger, 2010), 10–11.

100 Kgatle and Mofokeng, "Decolonial Hermeneutic," 6.
101 Ibid., 5; Mofokeng and Madise, "Evangelicalisation," 7, 10–11.
102 Niemandt, "Prosperity Gospel," 207.
103 Degbe, "Generational Curses," 264–65.
104 Ntozakhe Cezula, "Reading the Bible in the African Context: Assessing Africa's Love Affair with Prosperity Gospel," *Stellenbosch Theological Journal* 1, no. 2 (2015): 133; Clark, *Pentecostals Doing Church*, 45.
105 Kgatle, *The Fourth Pentecostal Wave*, 29–30.
106 Kgatle and Mofokeng, "Decolonial Hermeneutic," 3, 6–7.
107 Dube, "Desperation," 28; Niemandt, "Prosperity Gospel," 206.
108 Resane, "Eat Grass," 3.
109 Musa Dube, "Between the Spirit and the Word: Reading the Gendered African Pentecostal Bible," *HTS Teologiese Studies / Theological Studies* 70, no. 1 (November 20, 2014): 2; R. M. Gabaitse, "Pentecostal Hermeneutics and the Marginalisation of Women," *Scriptura* 114 (May 2015): 1–2; David Garrard, "African Pentecostalism," *African Pentecostalism: Journal of Beliefs & Values* 30, no. 3 (December 2009): 233; Marius Nel, "Pentecostal Hermeneutical Considerations About Women in Ministry," *Studia Historiae Ecclesiasticae* 43, no. 1 (August 17, 2017): 125.
110 Garrard, "African Pentecostalism," 233.
111 Kalu, *African Pentecostalism*, 42.
112 Clark, *Pentecostals Doing Church*, 16.
113 Degbe, "Generational Curses," 251–52; Pondani, "Prophets of Doom," 31, 37; Resane, "Eat Grass', 3.
114 Dube, "Desperation," 127.
115 Robins, *Pentecostalism in America*, 115.
116 Kgatle and Mofokeng, "Decolonial Hermeneutic," 6.
117 Clark, *Pentecostals Doing Church*, 16; Kgatle and Mofokeng, "Decolonial Hermeneutic," 3.
118 Degbe, "Generational Curses," 251.
119 Pondani, "Prophets of Doom," 37; Resane, "Eat Grass', 3.
120 Kgatle, *The Fourth Pentecostal Wave*, 66–71.
121 Mashau and Kgatle, "Culture of Greed," 1.
122 Dube, "Desperation," 29.
123 Dube, "Desperation," 27; Khanyile, "Virtualization," 16; Frahm-Arp, "Fourth Industrial Revolution," 5; Ramantswana, "Prophetic Ministry," 5.
124 Khanyile, "Virtualization," 95.
125 Dube, "Desperation," 27.
126 Khanyile, "Virtualization," 16.
127 Ibid., 17.
128 Dube, "Desperation," 27.
129 David Bosch, *Transforming Mission: Paradigm Shifts in Theology of Mission* (Maryknoll, NY: Orbis Books, 1991), 458, 464.
130 Khanyile, "Virtualization," 101; Kgatle and Mofokeng, "Decolonial Hermeneutic," 5.
131 Khanyile, "Virtualization," 101.
132 Garrard, "African Pentecostalism," 234.
133 "Prophet Dr Xaba," *Bay TV*, April 20, 2020.
134 *2nd Annual Commemoration of Ancient African Prophets* (The Dome, Johannesburg: African Hidden Voices, 2018).
135 "Prophet Dr Xaba."
136 Ibid.
137 Chimuka, "Contested Holiness," 130; Shale Matsepe and Mokhele Madise, "A New Phenomenon in Zionist Churches of Botswana? The Use of

Divination Bones and Sacred Places," 2005, 8, http://uir.unisa.ac.za/handle/10500/4356.

138 Ramabulana, *Church Mafia*.

139 Mashau and Kgatle, "Culture of Greed," 1.

References

2nd Annual Commemoration of Ancient African Prophets. The Dome, Johannesburg: African Hidden Voices, 2018. www.youtube.com/watch?v=5kibydwhRok.

Abraham, Vicky. "Bailed Ghanaian Pastor on the Run After Alleged Rape of 15-Year-Old." *City Press*, November 20, 2018. www.news24.com/citypress/news/bailed-ghanaian-pastor-on-the-run-after-alleged-rape-of-a-15-year-old-20181117.

Adedibu, Babatunde A., and Benson O. Igboin. "Eschato-Praxis and Accountability: A Study of Neo-African Pentecostal Movement in the Light of Prosperity Gospel." *Verbum et Ecclesia* 40, no. 1 (January 2019): 1–8. https://doi.org/10.4102/ve.v40i1.1987.

Anderson, Allan H. "The Newer Pentecostal and Charismatic Churches: The Shape of Future Christianity in Africa?" *Pneuma* 24, no. 2 (September 1, 2002): 167–84. https://doi.org/10.1163/15700740260388027.

———. "New African Initiated Pentecostalism and Charismatics in South Africa." *Journal of Religion in Africa* 35, no. 1 (2005): 66–92.

Ansah, Roland O. "The Usage of Anointing Oil in in Some Charismatic and Neo-Pentecostal Churches in Kumasi in the Context of Leviticus 8:1–12, and James 5:14–15." MPhil dissertation, Kwame Nkrumah University of Science and Technology, 2011. http://ir.knust.edu.gh/bitstream/123456789/3969/1/Final.pdf.

Bosch, David J. *Transforming Mission: Paradigm Shifts in Theology of Mission*. Maryknoll, NY: Orbis Books, 1991.

Botes, Lucius "South Africa's Landscape of Social Protests: A Way Forward for Developmental Local Government?" *Africa Journal of Public Affairs* 10, no. 4 (2018): 241–56.

Brown, Derren. "Miracles for Sale." *Sceptica TV*, 2011. www.youtube.com/watch?v=iuP5uOI7Xwc.

Chimuka, Tarisayi A. "Afro-Pentecostalism and Contested Holiness in Southern Africa." *Studia Historiae Ecclesiasticae* 42, no. 1 (September 28, 2016): 124–41.

Clark, Mathew. *Pentecostals Doing Church: An Eclectic and Global Approach*. Newcastle: Cambridge Scholars Publishing, 2019.

CRL Rights Commission. "Report of the Hearings of the Commercialisation of Religion and Abuse of People's Belief Systems." 2017. www.crlcommission.org.za/docs/Final%20redesigned%20for%20office%20print.pdf.

Daneel, Marthinus L. *Zionism and Faith-Healing in Rhodesia: Aspects of African Independent Churches*. The Hague: Mouton, 1970.

Degbe, Simon K. " 'Generational Curses' and the 'Four Horns': Illustrating the Shape of the Primal Worldview in Contemporary African Pentecostal-Charismatic Spirituality." *Journal of Pentecostal Theology* 23, no. 2 (October 16, 2014): 246–65. https://doi.org/10.1163/17455251-02301007.

Department of Higher Education and Training. "Register of Private Higher Education Institutions: Last Update 17 March 2020." www.dhet.gov.za/Registers_DocLib/register%20of%20private%20higher%20education%20institutions%2017%20March%202020.pdf.

"Documentary Winners: 1973 Oscars." Youtube, 2014. www.youtube.com/watch?v=UFh9u-4FKOA.

Dube, Bekithemba. " 'Go and Prophesy in Your Own Land': Foreign Prophets and Popularism in South Africa. Evoking the Need of Jonathanic Theology for Peaceful Resolution of Difference." *Religions* 11, no. 1 (January 2020): 42. https://doi.org/10.3390/rel11010042.

Dube, Elijah Elijah N. "Desperation in an Attempt to Curb Modern-Day Prophets: Pentecostalisation and the Church in South Africa and Zimbabwe." *Conspectus: The Journal of the South African Theological Seminary* 27, no. 1 (May 23, 2019): 25–34.

Dube, Musa. "Between the Spirit and the Word: Reading the Gendered African Pentecostal Bible." *HTS Teologiese Studies / Theological Studies* 70, no. 1 (November 20, 2014): 7.

Frahm-Arp, Maria. "Why at the Start of the Fourth Industrial Revolution Do We See a Rise in Cult-Type Pentecostal Churches in South Africa?" *The Thinker: A Pan-African Quarterly for Thought Leaders* 82 (2019): 4–9.

Gabaitse, Rosinah M. "Pentecsostal Hermeneutics and the Marginalisation of Women." *Scriptura* 114 (May 2015). https://doi.org/10.7833/114-0-1043.

Gangatharan, A. "The Problem of Periodization in History." *Proceedings of the Indian History Congress* 69 (2008): 862–71.

Garrard, David. J. "African Pentecostalism." *African Pentecostalism: Journal of Beliefs & Values* 30, no. 3 (December 2009): 241–44. https://doi.org/10.1080/13617670903371548. The Interdenominational Theological Centre-RSA. Facebook, August 2, 2013. https://web.facebook.com/itcrsa/posts/520991824656984.

———. Facebook, October 10, 2014. https://web.facebook.com/itcrsa/posts/718921338197364.

———. Facebook, March 16, 2018. https://web.facebook.com/itcrsa/posts/1696971553725666.

Kalu, Ogbu Uke. *African Pentecostalism: An Introduction*. Oxford: Oxford University Press, 2008.

Kgatle, Mookgo S. "The Unusual Practices Within Some Neo-Pentecostal Churches in South Africa: Reflections and Recommendations." *HTS Teologiese Studies / Theological Studies* 73, no. 3 (February 8, 2017). https://doi.org/10.4102/hts.v73i3.4656.

———. *The Fourth Pentecostal Wave in South Africa: A Critical Engagement*. Abingdon: Routledge, 2019.

Kgatle, Mookgo S., and Thabang R. Mofokeng. "Towards a Decolonial Hermeneutic of Experience in African Pentecostal Christianity: A South African Perspective." *HTS Teologiese Studies / Theological Studies* 75, no. 4 (2019): 9. https://doi.org/10.4102/hts.v75i4.5473.

Khanyile, Sphesihle Blessing. "The Virtualization of the Church: New Media Representations of Neo-Pentecostal Performance(s) in South Africa." MA dissertation, University of Witwatersrand, Witwatersrand, 2016.

Landman, Christina. "Faces of Religious Healing in Nkhoma, Malawi: An Exercise in Oral History." *Studia Historiae Ecclesiasticae* 44, no. 3 (2018): 1–17. https://doi.org/10.25159/24124265/5n5.

Larbi, Kingsley. "African Pentecostalism in the Context of Global Pentecostal Ecumenical Fraternity: Challenges and Opportunities." *Pneuma* 24, no. 2 (September 1, 2002): 138–66. https://doi.org/10.1163/15700740260388009.

Mandell, Nikki, and Bobbie Malone. *Thinking like a Historian: Rethinking Historical Instruction.* Madison, WI: Wisconsin Historical Society Press, 2007.

Mashau, Thinandavha D., and Mookgo S. Kgatle. "Prosperity Gospel and the Culture of Greed in Post-Colonial Africa: Constructing an Alternative African Christian Theology of Ubuntu." *Verbum et Ecclesia* 40, no. 1 (2019): 1–8. https://doi.org/10.4102/ve.v40i1.1901.

Mathole, Ezekiel M. "The Christian Witness in the Context of Poverty: With Special Reference to South African Charismatic Evangelicals." Doctoral thesis, University of Pretoria, Pretoria, 2005.

Matsepe, Shale S., and Mokhele Johannes S. Madise. "A New Phenomenon in Zionist Churches of Botswana: The Use of Divination Bones and Sacred Places." 2005. http://uir.unisa.ac.za/handle/10500/4356.

Maxwell, David. *African Gifts of the Spirit: Pentecostalism & the Rise of a Zimbabwean Transnational Religious Movement.* Oxford: James Curry, 2006.

Mgidi, Emily. "Gobela: I Give Pastors Powers!" *DailySun*, December 19, 2019. www.dailysun.co.za/News/gobela-i-give-pastors-powers-20191219.

Mkhwanazi-Xaluva, Thoko. "Money First, God Next: Commercialisation of Religion Report." Facebook, Department of Christian Spirituality, Church History and Missiology, UNISA, August 27, 2018. https://web.facebook.com/UnisaCollegeOfHumanSciences/videos/2104114849838761.

Mofokeng, Thabang, and Mokhele Madise. "The Evangelicalisation of Black Pentecostalism in the AFM of SA (1940–1975): A Turning Point." *Studia Historiae Ecclesiasticae* 45, no. 1 (March 13, 2019): 16. https://doi.org/10.25159/2412-4265/4050.

Molobi, Victor S. "Vanguard of African Culture: An Analysis of the Oral History of Selected AICs in Tshwane (Pretoria)." *Studia Historiae Ecclesiasticae* 35, no. 1 (2009): 1–9.

———. "Power Struggles, Poverty and Breakaways in the African Independent Churches in South Africa." *Studia Historiae Ecclesiasticae* 37, no. 2 (2011): 51–65.

Mvelashe, Phakamani. "This Is Why Winnie Mashaba Believes She Received Her Honorary Doctorate." *Channel24*, December 2, 2019. www.news24.com/channel/The-Juice/News/LocalSA/this-is-why-winnie-mashaba-believes-she-received-her-honorary-doctorate-20191202.

———. "Hlengiwe Mhlaba Awarded an Honorary Doctorate." *Channel24*, February 19, 2020. www.news24.com/channel/The-Juice/News/LocalSA/hlengiwe-mhlaba-awarded-an-honorary-doctorate-20200219.

"Nana Kwaku Bonsam Reclaims God from Church," Youtube. Accessed April 28, 2020. www.youtube.com/watch?v=aj1-yFzUhbM.

Ndabeni, Thandi. "Rape, Sex Assault Claims Pile Up Against Klerksdorp Pastor." *SowetanLive*, February 20, 2018. www.sowetanlive.co.za/news/south-africa/2018-02-20-rape-sex-assault-claims-pile-up-against-klerksdorp-pastor/.

Nel, Marius. "Rather Spirit-Filled Than Learned! Pentecostalism's Tradition of Anti-Intellectualism and Pentecostal Theological Scholarship." *Verbum et Ecclesia* 37, no. 1 (2016): a1533. http://dx.doi.org/10.4102/ve.v37i1.1533.

———. "Pentecostal Hermeneutical Considerations about Women in Ministry." *Studia Historiae Ecclesiasticae* 43, no. 1 (August 17, 2017): 122–37.

Niemandt, Nelus. "The Prosperity Gospel, the Decolonisation of Theology, and the Abduction of Missionary Imagination." *Missionalia: Southern African Journal of Missiology* 45, no. 3 (2017): 203–19. https://doi.org/10.7832/45-3-199.

Omenyo, C. N. "African Pentecostalism." In *The Cambridge Companion to Pentecostalism*, edited by C. M. (Jr) Robeck and A. Yong, 132–51. New York: Cambridge University Press, 2014.

Pondani, Simbarashe. " 'Prophets of Doom': The Phenomenon of Healing and Power Dynamics in Neo-Pentecostal African Churches." MTh dissertation, University of Stellenbosch, Stellenbosch, 2019.

"Prophet Shepherd Bushiri Answers on Alleged Money Laundering Claims 1." SABC News, 2018. www.youtube.com/watch?v=71zWFmN8GUE.

"Prophet Dr Xaba." Bay TV, April 20, 2020.

Ramabulana, Makhado Sinthumule. *Church Mafia – Captured by Secret Powers: An Untold African Narrative*. 1st ed. Pretoria: Makhado Freedom Ramabulana, 2018.

Ramantswana, Hulisani. "Prophets Praying for, or Preying on People's Faith: A Reflection on Prophetic Ministry in the South African Context." *Die Skriflig/ In Luce Verbi* 53, no. 4 (November 18, 2019): 8. https://doi.org/10.4102/ids. v53i4.2495.

Resane, Kelebogile T. " 'And They Shall Make You Eat Grass Like Oxen' (Daniel 4:24): Reflections on Recent Practices in Some New Charismatic Churches." *Pharos Journal of Theology* 98 (2017): 17.

———. "Commercialisation of Theological Education as a Challenge in the Neo-Pentecostal Charismatic Churches." *HTS Teologiese Studies / Theological Studies* 73, no. 3 (September 29, 2017): 7.

Robins, Roger G. *Pentecostalism in America*. Santa Barbara, CA: Praeger, 2010.

"Seer 1 Exposed?" YouTube. Accessed April 28, 2020. www.youtube.com/ watch?v=K_idrzB-Q6Q&feature=youtu.be.

Smith, Howard, and Sarah Kernochan. *Marjoe*. DVD. Docudrama, 1972.

Togarasei, Lovemore. "Modern Pentecostalism as an Urban Phenomenon: The Case of the Family of God Church in Zimbabwe." *Exchange* 34, no. 4 (2005): 349–75. https://doi.org/10.1163/157254305774851484.

———. "Cursed Be the Past! Tradition and Modernity Among (Modern) Pentecostal(s) Charismatics." *Boleswa Occasional Papers in Theology and Religion*, no. 1 (January 1, 2006): 109–18.

Van Dijk, Rijk. *Christian Fundamentalism in Sub-Saharan Africa: The Case of Pentecostalism*. Leiden, The Netherlands: Africa Studies Centre, 2000. www.ascleiden.nl/publications/christian-fundamentalism-sub-saharan-africa-case-pentecostalism.

3 The abuse of the Spirit

An immigration-imported new wave or a development of pre-existing local beliefs?

Elise B. Kisungu

3.1 Introduction

It must be admitted from the outset, that a title such as *the abuse of the Spirit in Pentecostal Christianity* may appear misleading, if not provocative. For some people in leadership positions, when it comes to the Holy Spirit, His power and His gifts, this may even seem like a pointing of the finger. As it is the custom with any new domain, it would ideally have been adequate to refer to the pioneers of the new movement in order to understand and assess their practices. In fact, those first shepherds who, in our times, were blessed to (re)discover and help (re)discover the long-buried crucial role (and person) of the Holy Spirit in Christianity were meant to remain authoritative and trustworthy references on the subject.

Sadly, so many seem to have fallen to abusing the Spirit which makes them the very last ones one can refer to when one needs pure and strictly Biblical insights into the person and work of the Holy Spirit.

It should be noted that the abuse of the Spirit in this study refers to any questionable practices that disturb the church in general as well as the society. The questionability of these practices lies in the fact that these practices and their proponents tarnish the image of Christianity and generally dehumanise people. In the South African context, the abuse of the Spirit includes, among others, outrageous acts such as making people eat grass and asking men and women to undress and masturbate in church. Shockingly, the church leaders who have resorted to these acts always claim to be led by the Holy Spirit. Given the fact that some foreigner pastors are involved in such appalling conduct, the abuse of the Spirit, some South Africans believe, are more a new wave imported by foreign migrants than a development of pre-existing beliefs.

Nevertheless, for a thorough, comprehensive and accurate analysis of this phenomenon occurring in South Africa, it is of critical importance to view it in its historical context. Such a historical and comparative approach to the abuses in South Africa will help tackling the root causes as they become evident through such a lens. What follows is therefore a brief review of South African Pentecostalism.

3.2 Brief description of South African Pentecostalism

Since its emergence, Pentecostalism in South Africa was influenced by global Pentecostalism with its theology of baptism of the Holy Spirit evidenced in the speaking of tongues and miraculous gifts. In classical Pentecostalism, these signs were, and still are today, firmly grounded on the preaching of the Word.[1] Even though classical forms of Pentecostalism are the oldest, they still have a huge following. The largest Pentecostal churches in South Africa are the Apostolic Faith Mission (AFM), the Assemblies of God (AOG) and the Full Gospel of God (FOG).[2]

However, other waves such as the African Independent Churches (AICs), Charismatics and the neo-Charismatics/ Pentecostals emerged, each having distinct characteristics. The AICs (also called "Churches of the Spirit") were born as a response to the inequalities between races in missionary Pentecostal churches and the concern for a relevant Christianity in African terms. The appellation "Churches of the Spirit" refers to their emphasis on the manifestation of the Spirit such as the practices of speaking in tongues, healing and prophecy.[3] According to Muller Retief, AICs are prevalent in South Africa, and are certainly not eclipsed by the success of the new Charismatic and Pentecostal movements as is the case in West Africa.[4]

As for the Charismatics, they accept the gifts of the Holy Spirit and believe in miracles through prayer; they have also introduced the prosperity gospel in South Africa.[5] New Prophetic churches (NPC) are also growing rapidly in South Africa. They give much prominence to "prophecy" and "miracle" services brandished as proof of a leader's divine calling and empowerment by the Spirit.[6] Pentecostalism, as we can see, has quite a broad scope in South Africa. For our purpose we will focus on the NPC. Nonetheless, two things need to be said before closing this section.

First, as supported by a number of researchers, ever since its groundbreaking upswing, global Pentecostalism in general, and South African Pentecostalism in particular, has consistently shown its impact on different areas of peoples' lives. Its impact has reached far beyond denominational borders – to the extent that even non-Pentecostal Christians have been reached, or rather, challenged. As a matter of fact, Mashau explains that,

> Pentecostalism, with its theology of the resurgence of the charismata in the life of the church today, has given birth to the renewal vigour in worship, renewed interest in realising spiritual gifts in congregational life, and new motivations for evangelism and missions.[7]

Secondly, the features developed within the different waves of Pentecostalism are not entirely independent, as preceding waves undoubtedly influence subsequent ones. Sometimes the reverse can also be observed in that subsequent waves can influence the preceding ones.

3.3 Migrant Pentecostal churches in South Africa

The fall of apartheid in South Africa had indeed brought about a new era for internal and international migration. South Africa's economic position on the continent and other factors such as democracy, better education and health care systems than some other countries, and easy domestic travel, truly positioned South Africa as a preferred destination for many Africans and other foreigners. The deterioration of living conditions in many countries has also contributed to making South Africa a net for migrants, particularly Africans. Regarding South Africa's emergence as an attractive option, Castles et al. assert:

> Since the end of Apartheid in 1994, South Africa has attracted migrants from an increasingly diverse array of African countries. In the post-apartheid era, Africans from as far away as Ghana, Nigeria, Kenya, and DR Congo have migrated to South Africa. Many brought with them qualifications and experience in medicine, education, administration and business. Other joined the informal economy as hawkers, street food-sellers or petty traders.[8]

Furthermore, Statistics South Africa reported that South Africa moved from being the 8th to the 6th highest migrant-receiving country in the periods 1990–2000 and 2000–2010, ahead of countries like Canada, the United Kingdom, Saudi Arabia and Australia.[9]

Nonetheless, South Africa at present faces many challenging realities like unemployment, poverty, crime, and homelessness. These challenges have certainly given rise to xenophobic sentiments towards foreigners, and migrants in South Africa have been subjected to multiple attacks from South Africans.[10] At every rise of xenophobic attacks, migrants undergo significant loss of lives and belongings. In such a general xenophobic context, most immigrants feel like outcasts, devalued and frustrated – living in constant fear of possible persecution. Akinola explains these xenophobic attitudes as follows:

> When societies are frustrated and undergoing socio-economic crises, a particular group, or groups tend(s) to be blamed. This is at the centre of the scapegoating theory. In many instances, immigrants are scapegoated when societies and governments are confronted with daunting socio-economic and political difficulties.[11]

As a consequence of xenophobic attacks, migrants actively seek opportunities to leave South Africa and relocate to countries where they will be able to live peacefully. Generally, only a small number of migrants return to their country of origin.

However, migrants do not only bring with them qualifications and experience in different fields as mentioned above by Castles et al., they also bring their faith. Hence, post-apartheid South Africa's migrant's inflow also had religious ramifications. These foreign nationals have planted and headed a steadily growing number of churches, with most of them as Pentecostal churches.[12] For instance, Ukah states that "there were well over a million Nigerian nationals (both documented and undocumented) living in South Africa in 2014".[13] And, "in mid-2014," continues Ukah, "there were well over 600 Pentecostal-Charismatic formations and ministries founded and led by Nigerians in South Africa".[14] This researcher is presently conducting research on Congolese churches in the South African province of Gauteng.[15] Not yet published, the findings reveal that there are more than 400 churches and "ministries" planted and headed by Congolese nationals in the province of Gauteng alone. In the suburbs of Yeoville in Johannesburg and Sunnyside in Pretoria, to mention but two, one could find more than five Congolese churches on one street. These specific suburbs are known to be populated by migrants.[16] Many other similar churches are also planted in cities like Cape Town, Durban, etc. Most of these Congolese churches are Pentecostal and mono cultural.

Foreign-led Pentecostal churches in South Africa originate from various nations such as Brazil, Nigeria, Democratic Republic of Congo, Nigeria and many others. The following are among the most popular foreign-led churches:

- The Enlightened Christian Gathering (ECG) with the Malawian Prophet Shepherd Bushiri named "Major One"
- Alleluia International Ministries led by a Congolese national, Alph Lukau
- Jesus Dominion International, led by a Nigerian national, Timothy Omotoso
- The Christ Embassy, a Nigerian originated Church globally pastored by the well-known pastor Chris Oyakhilome
- Universal Church of the Kingdom of God, Brazilian origin

Membership of these churches varies from tens to tens of thousands. Those with tens or hundreds of members are typically monocultural. Members of the really big churches consist of different nationalities – South Africans included – of which the majority are black. One such example is the ECG which draws thousands of people from Southern Africa and other parts of the world.[17]

Like countless migrants across the world, migrants in South Africa consider the Pentecostal church with its different liturgies as one of the main survival tools to negotiate their livelihoods in host countries.[18] Asamoah-Gyadu observes that prayers for legal documentation, employment and security are the kinds of prayers heard in the African churches in the diaspora.

According to Asamoah-Gyadu, these kinds of prayers display migrants' fears and anxieties. Often under uncertain circumstances, these Pentecostal churches "provide a social net for immigrants whose future remains uncertain by the minute."[19] Asamoah-Gyadu's observation was made in the European and American contexts, but the same reality is found in South Africa. The factors that favor the immigrant Pentecostal church planting phenomenon are best captured in Kalu's statement:

> The reasons of the larger presence are that they are easier to form without the burden of formality, official permission and trained leadership. The evangelical impulse in Pentecostalism ensures that leaders are very motivated and encourage immigrant members to form churches. Such members have been socialized in evangelism and leadership roles.[20]

Kalu's statement offers the right picture of Pentecostal leadership that generally varies from ordained pastors to zealous members. A close observation reveals that a considerable number of these Pentecostal churches do not have any mandate from their home-affiliated church to plant a church in South Africa. The challenges in host countries seem to be a trigger that awakens the missionary impulse and push some individuals to fulfil a leadership role in such an "informal" way. This brings us to the next section, about the abuse of the Spirit in South Africa.

3.4 The abuse of the Spirit in South Africa

After long years of oppression and poverty, South Africans (mostly black) expected major changes regarding their socio-economic conditions. Unfortunately, according to Kgatle, "the economic policies of a democratic South Africa are unable to resolve the issues of unemployment, poverty and inequality".[21] It is within such a context where citizens are feeling hopeless for the future and migrants fight for their survival that the neo-Prophetic movement is emerging and growing. Since the new movement has put much emphasis on prophecy, deliverance, and different kinds of miracles, these churches have found fertile ground in the African worldview of mystical causalities. Consequently, numerous communities living in South Africa consider these churches as a solution for the various challenges they have to endure, as governments have seemingly failed them.

Regrettably, over recent years, these churches considered the "Biblical Bethesda pool" where everyone could expect their possible miracle,[22] have also become places where members are abused and stripped of any discernment. Outrageous acts, mostly performed during prophetic, deliverance and miracle services, have become commonplace. Paradoxically, these acts are on the one hand performed in the name of the Holy Spirit, and on the other hand they are supported by a misunderstanding of the freedom of religion championed by the South African constitution.[23] Kelebogile T. Resane lists some of the practices and underlines their connection with the glory of God as comprehended within the NPC:

> In recent past, incidents such as people made to eat grass, rats, snakes and drinking petrol had mistakenly become a *theatrum gloriae Dei* by which the glory of God should be discerned and recognized. Preachers are watched standing on prostate bodies of people, licking naked women, etc. to demonstrate the *dunamis* of the gospel by the celebrity preachers had shocked many of the household of faith.[24]

These indignities are claimed to be happening under the power and the guidance of the Holy Spirit.[25] Shockingly they include, among others, pastors asking church members – men and women – to undress and masturbate in the church as a way of making the church floor as sacred as heaven by their fluid.[26] Another shocking example is where a prophet made his church members to drink the antiseptic Dettol, promising they will be healed from their sicknesses.[27] There has also been an instance whereby a pastor, after declaring that God was working in the church service by the power of the Holy Spirit, kissed a woman live on Tshwane TV.[28]

In the NPC, congregants and leaders express a strong desire for miracles, to the extent that some even falsify miraculous acts. The scandalous resurrection of a presumed dead man at Alleluia Ministries in 2019 by the overseer Alph Lukau, a Congolese national, is an example of such a burning desire for miracles. Prior to this scandal, Lukau organised a meeting to pray for women's ring fingers, promising them that they would be receiving marriage proposals within 90 days of that "miracle prayer". Tickets to this meeting were sold at prices varying between R450 and R5000.[29]

Regrettably, this ardent desire for miracles has also led to syncretism. Some congregants do not hesitate to consult traditional healers when promises of happiness received in the church are delayed or fail to occur. Mashau notes, "The development of secularism and pluralism in Africa, especially in South Africa, is one of the contributory factors toward the syncretism of African Christianity and the revival of Traditional African Religion".[30]

In the NPC, prophets are portrayed as individuals God has chosen merely to enlighten people about their future, make them prosperous, or deliver them from satanic bondages. It is deeply troubling, as observed by Mashau and Kgatle, that pastors often have a materialistic lifestyle filled with luxury while church members are continuously struggling with life challenges, which, in many cases, were the main reasons that had led them to these churches in the first place.[31] In spite of the fact that some churches and the public have openly decried these disturbing practices, congregants have generally and alarmingly shown more loyalty to their church leaders than to God and His Word.[32] Most congregants trust their church leaders' prophecies and strange rituals without any discernment because these leaders somehow inspire confidence. For this reason, when accused of misconduct, most church leaders have the loyal and full support of their congregations. Dube et al. explain congregants' gullibility as follows: "In many cases, oppressive religious practices go unreported to the police; usually because people fear the religious leader, or believe that unusual religious practices are a manifestation of the presence of God".[33]

In reference to church members' loyalty to rituals, Asamoah-Gyadu points out that the therapeutic effect of African religious rituals cannot be denied. Nevertheless, there is a danger in rituals leading to what may be described as "obsessive-compulsive behaviour".[34] Asamoah-Gyadu's observations revealed the serious consequences of such behavior. This should be addressed with much urgency. Our main question, however, remains: what is the relationship between the abuse of the Spirit and migration? This is the point of discussion in the next section.

3.5 The abuse of the Spirit and migration

In regard to existing links between foreigners and the abuse of the Spirit in South Africa, it should be highlighted that not only are foreign church leaders often involved in the abuses described in the previous section, they appear to even be pioneers therein. For instance, forensic prophecy and money miracles have been promoted in South Africa by the Pretoria-based Malawian Prophet Bushiri, a leading figure and senior pastor of ECG. The latter draws thousands of people, who do not hesitate to camp for hours and pay exorbitant amounts of money to meet with the prophet personally.[35] This tantalising forensic prophecy involves, among others, the prophet revealing personal, hidden information about the prophecy recipient, from personal or relatives' names to physical address, phone, bank account number or vehicle registration plates, and so on.[36] Money miracles entail cash being deposited in people's bank accounts in mysterious ways.

Likewise, several other NPC prophets of foreign nationality have built a reputation with similar performances. Among them is Congolese Pastor Alph Lukau, famous for his highly detailed "visions" which he refers to as "accurate prophecy". By way of illustration, during the course of a live stream on his YouTube channel, Pastor Lukau claimed to be transported "in the spirit" from Johannesburg to prophesy to a woman in Melbourne, Australia. He provided details including the name of the woman, the year of her wedding and even spoke of a miscarriage she had suffered after two months of pregnancy. The woman later sent a video to testify to the accuracy of the prophecy.[37] Another video shows him prophesying during a service about the failure of relationships in a man's life and then claiming to have prophetically seen his "God-chosen" wife right there in the church. He walked around, finally found *the* lady and offered her to the man to the applause of an excited crowd while the service reporter subsequently enthroned pastor Lukau as "God's oracle. The facilitator of your miracle".[38] Such "miracle" performances have often been debunked with people telling how they have been bribed to fake an illness or disability and the miraculous healing thereof on stage.[39]

All of the above acts are claimed to be totally performed under the "guidance of the *Holy* Spirit" by these pastors. It remains however curious how the same pastors seem to share *quite unholy* traits, namely an extravagant, pompous, luxurious lifestyle, with accusations of suspicious activities such as money laundering, women abuse, and exchange control irregularities.[40] This has led South African nationals to charge them with bringing *new* beliefs that are nothing more than various means for amassing wealth, profiting off South Africans, abusing women and transforming religious entities into commercial enterprises.[41] Unfortunately, this South African context of "prophetic ministry" and "miracle service" is henceforth becoming a new area of tension between, on the one hand, local citizens and church leaders and, on the other, their counterparts of foreign nationalities. Dube asserts that the particular area of prophecy in South Africa is both interesting and disturbing, and explains it in the following words:

> It is interesting, because innovations are emerging in the prophetic space, which we, or, at least, people with an orthodox or conventional theological orientation, would not have imagined. It is disturbing, because prophetic movements have evoked wars through their prophets based on nationality, popularity, and, in some cases, jealousy.[42]

This same issue of growing tension between South African nationals and foreigners triggered by religious abuse is also raised by Ukah within the specific framework of Nigerian immigrants in South Africa:

> As religion has become a strong and important structure of identity politics for Nigerian migrants in South Africa, so also it has become a site of contestation with South Africans for Nigerians church owners and leaders, a different segment of the local society perceives them with generalized feeling of hostility.[43]

Amidst the aforementioned tensions, the global slogan "foreigners go back home" now appears to have an additional precise connotation against foreign church leaders and their congregations. This implication is clearly expressed in the following petition post in support of Cheryl Zondi, a South African woman who has accused Nigerian televangelist Timothy Omotoso of rape:

> As citizen of South Africa, we stand together in one voice requesting our government to please close down all these foreign prophetic churches based in South Africa with immediate effect to avoid victimization of our citizens, whether sexually, financially, emotionally, or otherwise in the name of miracles. We request that our government regulate our

churches and monitor and evaluate their activities. We believe that they can perform miracles in their countries and groom their girls as well contribute positively to the growth of their economy. Enough is enough.[44]

As of April 2020, the petition has accumulated 6,593 signatures. Furthermore, Fisher reports that Omotoso and two women are accused of recruiting girls and women for sexual exploitation.[45] Distressingly, there are similar cases involving foreign pastors that we can't go into here for the sake of space.

Undeniably, South Africans' appeals to authorities for the closure of foreign-led churches and the expulsion of their leaders, cannot be seen as separate from a general attitude of rejecting foreign migrants. The category of South Africans who vehemently advocate in favour of deportation believe that immigration is one of the major factors of poverty, unemployment, abuse in churches, and other vices. In their perspective, foreigners are more perceived as competitors than contributors.

Under such circumstances, how have the South African authorities responded to the calls by citizens for the closure of foreign-led churches? Therefore, what should be the appropriate missiological approach and response to calls that advocate *deporting* as a way to help curb such spiritual abuses in South Africa? These are the questions addressed in the next two sections.

3.6 Government intervention/regulation and migration

The new-prophetic controversial acts attracted the attention of the authorities and made headlines in the media. All kinds of controversial behaviour besides reprehensible acts were widely reported, including superfluous expenditure and financial mismanagement. Following media reports and public complaints lodged with the Commission for the Promotion and Protection of the Rights of Cultural, Religious and Linguistic Communities (the CRL Rights Commission), the Commission decided to investigate the commercialisation of religion and the abuses of people's belief systems.[46] Numerous deviations that shamed Christianity have been documented in the CRL's final report.[47] For the sake of space, we list only some of the CRL's final report findings:

- People pay substantial amounts of money before blessings and prayers can be said over them.
- Access to the spiritual leader or traditional healer is only guaranteed by paying a fixed amount.
- Blessed water and oils are sold to congregants at a high mark-up price.
- In some cases, money collected from church members is never banked with any commercial bank.

- Some religious organisations operate freely without registration or a licensing certificate.
- In some cases, instead of depositing money in the institution's account, the money is deposited in the spiritual leader's account, whereby the pastor effectively becomes the treasurer.
- There is an established and exponential increase in religious organisations and leaders of foreign origin with evidence that they unfortunately often display a propensity for amassing money.
- Some religious institutions tell their congregants that money has to be paid to their head offices whilst most of these head offices are based outside the country.

Admittedly, the CRL Rights Commission did not only focus on churches, but also on traditional religions. However, most of the abuses as listed above are found among the NPC as described in the previous sections. The CRL Rights Commission investigated both local and foreigner-headed religious institutions. As a result of their findings, the CRL Rights Commission formulated recommendations in order to limit abuses. Following are some of the general recommendations for churches and those specifically related to foreigner-headed churches:

> Each worship center should have an umbrella organization that will support and guide them in their spiritual work; Existing legislation affecting the various aspects of religious organisations (training/education, employment, registration, immigration legislation, etc.) needs to be enforced with due diligence because the hearings revealed many existing loopholes that create opportunities for abuse; The Department of Home Affairs should play a crucial role in curbing this abuse when considering visa applications. Under the Immigration Act, foreign pastors who do not have the necessary visas to reside or work in South Africa may be arrested, deported, fined, imprisoned, etc.[48]

In closing this section, we need to point out that the CRL Rights Commission's recommendations were deemed unacceptable by many. For instance, Freedom of Religion South Africa filed a petition against the CRL Rights Commission's recommendations. One of the arguments in the petition states: "It is not for the State, or any other body, to decide which religions qualify as a 'religion', or to sit as 'judge' over the doctrines of religious institutions, and decide whether they can operate".[49] As for the call by South Africans to shut down foreigner-led churches and repatriate their leaders, there has not been a single foreigner-led church, at least those that have been accused to be involved in these practices, that has been closed. Nonetheless, the trials that some local and foreigner leaders go through after evidence of their alleged misconduct started to surface, seem to indicate that local authorities are now trying to regulate freedom of religion.

3.7 Abuse of the Spirit: foreign or local

In trying to assess whether the immediate causes of the abuse of the Spirit phenomenon in South Africa are of a foreign *or* a local nature, the following points need to be factored in. Firstly, South Africans protesting against the misconduct of church leaders from other countries is legitimate and justifiable. These abuses not only pose a serious threat to the congregants, but also to South African society as a whole. However, it is equally imperative to keep in mind that these questionable practices are not only found in foreigner-led churches. As a matter of fact, it is no secret to anyone familiar with spiritual abuse in the country that a number of South African spiritual leaders are also involved in promoting such deviant practices. Prophet Paseko Motsoeneng, otherwise known as Prophet Mboro, for example, found himself in the spotlight years ago for ordering his congregants to remove their underwear during a Sunday service. He then went further, instructing the congregants to wave their underwear in the air whilst touching their private parts as he was praying and chasing evil spirits from the altar.[50] When interviewed on this practice, Prophet Mboro argued that when the underwear is touched by the power of God through his prayers, they are blessed and no evil spirit can visit congregants and have sexual relations with them in their sleep as sometimes experienced by them.[51]

South Africans protesting against non-South African church leaders involved in spiritual abuse may therefore embody a *simplistic way* of viewing a complex issue that is not only socially and economically rooted, but also theologically embedded.

Secondly, immigrants bring their beliefs with them as stated earlier; and also, the immigrant church planting phenomenon is a global reality. In most cases, immigrant churches are characterised by the kind of religious experiences immigrants have brought with them from their home countries.[52] Nevertheless, the immigrant churches that are more *multiculturally* oriented often take into consideration the religious trends of their host countries to find common ground so as to more seamlessly and surreptitiously enforce their "imported" beliefs and practices. With some exceptions, Africans generally find it difficult to undertake this immigrant church approach in Western countries. This is surely due to the divergence between African and Western worldviews.[53] It does seem however easier for African immigrant Pentecostal churches to implement their own expression of faith in other African host countries due to religious commonalities. Unfortunately, that easier implementation in the African host country includes both the strengths and weaknesses of the "imported" beliefs. This is what we see when we look at the impact of the new wave of foreigner-headed Pentecostal churches in the context of South Africa as a host country.

Thirdly, spiritual movements are characterised by how they precede and bring about the emergence of subsequent ones. This global phenomenon can be viewed as an inevitable cycle. In his article addressing new Charismatic

Churches with their African-initiated Pentecostalism – which he considered the newer Pentecostal movement at the time – Anderson highlights this reality in the South African context. He states that despite the tension between the AICs and the newer Pentecostal movement, the latter is not *fundamentally* different from the former; it simply is a continuation of AICs in a different situation. As for the classical Pentecostal churches, Anderson says they played a significant role in the emergence of the Charismatic movement. According to Anderson all three waves offered a personal encounter with God through the power of the Holy Spirit, healing from sickness and deliverance from evil in all its manifestations.[54]

In conclusion: Aligning with Anderson's perspective, our view is that immigrant Pentecostals found the South African complex religious landscape littered both with the *strengths* and *weaknesses* of the theology of the Spirit from the pre-existing classical Pentecostalism, AICs and Charismatics. Thus, the new form of Pentecostalism that these foreigners brought could easily be adopted in their host country.

This phenomenon can thus be regarded as a threat against Christianity in Africa, and not only Christianity in South Africa. Therefore, while the recommendations in the next section are specifically intended to address the challenges in the South African context, they nonetheless also apply to African Christianity in general.

3.8 Recommendations to address the abuse of the Spirit in South Africa

3.8.1 Theological training of church leaders

One important reason for the abuse of the Spirit is a lack of theological training, and even more from biased exegesis of the Scriptures. It is not a secret that most of the leaders of the NPC have not received theological training and do not even accept it. Mindful of critics, some however choose short-term training. Unfortunately, their choice of training depends more on their own criteria than on biblical doctrine. Biwul proposes that African church leaders should receive the same high-quality training as their former African spiritual fathers. He argues that the apostles laid the foundation upon which former African spiritual fathers were grounded. As a result, faced with persecution and the heresies of their time, former African church leaders fervently defended the Christian faith.[55]

In the light of contemporary missiological challenges, the church leadership, regardless of a congregation's membership size, should give serious consideration to theological training. Congregants will stand firm in their faith and those who migrate and find themselves in positions of leading people in a host country will do so in this same spirit guided by solid teaching. It is however pivotal for African theological training to be decolonized from the dominant Western curriculum in order to be relevant in the African context.[56]

3.8.2 *Partnership and dialogue between local and foreign faith communities*

South Africans' demands for the closure of foreign-led churches often mask their general pervasive rejecting attitude towards foreigners. In addition, it also masks the concealed tension between foreign and local pastors. Often-times congregants are the victims, as they find themselves involved in conflicts, they cannot define nor justify. Dube, one the few researchers who address the tension between foreign and local prophets in South Africa, suggests that the Jonathanic theology is a model that could smooth out these tensions and construct sustainable peace. The Jonathanic theology has been developed from Jonathan's initiative to protect, defend, and make peace with David in the face of his father Saul's brutality towards David. In reference to this biblical story, Dube develops four tenets to define this Jonathanic theology: Brotherly love greater than the throne, defence for the afflicted in society, sincerity to power, and commitment to purpose.[57]

One can conclude that it is the obligation of church leaders to set aside their differences and foster communities' cohesion and peace. In this way the Kingdom of God which they claim to be serving will expand.

3.8.3 *Foreign pastors should seek the peace of their host cities*

Urban challenges can be overwhelming and are too big for a single entity like the government to address alone, hence contributions from various sources are indispensable. According to Jeremiah's letter addressed to the exiles (Jeremiah 29), in spite of their hardships Israelites were called to consider Babylon their home and seek the peace and welfare of the city. This is a message that should be known and taken to heart by foreign church leaders and immigrant churches as a message from God who recommends that they act as the Israelites did in a foreign land, Babylon.[58]

Only when local people see foreign-led faith communities working diligently to foster peace and show concern about local issues will trust be built to the degree that foreigners will be considered as brothers and sisters. Similarly, South African ministers should embrace foreigners, in remembrance of the fact that immigrant church planting is a global phenomenon. South Africans are themselves planting churches in other countries. As long as immigration continues, host countries will always have faith communities in the diaspora.

3.8.4 *Enhance biblical knowledge*

The lack of solid biblical teaching is one of the main criticisms of Pentecostalism, particularly the new movement. There is enough space for different kinds of prayers and other kinds of services, such as the prophetic service, but there is less commitment to the study of the Scriptures.[59] For this reason, church members in most cases remain spiritually immature and vulnerable to abuse. The lack of Bible study is mainly linked to the lack of biblical training of leadership.

3.9 Conclusion

The fall of apartheid had ignited South Africans' hope for equality and better socio-economic conditions, especially among black people who had lived under so much oppression for so long. Urban migration increased in the quest for opportunities that cities could offer. The hope of a great future in post-apartheid South Africa also attracted hundreds of thousands of foreign nationals who left their countries because of dictatorial regimes, poverty, war, etc. Kgatle points out that political freedom with the fall of apartheid also implied religious freedom. Consequently, as Kgatle reports, "there was an increase of Pentecostal churches in cities, townships, and villages that could not start during apartheid."[60] Hence, the planting of post-apartheid churches was not only undertaken by South Africans, but also the foreign nationals.

Nevertheless, the promises made in post-apartheid South Africa were often not kept, crippled by various appalling crises which left many people disillusioned. The majority of South Africans are still unemployed and live in poverty with a lack of decent housing. As a result, South Africa is ridden with problems such as a very high crime rate including one of the highest murder rates in the world, prostitution and human trafficking, to name but a few. Amid these challenges, there is often a lot of tension within various local communities. Local people suffer where poverty and unemployment abound and foreign nationals are often scapegoated as a major cause for this hardship because they are perceived to take jobs away from locals, etc.

In the context of socio-economic hardship, the abuse of the Spirit usually increases because it seems to bring relief to people. Many spiritual abuses have come under the spotlight and regrettably some foreign church leaders have been implicated in these abuses. This has in recent years contributed to xenophobic attacks that have also been directed against many faith communities headed by foreigners.

It is clear that within such a complex and volatile context, responses to abuses of the Spirit cannot be left to the public alone. While the public has a legitimate right to react to what can be perceived as outrageous acts, it doesn't have the capacity to deal with such a complicated and multi-faceted problem. Better equipped institutions with analytical capacity such as ecclesiastical authorities, academic structures and local authorities should rather be invited to get involved, and where necessary, collaborate to understand the source of these deviations in order to address it in a way that is adequate and effective.

Notes

1 Hulisani Ramantswana, "Prophets Praying for, or Preying on People's Faith: A Reflection on Prophetic Ministry in the South African Context," *In die Skriflig / In Luce Verbi* 53, no. 4 (2019): 3.

2 Solomon Kgatle, *The Fourth Pentecostal Wave in South Africa. A Critical Engagement* (Abingdon: Routledge, 2020), 2.

3 Retief Muller, *African Pilgrimage: Ritual Travel in South Africa's Christianity of Zion* (Farnham: Ashgate, 2011), 65–67.

4 Ibid.

5 Allan Anderson, "New African Initiated Pentecostalism and Charismatic in South Africa," *Journal of Religion in Africa* 35, no. 1 (2005): 80.

6 Kgatle, *The Fourth Pentecostal Wave*, 59.

7 Derrick Mashau, "Ministering Effectively in the Context of Pentecostalism in Africa: A Reformed Missional Reflection," *In die Skirling* 47, no. 1 (2013): 10–17.

8 Stephen Castles, et al. *The Age of Migration: International Population Movements in the Modern World* (New York: The Guilford Press, 2015), 185.

9 Statistics South Africa, "Census 2011: Migrations Dynamics in South Africa," 2015, 215, www.statssa.gov.za/publications/Report-03-01-79/Report-03-01-792011.pdf.

10 Elizabeth Chinomona and Eugine Maziriri, "Examining the Phenomenon of Xenophobia as Experienced by African Immigrants Entrepreneurs in Johannesburg, South Africa: Intensifying the Spirit of Ubuntu," *International Journal of Research in Business Studies and Management* 2, no. 6 (2015): 24.

11 Adeoye Akinola, "The South African Xenophobic Question: A Reflection on the Complicity of State Actors," *Ubuntu: Journal of Conflict and Social Transformation* 7, no. 1 (2018): 60.

12 Asonzeh Ukah, "Re-Imagining the Religious Field: The Rhetoric of Nigerian Pentecostal Pastors in South Africa," in *Bourdieu in Africa. Exploring the Dynamics of Religious fields* (Leiden and Boston, MA: Brill, 2015), 78.

13 Ibid., 70.

14 Ibid., 71.

15 From Democratic Republic of Congo (DRC). No to be confused with the Republic of Congo which actually is a neighboring country of DRC.

16 Vedaste Nzayabino, "The Role of Refugee-Established Churches in Integrating Forced Migrants: A Case Study of Word of Life Assembly in Yeoville, Johannesburg," *HTS Teologiese Studies / Theological Studies* 66, no. 1 (2010): 2.

17 Steve Mochechane, "Dealing with Fear and Anxiety in Pentecostalism: The Bushiri Phenomenon in Pretoria." A CHSSA paper presented on July 11–15, 2016 at the Third Conference of Academic Societies in the Fields of Religion and Theology, University of Pretoria, Pretoria.

18 Nzayabino, "The Role of Refugee," 1.

19 Kwabena Asamoah-Gyadu, "To the Ends of the Earth: Mission, Migration and the Impact of African-led Pentecostal Churches in The European Diaspora," *Mission Studies* 29, no. 1 (2012): 24.

20 Ogbu Kalu, "African Pentecostalism in Diaspora," *Pentecostudies* 9, no. 1 (2010): 21.

21 Mookgo Kgatle, "The Relationship Between Economic Strand of Contemporary Pentecostalism and Neo-Liberalism in post-1994 South Africa," *Religions* 11, no. 4 (2020): 156.

22 John 5:2–9. New King James Version.

23 Bekithemba Dube, Milton Nkoane, and Dipane Hlalele, "The Ambivalence of Freedom of Religion, and Unearthing the Unlearnt Lessons of Religious Freedom

from the Jonestown Incident: A Decoloniality Approach," *Journal for the Study of Religion* 30, no. 2 (2017): 331.

24 Kelebogile Resane, " 'And They Shall Make You Eat Grass Like Oxen' (Daniel 4: 24): Reflections on Recent Practices in Some New Charismatic Churches," *Pharos Journal of Theology* 98, no. 1 (2017): 5.

25 Ramantswana, "Prophets Praying," 4.

26 Inemesit Udodiong, "South African Pastor Tells the Church Members to Masturbate, They Obey," www.pulse.ng.

27 Joshua Sebola, "From Pastor Doom to Pastor Disinfectant," 2016, www.dailysun.co.za/.

28 Citizen Reporter, "Yes Lord. Says Interpreter as Pastor Kisses Woman in Church," https://web.facebook.com/salatestnews/posts/1950283848583090?_rdc=1&_rdr.

29 Check Point, "Marriage Miracle," 2016, accessed April 11, 2020, www.enca.com/south-africa/checkpoint-marriage-miracle.

30 Derrick Mashau, "A Reformed Missional Perspective on Secularism and Pluralism in Africa. Their Impact on African Christianity and the Revival of Traditional Religion," *Calvin Theological Journal* 44, no. 1 (2009).

31 Derrick Mashau and Mookgo Kgatle, "Prosperity Gospel and the Culture of Greed in Post-Colonial Africa: Constructing an Alternative African Theology of Ubuntu," *Verbum et Ecclesia* 40, no. 1 (2019): 3.

32 Mookgo Kgatle, "The Unusual Practices Within Some Neo-Pentecostal Churches in South Africa: Reflexions and Recommendations," *HTS Theologiese Studies/ Theological Studies* 73, no. 3 (2017): 3.

33 Dube, et al., "The Ambivalence of Freedom," 342.

34 Kwabena Asamoah-Gyadu, "Unction to Function. Reinventing the Oil' Influence in African Pentecostalism," *Journal of Pentecostal Theology* no. 13 (2005): 231–56.

35 Mochechane, "Dealing with Fear," 4.

36 Mookgo Kgatle, "Reimagining the Practice of Prophecy in Southern Africa: A Critical Engagement," *HTS Theologiese/Theological Studies* 75, no. 4 (2019): 3.

37 "Right in Melbourne, Australia in Her House, She Received a Prophetic Word from Pastor Lukau," accessed April 10, 2020, www.youtube.com/watch?v=3pjpjL-GcfM.

38 "Pastor Lukau Gives a Man a Wife Right in the Church," accessed April 10, 2020, www.youtube.com/watch?v=HrXSw2wzQpc.

39 Maageketla Mohlabe, "Alleluia Ministries Congregants Fake Illnesses to Stage Miracles," www.sabcnews.com/sabcnews/alleluia-ministries-congregants-fake-illnesses-to-stage-miracles/.

40 Ilana Van Wyk, "Why Money Gospel Followers Aren't Simply Credulous Dupes," https://theconversation.com/why-money-gospel-followers-arent-simply-credulous-dupes-111838.

41 Ukah, "Re-Imagining the Religious Field," 72.

42 Bekithemba Dube, "Go Prophesy in Your Land: Foreign Prophets and Popularism in South Africa," *Religions* 11, no. 1 (2020): 42.

43 Ukah, "Re-Imagining the Religious Field," 71–72.

44 Sibongile Kunju, "Total Shutdown of Foreign Prophetic Churches in SA," *Petitions.net*, 2018, www.petitions.net/total_shutdown_of_foreign_prophetic_churches_in_sa.

45 Shamiela Fisher, "Sheryl Zondi Will Have to Testify Again as More Witnesses Due in Omotoso Trial," 2020, https://ewn.co.za/2020/01/29/cheryl-zondi-will-have-to-testify-again-as-more-witnesses-due-in-omotoso-trial.

46 "CRL Rights Commission's Preliminary Report of the Hearings on Commercialization of Religion and Abuse of People's Belief Systems," CRL Rights Commission, 2016, 1, https://synapses.co.za/uploads/CRLReport.pdf.
47 "CRL Rights Commission's Final Report of the Hearings on Commercialization of Religion and Abuse of People's Belief Systems," CRL Rights Commission, 2017, 31–34, www.crlcommission.org.za/docs/Final%20Report%20on%20 the%20Commercialisation%20of%20Religion.pdf.
48 "CRL Rights Commission's Final Report," 34–36.
49 "Freedom of Religion South Africa. CRL Rights Commission: Keep Religion Free from Regulation in South Africa," 2017, accessed April 11, 2020, www.change. org/p/crl-rights-commission-keep-religion-free-from-regulation-in-south-africa.
50 Daily Active, "Taking Off Underwear and Other Weird Things Congregates Do in Church," https://dailyactive.info/2020/02/24/taking-off-underwear-and-other-weird-things-congregates-do-in-church/#:~:text=Taking%20Off%20 Underwear%20and%20Other%20Weird%20Things%20Congregates %20Do%20in%20Church,-24%2F02%2F2020&text=A%20section%20 of%20gullible%20congregants,that%20they%20can%20receive%20miracles.
51 "News 24 Video. Holy Underpants," Prophet Mboro Explains Blessing Panties, 2016, www.news24.com/news24/video/southafrica/news/holy-underpants-prophet-mboro-explains-blessing-panties-20160419.
52 Ukah, "Re-Imagining the Religious Field," 85.
53 Werner Khal, "Migrants as Instruments of Evangelization: In Early Christianity and in Contemporary Christianity," in *Global Diasporas and Mission* (Regnum Books International, 2014), 84–85.
54 Anderson, "New African," 69–70.
55 Joel Biwul, "Will Christianity Survive in Africa? Seven Predators Devouring Christianity in Africa and Four Proposals for Surviving Them," *Africa Journal of Evangelical Theology* no. 35 (2016): 102–3.
56 Marilyn Naidoo, "Overcoming Alienation in Africanising Theological Education," *HTS Theologiese Studies/ Theological Studies* 72, no. 1 (2016): 6.
57 Dube, "Go Prophesy," 7–8.
58 Derrick Mashau, "Seek the Shalom of the City: Homelessness and Faith Communities in Diaspora," *Stellenbosch Theological Journal* 5, no. 1 (2019): 239–61.
59 Acts 17: 10–11. New King James version.
60 Kgatle, "The Fourth Pentecostal Wave," 24.

References

Akinola, Adeoye O. "The South African Xenophobic Question: A Reflection on the Complicity of State Actors." *Ubuntu: Journal of Conflict and Social Transformation* 7, no. 1 (2018): 53–79.

Anderson, Allan. "New African Initiated Pentecostalism and Charismatic in South Africa." *Journal of Religion in Africa* 35, no. 1 (2005): 66–92.

Asamoah-Gyadu, J. Kwabena. "To the Ends of the earth: Mission, Migration and the Impact of African-led Pentecostal churches in The European Diaspora." *Mission Studies* 29, no. 1 (2012): 23–44.

———. "Unction to Function: Reinventing the Oil Influence in African Pentecostalism." *Journal of Pentecostal Theology* 13, no. 2 (2005): 231–56.

Biwul, Joel. "Will Christianity Survive in Africa? Seven Predators Devouring Christianity in Africa and Four Proposals for Surviving Them." *Africa Journal of Evangelical Theology* 35, no. 2 (2016): 91–108.

Castles, Stephen, de Haas Hein, and Mark J. Miller. *The Age of Migration: International Population Movements in the Modern World*. New York: The Guildford Press, 2014.

Check Point: "Marriage Miracle." 2016. Accessed April 11, 2020. www.enca.com/south-africa/checkpoint-marriage-miracle.

Chinomona, Elizabeth, and Eugine T. Maziriri. "Examining the Phenomenon of Xenophobia as Experienced by African Immigrant Entrepreneurs in Johannesburg, South Africa: Intensifying the Spirit of Ubuntu." *International Journal of Research in Business Studies and Management* 2, no. 6 (2015): 20–31.

Citizen Reporter, "Yes Lord! Says Interpreter as Pastor Kisses in Church." Accessed April 9, 2020. https://citizen.co.za/news/news-eish/1521927/watch-yes-lord-says-interpreter-as-pastor-kisses-woman-in-church/.

CRL Rights Commission's Final Report of the Hearings on Commercialization of Religion and Abuse of People's Belief Systems, CRL Rights Commission. 2017. www.crlcommission.org.za/docs/Final%20Report%20on%20the%20Commercialisation%20of%20Religion.pdf.

CRL Rights Commission's Preliminary Report of the Hearings on Commercialization of Religion and Abuse of People's Belief Systems, CRL Rights Commission. 2016. Accessed May 10, 2020 www.crlcommission.org.za/docs/Preliminary%20Report%20of%20the%20hearings%20on%20Commercialization%20of%20Religion.pdf.

Daily Active. "Taking Off Underwear and Other Weird Things Congregates Do in Church." 2020. Accessed April 27, 2020. https://dailyactive.info/2020/02/24/taking-off-underwear-and-other-weird-things-congregates-do-in-church/.

Dube, Bekithemba. "Go Prophesy in Your Land: Foreign Prophets and Popularism in South Africa. Evoking the Need of Jonathanic Theology for Peaceful Resolution of Difference." *Religions* 11, no. 1 (2020): 42.

Dube, Bekithemba, Nkoane Milton Molebatsi, and Hlalele Dipane. "The Ambivalence of Freedom of Religion, and Unearthing the Unlearnt Lessons of Religious Freedom from the Jonestown Incident: A Decoloniality Approach." *Journal of the Study of Religion* 30, no. 2 (2017): 330–49.

Fisher, Shamiela. "Cheryl Zondi Will Have to Testify Again as More Witnesses Due in Omotoso Trial." *Eyewitness News*, January 29, 2020. Accessed April 11, 2020. https://ewn.co.za/2020/01/29/cheryl-zondi-will-have-to-testify-again-as-more-witnesses-due-in-omotoso-trial.

Freedom of Religion South Africa. CRL Rights Commission: Keep Religion Free from Regulation in South Africa, 2017. Accessed April 11, 2020. www.change.org/p/crl-rights-commission-keep-religion-free-from-regulation-in-south-africa.

Kalu, Ogbu O. "African Pentecostalism in Diaspora." *Pentecostudies* 9, no. 1 (2010): 9–34.

Kgatle, Mookgo S. "The Unusual Practices Within Some Neo-Pentecostal Churches in South Africa: Reflexions and Recommendations." *HTS Theologiese Studies/ Theological Studies* 73, no. 3 (2017): 1–8.

———. "Re-Imagining the Practice of Pentecostal Prophecy in Southern Africa: A Critical Engagement." *HTS Theologiese Studies/ Theological Studies* 75, no. 4 (2019): 1–7.

———. *The Fourth Pentecostal Wave in South Africa. A Critical Engagement*. Abingdon: Routledge, 2020.

———. "The Relationship Between Economic Strand of Contemporary Pentecostalism and Neo-Liberalism in Post-1994 South Africa." *Religions* 11, no. 4 (2020): 156.

Khal, Werner. "Migrants as Instruments of Evangelization: In Early Christianity and in Contemporary Christianity." In *Global Diasporas and Mission*, edited by Chandler H. Im and Amos Yong, 71–88. Oxford: Regnum Books International, 2014.

Kunju, Sbongile. "Total Shutdown of Foreign Prophetic Churches in SA." *Petitions.net*, 2018. Accessed April 17, 2020. www.petitions.net/total_shutdown_of_foreign_prophetic_churches_in_sa.

Mashau, Derrick. "A Reformed Missional Perspective on Secularism and Pluralism in Africa. Their Impact on African Christianity and the Revival of Traditional Religion." *Calvin Theological Journal* 44, no. 1 (2009): 108–26.

———. "Ministering Effectively in the Conetxt of Pentecostalism in Africa: A Reformed Missional Reflection." *In die Skirling* 47, no. 1 (2013): 10–17.

———. "Seek the Shalom of the City: Homelessness and Faith Communities in Diaspora." *Stellenbosch Theological Journal* 5, no. 1 (2019): 239–61.

Mashau, Derrick, and Mookgo S. Kgatle. "Prosperity Gospel and the Culture of Greed in Post-Colonial Africa: Constructing an Alternative African Theology of Ubuntu." *Verbum et Ecclesia* 40, no. 1 (2019): 1–8.

Mochechane, Steve. "Dealing with Fear and Anxiety in Pentecostalism: The Bushiri Phenomenon in Pretoria." A CHSSA paper presented on July 11–15, 2016. at the Third Conference of Academic Societies in the Fields of Religion and Theology, University of Pretoria. www.academia.edu/28226346/Dealing_with_Fear_and_Anxiety_in_Pentecostalism_The_Bushiri-_Phenomenon_in_Pretoria.

Mohlabe, Maageketla. "Alleluia Ministries Congregants Fake Illnesses to Stage Miracles." Accessed April 11, 2020. www.sabcnews.com/sabcnews/alleluia-ministries-congregants-fake-illnesses-to-stage-miracles/.

Muller, Rietif. *African Pilgimage: Ritual Travel in south Africa's Christianity of Zion.* Farnham: Ashgate, 2011.

Naidoo, Marilyn. "Overcoming Alienation in Africanising Theological Education." *HTS Theologiese Studies/ Theological Studies* 72, no. 1 (2016): 1–8.

News 24. "Holy Underpants! Prophet Mboro Explains Blessing Panties." 2016. Accessed April 27, 2020. https://m.news24.com/Video/SouthAfrica/News/holy-underpants-prophet-mboro-explains-blessing-panties-20160419.

Nzayabino, Vedaste. "The Role of Refugee-Established Churches in Integrating Forced Migrants: A Case Study of Word of Life Assembly in Yeoville, Johannesburg." *HTS Teologiese Studies / Theological Studies* 66, no. 1 (2010): 1–9.

Pastor Lukau Alph YouTube Channel. "Not Seen Before: Pastor Lukau Gives a Man a Wife Right in the Church." Accessed April 10, 2020. www.youtube.com/watch?v=HrXSw2wzQpc.

———. "Right in Melbourne, Australia in Her House, She Received a Prophetic Word from Pastor Lukau." 2020. Accessed April 10, 2020. www.youtube.com/watch?v=3pjpjL-GcfM&t=285s.

Ramantswana, Hulisani. "Prophets Praying for, or Preying on People's Faith: A Reflection on Prophetic Ministry in the South African Context." *In die Skriflig* 53, no. 4 (2019): 1–8.

Resane, Kelebogile T. "'And They Shall Make You Eat Grass Like Oxen' (Daniel 4: 24): Reflections on Recent Practices in Some New Charismatic Churches." *Pharos Journal of Theology* 98, no. 1 (2017): 1–17.

Sebola, Joshua. "From Pastor Doom to Pastor Disinfectant!" 2016. Accessed April 17. www.dailysun.co.za/News/National/from-pastor-doom-to-pastor-disinfectant-.

Statistics South Africa. "Census 2011: Migrations Dynamics in South Africa." 2015. www.statssa.gov.za/publications/Report-03-01-79/Report-03-01-792011.pdf.

Udodiong, Inemesit. "South African Pastor Tells the Church Members to Masturbate, They Obey." Accessed April 9, 2020. www.pulse.ng/commu nities/religion/penuel-mnguni-sa-pastor-tells-church-members-to-masturbate-they-obey-photo/7w70fe3.

Ukah, Asonzeh. "Re-Imagining the Religious Field: The Rhetoric of Nigerian Pente-costal Pastors in South Africa." In *Bourdieu in Africa. Exploring The Dynamics of Religious Fields*, edited by Magnus Echtler and Asonzeh Ukah, 70–93. Leiden and Boston, MA: Brill, 2015.

Van Wyk, Ilana. "Why Money Gospel Followers Aren't Simply Dupes. Times-live." Accessed April 12, 2020. www.timeslive.co.za/news/south-africa/2019-02-23-why-money-gospel-followers-arent-simply-credulous-dupes/.

4 Whence have all the prophets come?

A reflection on neo-prophets and their oracular forms

Hulisani Ramantswana and Ithapeleng Sebetseli

4.1 Introduction

In 1997, J.G. Strydom pondered the question, where have all the prophets gone?[1] His was a bemoaning of the silence of the "black" prophets that crept in when the African National Congress took over political power in 1994. In 2000, he reflected again on the issue of being a prophet in the new South Africa, and he asked the question, can we learn from the Old Testament prophets?[2] For Strydom, once the oppressed black populace attained freedom from the apartheid regime, black theologians saw their task as fulfilled. Instead of continuing to sound the prophetic voice, the prophets sought for themselves positions in government.[3] In our view, it was a bit premature for Strydom to accuse the black prophets of silence in 1997, considering that the new democratic government at the time had only been in power for three years. Furthermore, moving into government positions did not necessarily have to be viewed as betraying the prophetic course; it could be seen instead as working towards its realisation. The black prophets/black theologians[4] were not merely prophets of doom – prophesying the fall of an oppressive colonial-apartheid regime – but like the Isaianic prophecy of a new creation, the black prophets also envisioned something new: a new South Africa. Reflecting on ten years of democratic South Africa, Kumalo argued that the black prophets had to realise that with the transition to democracy, their role also changed to that of nation-building. He went on to say,

> [T]heir theology is no longer prophetic[;] it is concerned with building and constructing the status quo as they see it. No longer can they claim to be part of the prophetic tradition. They must leave it to those who have emerged and taken that role. This does not mean that they can no longer prophesy. Now and again, they can have prophetic impulses, simply because God can use anyone to prophesy. Now that they are in government, they can see things that those outside cannot see. This puts them in a better position to challenge certain policies.[5]

Strydom may have asked the question prematurely, but scholars have pondered the matter again and again. Some in the church lament the church's silence in democratic dispensations,[6] whereas, from academia, some scholars mourn the silence of Black Theology,[7] and yet other scholars have argued for the relevance of Black Theology in the current context.[8] However, where there is a vacuum, something else or someone else comes in and takes that place. We are past the point of merely pondering whether we should be making "funeral arrangements" or "a quantum leap towards resuscitation," to use Slater's words. There is a new movement on the block, the "neo-prophetic movement" sweeping across the nation, and from the look of things, the nation is in love with it. Therefore, the relevant question to ask is no longer, where have all the prophets gone? Rather, it is, whence have all the prophets come? This study, therefore, focuses on the neo-prophetic movement with a specific focus on the prophetic/oracular types which neo-prophets use to deliver their messages, which we reflect on in light of the oracular types used by the Old Testament prophets as *rûaḥ*-filled agents of YHWH.

This chapter is structured as follows: First, we ponder on the notion of saying goodbye to Black Theology considering the emergence of the neo-prophetic movement; and second, we reflect on the neo-prophetic movement with a focus on the oracular types which the neo-prophets use in delivering their messages. The reflection of oracular types is done in the light of those oracular forms, wich Old Testament prophets as *rûaḥ*-filled agents of YHWH utilised.

4.2 Goodbye, black theology – there is a new movement on the block: the neo-prophetic movement

On Saturday, 28 April 2018, the Reverend James H. Cone, who is credited as the founder of the "Black Theology of Liberation," joined the company of black bodies in their eternal rest. As we said goodbye to the Reverend Cone, we wondered, does it necessarily follow that we are also saying goodbye to Black Theology? Can it be that the Tshivenda saying *mufu o ṱuwa na zwithu zwawe* (literally rendered, "the dead went with what is his/hers") applies in this instance? Did Reverend Cone take Black Theology with him, or has he left us a legacy to build on?

In *The Cross and the Lynching Tree*, Cone draws a connection between the death of Christ on the cross and the death of countless black bodies who were lynched on lampposts or trees.[9] Cone lamented that the cross had become a harmless symbol which Christians put around their necks without consideration of the "cost of discipleship," arguing, until we can see the cross and the lynching tree together, until we can identify Christ with a "recrucified" black body hanging from a lynching tree, there can be no genuine understanding of Christian identity . . . and no deliverance from the brutal legacy of slavery and white supremacy.[10]

Within the framework of Black Theology as propagated by Cone, the prophets stand in solidarity with the black bodies and allow blackness to shape their prophetic utterances. During the apartheid era, the Black Theologians of liberation in opting for a prophetic theology took a position to be prophets who stand on the side of the poor and the oppressed. As Cone argues, "The gospel is found wherever poor people struggle for justice, fighting for their right to life, liberty, and the pursuit of happiness."[11]

In our current South African context, the newness of the new South Africa did not obviate the need for the struggle for justice, non-racialism, an inclusive economy, freedom of movement, the return of stolen land, and so on. In our current context, corruption, joblessness, inequality, and poverty undermine the people's right to life, freedom, and justice. The xenophobic attacks which continue to tarnish the image of our country are characteristic of those who live in the zone of poverty – townships, squatter camps, poor urban neighbourhoods. As de Gruchy notes, "If 1994 was a *Kairos* moment, it was not one that called for uncritical solidarity with the newly elected government and the task of the nation-building, but for the ongoing confession of Christ as Lord."[12] De Gruchy argues that instead of prophetic theology continuing into the new South Africa, a new form of "state theology" in support of the state and its policies started to emerge within both white and black churches.[13] Politicians' frequent visits to churches, especially during election time, are further evidence of state and church collusion.[14] Besides, the church's voice is hardly heard in the face of xenophobic attacks on the lives of foreign nationals and foreign-owned businesses. The church for the most part has become apolitical and is no longer actively taking the side of the cross – the side of the suffering, the persecuted, the oppressed, the poor, the lynched, the stoned, the burned, and now in the face of COVID-19 the many who are losing their jobs in the face of the lockdown. Thus, the church is retreating to what the *kairos* theologians termed "church theology" – a theology which does not want to offend the powers that be.

In our view, the waning influence of Black Theology in South Africa, and the church's return to a state of comfort in state theology and church theology created a theological gap within the South African context. Where one thing leaves a gap, another comes in and fills it. The neo-prophetic movement, when it came to South Africa, filled the theological and religious gap. Since the late 1990s, the neo-prophetic movement has snowballed in South Africa. The prophets are drawing audiences both locally and internationally due to the ease of movement and the media. It is an open secret that South Africans travel to Nigeria regularly for a spiritual encounter with the Prophet T. B. Joshua.[15] Our world is now a global village.

The media provides platforms through which religious ideas are disseminated and new religious institutions and movements enter into the public realm.[16] The neo-prophets are also utilising the media to spread information and to draw people. They are making their presence felt in South Africa not only through Facebook, Twitter, and YouTube, but also through television programming. In essence, one simply has to browse through the religious channels and public channels on DSTV (channels such as Trace Urban, TRACE Africa, Sound City, One Gospel, Dove TV, GOD TV, Dumisa, FAITH, Day Star, TBN, iTV Networks, SABC 1, SABC 2, SABC 3, e.tv, Soweto TV, Bay TV, 1 KZN, Tshwane TV, Cape Town TV, GauTV, and Lesotho TV) to observe the sheer number of those who regard themselves as prophets. The prophets are many. They fill up stadiums and large auditoriums, and they have a broad reach – across the country, across the African continent, and around the world.

The neo-prophets are men and women who claim to be filled with the *rûaḥ* of YHWH, which enables them to prophesy and do wonders and miracles. As we will indicate subsequently, the neo-prophets regard themselves as standing in the long tradition of prophecy which has its roots in biblical times as projected in the Old Testament.

4.3 Neo-prophets and their oracular forms

The neo-prophets: who are they, and where do they come from? The neo-prophets mainly operate within the Pentecostal-Charismatic Movement and Churches. This is a dynamic movement, which has had different emphases such as the baptism of the Holy Spirit, a born-again experience, speaking in tongues, miracles, healing, deliverance, use of spiritual gifts, prosperity, and contemporary worship music. The neo-prophetic movement represents a development and a continuity of the Pentecostal movement which believes that Pentecost ushered in a new era in which prophecy is revived, as promised in Joel's prophecy (Joel 2:28–38). In this movement, the events of Pentecost are regarded as having inaugurated the age of the Spirit – a view which many within the Christian circle will concur with. However, there is disagreement among the Christian groups or movements on how the Spirit operates post the finalisation of the biblical canon (Old and New Testament). Some hold the view that prophecy has ceased as a mode of revelation that carries the same authority as the written Word of God, whereas some in the neo-prophetic movement believe that today's prophecies carry the same weight as far as they are inspired by the Holy Spirit.

Thus, the neo-prophetic movement is characterised by openness to the outworking of the Holy Spirit, thereby allowing for new spiritualities, manifestations, and practices to emerge. In the South African context this movement has been gaining momentum since the 1990s.[17] The prophetic dimension is drawing more and more people to the so-called "prophetic churches" in which prophecies take the central role. Collins regards the modern prophetic movement as a culture and lifestyle.[18] It is a culture which frames a believer's behaviour, values, paradigms, beliefs, and worldviews. A prophetic lifestyle, as Collins states it, is "a culture that believes in the supernatural, modern-day prophets, prophecy, apostles and the gifts of the Spirit."[19] This view sees a direct continuity in the function of the Holy Spirit, implying that just as the Spirit was operating during the first century AD, the Spirit is still working today, enabling people to prophesy. Hermeneutically, the way that the Holy Spirit operated in biblical times serves as a model for the church.[20] However, within the African context, as Nel highlights, Pentecostal prophetism appropriates the holistic African worldview by focusing on how the spirit world impinges on the visible world to hinder or foster human flourishing because unemployment, poverty, the challenges of barrenness and an unhappy marriage, sickness, and death are problems that have their provenance in the spirit world – and not physical problems that need secular analysis, as viewed by Western society.[21]

Alph Lukau, who in 2019 was embroiled in the resurrection scandal, in his book *The Rise of the Prophetic Voice*, claims that he wrote the book "under the prophetic guidance of the Holy Spirit" and also declares himself to be a prophet of God.[22] He contends that prophecy is God's "last" weapon and that it is through this that he wants to demonstrate his power to the world.[23] He claims divine inspiration and regards his book as a tool of the Holy Spirit, arguing further that the prophetic ministry today is supernatural and biblical. In his view, just as the biblical writers were supernaturally inspired to receive divine revelation, therefore making the Bible a prophetic book, today's prophetic ministry stands in continuity with the Bible. This implies that the words of the prophets today carries the same authority as the Bible itself.

In the context of the neo-prophetic movement, the gift of "prophecy" is an extraordinary gift to be desired in the life of the church, and a text such as 1 Corinthians 14:1 provides the biblical base for desiring the gift of prophecy: "Follow the way of love and eagerly desire spiritual gifts, especially the gift of prophecy" (NIV). However, this does not necessarily amount to the idea of "everyone prophesying"; instead, there are those appointed individuals who are endowed with the gift of prophecy. These are the Moses-type figures who continue Moses's prophetic tradition:

> The Lord, your God, will raise up for you a prophet like me from among your own brothers. You must listen to him. . . . I will raise up for them a prophet like you from among their brothers; I will put my words in his mouth, and he will tell them everything I command him.
>
> (Deut18:15, 18, NIV; cf. Acts 3:22)

Thus, the neo-prophets see themselves standing in the long tradition of *rûaḥ*-filled prophets from Old Testament times. Therefore, it is necessary to provide a brief description of the Old Testament prophetic movement which they claim as the foundation on which they continue.

In the Old Testament, the prophets were people called by YHWH to communicate their messages to individual Israelites, to Israel as a nation, and to foreign nations. They were receptors of YHWH's message and had to deliver the message using various oracular styles and techniques. The Old

Testament/Hebrew Bible makes use of the following terms for prophets: *nābî* ("the one who invokes God"), *ḥōzeh* ("to see" or "seer"), *rō'eh* ("to see" or "seer"), *qōsēm* ("to divine" or "to predict"), *'îš hā'ĕlōhîm* ("man of God"), and *bĕnê hannĕbî'îm* ("sons of the prophets"). However, sometimes a person may perform the prophetic function without necessarily using these terms or refusing to be referred to as such. In addition, prophetic function was not limited to individual prophets operating in silos. We find examples of families of prophets: Mariam, Aaron, and Moses (Exod 15:20; Num 12); Azariah and Oded (2 Chron 15:8),[24] as well as circles or schools of prophets.[25] Furthermore, the prophetic function does not have to be viewed simply as an informal ministry; instead, people trained to be prophets. The prophetic circles operated under their leading prophets, and within these circles, the metaphor of fatherhood and sonship was used to express the relationship between the leader and the trainees and attendants (1 Kgs 13:11; 20:35; 2 Kgs 2:3, 5, 7, 15; 4:38; 5:22; 5:22; 6:1).[26] Prophetic circles should also be viewed as communities which had distinctive ways of life, including specific dietary regulations, and they were also characterised by prophetic ecstasy (Jer 35).[27] It is essential to note that prophetic communities were male-dominated, though there are a few references to women as prophets (Miriam, Deborah, Hulda, and Noadiah).[28] However, we are not here interested in the development of prophecy in ancient Israel or the historicity of the prophetic movement in ancient Israel.

In the Old Testament, the *rûaḥ* of Elohim (מִיהֹלֱאַ חוּר)[29] or the *rûaḥ* of YHWH (הֹוהי־חוּר)[30] enabled prophets to fulfil their prophetic function. The prophetic spirit in the prophet took various modes of operation: First, the prophetic spirit dwells in the prophet's life from the time the prophet assumes office until the end of the prophetic ministry; however, this spirit can be shared with others or transferred to a successor (Num 11:6–30; 2 Kgs 2:15). Second, the prophetic spirit possesses the prophet, and the prophet prophesies, "Thus says the Lord/God." While prophecy may come from an indwelling of the prophetic spirit, there are also those spontaneous prophetic moments in which the *rûaḥ* possesses the prophet, and therefore, the prophet prophesies (see 2 Chron 24:20). Third, the *rûaḥ* speaks to the prophet, and the words spoken are recorded as the words of the *rûaḥ*. In such instances, the prophet is the receptor of the message, thus the references "to me" (Ezek 3:34; 11:5). Fourth, the prophetic spirit enables the prophet to receive the prophetic message. The *rûaḥ* of YHWH, in this case, functions as an agent of God to enable the prophet to receive the message from divine revelation (Ezek 2:1–5). Fifth, the prophetic spirit is the one who makes prophets see visions; thus, the *rûaḥ* of YHWH acts supernaturally by revealing visions to the prophets (see Ezek 8:3–4; 11:1–4; 11:24–25; 37:1; 43:5).

The prophetic spirit in the Old Testament is contrasted with the *rûaḥ* of lies/deception/falsehood (רֶקָשׁ חוּר; 1 Kgs 22:21, 24; 2 Chron 18:22), which is associated with false prophets. In the Old Testament perspective, false prophets are those who prophesy "according to the own spirits" (אחַר חוּרֵמ,

see Ezek 13:1–6). False prophecy in the Old Testament, as Crenshaw points out, reveals the conflict which existed within the prophetic circle.[31] The existence of false prophets even in the prophetic movement as projected in the Old Testament should also serve as a warning in our current context wherein there are those who claim to be prophets. If prophetic conflict is, as Crenshaw argues, an inevitable component of prophetic ministry, then it is incumbent upon the modern audience to exercise their judgment to determine the true prophets from the false prophets.[32]

4.4 The prophetic/oracular forms used by neo-prophets

In this section, we reflect on the prophetic/oracular types within the neo-prophetic movement, considering that prophecy plays a central role in the movement, howbeit accompanied by other elements such as healing and deliverance. Some tend to view the neo-prophets with suspicion, equating them with traditional healers in the African context and even regarding their prophetic practices as divination.[33] Pondani regards the neo-prophets as "prophets of doom" not so much because they prophesy a message of judgment; rather, drawing from an incident in which a South African prophet used Doom, a pesticide spray, as an instrument of healing. He therefore gives the label to prophets who utilise dangerous healing practices,[34] without dismissing, the negative view that is there about neo-prophets and some of their activities. It is necessary to assess their practices in light of the biblical tradition which they regard themselves as continuing. Therefore, before turning to the oracular forms used by the neo-prophets, we briefly outline some of the oracular forms which the Old Testament prophets used in their prophetic communication:

Judgment oracles: The judgment speech could be against an individual (e.g., 1 Sam 2:27–36; [3:11–14]; 13:11–14; 15:10–31; 2 Sam 12; 1 Kgs 11:29–40; 13:1–3; 14:7–14; 17:1; 20:35–43; 21:17–22; 22:13–23; 2 Kgs 1:6 [16]; 20:14–19; 21:10–15; Amos 7:14–17; Isa 7:10–16; 22:15–25; 37:22–30; Jer 20:1–6; 22:10–12, 13–19, 24–27 [28], 30; 28:12–16; (29:21–23); 29:24–32; 36:29–30; 37:17; Ezek 17:11–21) or the nation of Israel (Isa 8:5–8; 9:7–11, 17–20; 22:8b – 14; 28:7–13; 29:13–14; 30:12–14, 15–17) or foreign nations (Isa 13:1–23:18; Ezek 25–32, Amos 1–2; Nahum, Jonah). The structure of the prophetic judgment speech commonly includes the following two elements: the accusation or reasons for judgment and the announcement of punishment.[35] However, there is flexibility as other aspects may be incorporated into the structure as well:[36] introduction with a commissioning,[37] transitional elements from accusation or reasons of judgment to announcement of punishment.[38]

Woe (יוֹה or יְלָלָא) *oracle:* A woe oracle, while it may be viewed as a subcategory of judgment oracle,[39] has its unique features: vocative of address, accusation, and judgment. The woe oracles are easily identifiable by the introductory woe particle, יוֹה or יְלָלָא, and the language of lament (Isa 1:4,

24; 5:8, 11, 18, 20; 10:1, 5; 16:4; 17:12; 18:1; 28:1; 29:1, 15; 30:1; 31:1; 33:1; 45:9; 55:1; Jer 22:13, 18; 23:1; 30:7; 47:6; 48:1; 50:27; Ezek 13:3, 18; 34:2; Amos 5:18; 6:1; Mic 2:1; Nah 3:1; Hab 2:6, 9, 12, 15, 19; Zeph 2:5; 3:1; Zech 2:10; 11:17). The particle *Hôy!* functions not merely as a call to listen but also as an exclamation that evokes strong emotions against actions that would potentially lead to devastation.

Salvation oracles: The prophets were not merely messengers of doom; they were also messengers of a message of salvation and hope. For Koch, the oracles of salvation follow a pattern similar to that of the judgment oracles: first, description of the situation; second, the promise of salvation; and third, the authorisation of the promise by YHWH (e.g., Jer 28:24; 32:14–15, 36–41; 34:4–5; 35:18–19; 1 Kgs 17:14; 2 Kgs 3:16–19).[40] The oracles of salvation could be addressed to individuals or people, or one or more nations (e.g., Isa 7:7–9; Jer 28:2–4; 31:2–6; 34:4; Amos 9:11–12, 13–15; Mic 5:10–20).[41] The prophets offered a message of hope, especially following the judgment on the people. This type is mainly future oriented as inspiring hope. In the prophetic scheme, hope lies in the future – near or distant – not in the past. The past was useful inasmuch as it reminded the people of the mighty acts of YHWH and gave hope that YHWH would act in the future for the sake of his people. Considering the covenantal arrangement between YHWH and Israel, the oracle of salvation presumed a reversal of judgment or covenantal curses as the people of God returned and blessings were restored. In a sense, prophets were "covenant prosecutors" whose oracles were part of the prosecution case as the prophets charged the people on behalf of YHWH. Therefore, the oracles of judgment and oracles of salvation were projected in terms of the demands of the covenant. Covenantal unfaithfulness invited YHWH's judgment and curses, while covenantal faithfulness invited salvation and blessings.[42]

Oracle of instruction: An oracle of instruction or prophetic instruction is didactic in form. The prophet, as a teacher, instructs the people to keep the law (Torah) and on matters relating to cultic purity and practices (e.g. Isa 1:10–17; Jer 7:21; Amos 5:21–24; Micah 6:6–8; Hag 2:11–12; Mal 2:10–3:12).[43] For Sweeney, the oracle of instruction should be viewed as derived from the wisdom tradition, which used various forms such as commands, prohibitions, rhetorical questions, calls to attention, exhortations, admonitions, and parables.[44]

Sign as oracle: The giving of a "sign" (אוֹת) features as an oracle form in the prophetic announcement (Deut 13:1–6); however, it is not limited to the prophetic activity.[45] When the prophets gave signs, three elements commonly formed part of each oracle: first, the declaration of an event that would be a sign accompanied by the words, "This shall be a sign to you from YHWH"; second, a clause indicating the significance of the sign; and third, a description of the event that would be a sign (see 1 Kgs 13:3; Isa 37:30–32 [2 Kgs 19:29–31]; Isa 38:7–8 [2 Kgs 20:9–10]; Jer 44:29–30). In Deuteronomy 16:1–6 the measure of a legitimate prophet is in the discernment of what the prophet instructs the people to do once the sign is fulfilled: if the sign is fulfilled, but the prophets instruct the people to follow other gods, such a prophet is not a true prophet.[46] Therefore, prophets could give signs which could be fulfilled immediately or soon after or within their prophetic span. The practice of giving a sign could be an initiative from the side of the prophet (Isa 7:14; 20:3, 37:29–30; 38:7–8), but it could also arise from an inquiry from the people (Isa 7:11).

Now turning to the neo-prophets, the following oracular forms are identifiable in the Old Testament: The neo-prophets tend to have their preferences in terms of their oracular types, mainly prophetic telling, prophetic predictions or foretelling, prophetic contests with forces of evil, and the prophet as a bridge between the living and the dead.

4.4.1 Forthtelling oracles

The neo-prophetic prophets often use forthtelling oracles,[47] of which there are three types commonly in use. The first tells about the situation that the individual is experiencing in his or her own life, whether good or bad. The prophet may tell or describe situations which individuals are going through in their personal lives relating to family, work, business, witchcraft, relationships, and so on. The forthtelling usually takes two forms: one is where the individual presents him/herself to the prophet and the prophet then tells what the individual is going through; the other is where the prophet calls the individual out from the crowds by telling their name or their life circumstances, for example a sickness or pain or troublesome situation. The telling of oracles projects YHWH as omniscient and the prophet as his instrument. Such oracles may reveal even secret things or things that the prophet could not have known about if not through revelation.

In the Old Testament, an example of a prophetic forthtelling in the Old Testament is Nathan using a parable to tell David about his adulterous act with Bathsheba and his killing of Uriah (2 Chron 12). The telling of David's iniquity sets YHWH as the one who knows even the iniquities done in secret and who is able to bring them to light (see Ps 90:8; Jer 23:24).

The second type of forthtelling oracles focuses on narrating what the prophet was told by God. It is common to find prophets claiming, "the Lord told me" or "the Lord revealed to me" or "the Lord showed me," and then proceeding to tell what he/she was told or shown. This portrays the neo-prophets as people who have divine encounters uncharacteristic of other people. The forthtelling oracles of the neo-prophets to some extent follow the formula of instruction from YHWH, "go say" or "go and say," as found in the Old Testament. In these cases, the prophet may be responding to an enquiry from an individual, thereby telling what the Lord has shown the prophet (1 Kgs 8:10). Or else the prophet goes and speaks to an individual without necessarily having received an enquiry but as instructed by YHWH (2 Sam 24:12; 1 Chron 21:10; Isa 6:9; Isa 38;5; Jer 35:13; 39:16).

The third type of forthtelling oracle is diagnostic in nature. The diagnosticians tend to focus on revealing causes of sickness, misfortunes, conflicts, and so on. The diagnostic form of forthtelling oracles in some sense is inherited from the Zionist churches which has used this form of prophecy.[48] The diagnostic oracles are tied to the belief that nothing happens without a cause. Therefore, in the African context, where belief in witchcraft is serious, the diagnostic oracles thus serve to solve the mystery behind misfortunes. However, the diagnostic oracles have the potential of stirring up enmity and strife within families, in workplaces, and in the community.

4.4.2 Foretelling oracles

In the neo-prophetic movement there has been a dramatic rise in the number of people who claim the power to foretell things or events. This arises from the sense of openness to the experience of dreams and visions which in some instances foretell the future.[49] The neo-prophets, therefore, can predict or foretell things before they happen. In the current era of television and livestreaming via social media platforms such as YouTube, if the prophet has predicted something correctly, it becomes a big marketing tool, while the predictions which go unfulfilled are quickly forgotten. Now, with the easy access to old recordings, it is also becoming common for them to be retrieved and presented as evidence for or against the claim of successful foretelling.

Neo-prophets utilise a variety of foretelling oracles. The first are predictions of something, good or bad, that will happen or is about to happen in an individual's life. However, there is also an inclination towards offering positive messages, this mainly for those aligned with the prosperity gospel. The second are predictions of secular events or incidents, such as the disappearance of an airplane which is about to happen. However, the coronavirus has caught most of these neo-prophets off guard, as prophecies regarding the current health disaster were hardly uttered, and neo-prophets hardly prophesied about the remedies which could help avert a disaster. Third are predictions relating to high-profile people or celebrities in their absence, such as illness or maybe even the death of a president. Fourth are predictions relating to the results of elections or sports. Such prophecies serve to bolster the image of a prophet as a true prophet. If the prophet has the power to predict what will happen in the future, people in turn believe that the prophet can turn things in their favour.

The Old Testament prophets predicted events in the future. However, as we have noted, when the prophets prophesied about the future, it could be about judgment or salvation. However, future hope also depended on the people's change and return to YHWH. This, however, does not discount prophecies which did focus on individuals. Furthermore, in dealing with Old Testament prophecies, we do not have to discount the fact that the received text is an edited text.

4.4.3 Oracles of confrontation

Neo-prophets often get into contests with forces of darkness – demons. Demonic manifestations are a common feature warranting confrontation and casting out. Therefore, the neo-prophets in their contests with forces of darkness cast out demons.

The concept of engagement with demonic forces is one which is mainly derived from the New Testament. In the Old Testament, the prophetic contests do not venture into the invisible world. Whenever the invisible world comes into view, it is in visions. The stories of dream interpretations do not necessarily venture into confrontations; rather, in those stories YHWH projects himself as the one in charge through those whom he has endowed with wisdom – Joseph (Gen 41) and Daniel (Dan 2; 5; 5). The prophetic contests encountered within the Old Testament are between prophets and magicians (Exod 7:8–9:35)[50] or between YHWH's prophets and the prophets of Baal (1 Kgs 18:20–40) or among the prophets themselves (Jer 28).

4.4.4 Declarative oracles

Because in them resides the power of God, the neo-prophets have the divine power to bless, restore stolen blessings, curse, reverse curses, and declare prosperity, favour, and special privileges. The formula that is commonly used in the declarative oracles is "I declare." It is common in South Africa to come across posters of prophets whose focus is on praying that one finds the right partner or has a happy marriage, that couples reunite, for conception, the breaking of curses, and so on.

While the "I declare" formula is also found in the Old Testament prophets, when the first person is used in the formula, the referent is YHWH, not the prophet (Isa 45:19; Jer 18:7, 9; Ezek 38:19; Hos 5:9; Zech 9:12). Further, when it appears, it is in oracles that concern judgment on and salvation of Israel as a nation, not in oracles that concern the health and prosperity of an individual.

4.4.5 Mediatory oracles

Some of the neo-prophets act as mediums who can link the living and the dead. This form of prophetic dimension focuses on what the ancestors are communicating and what the living can say to the deceased. In this sense, neo-prophets become mediators between the divine world, the ancestors' world, and the human world. The floating of the neo-prophets between the three worlds gives them the power to instruct the ancestors to protect and open doors of wealth to an individual or to stop tormenting the living. They use the African belief system regarding ancestors to gain the trust of their followers. As Anderson notes, "Pentecostalism has been successfully incarnated into a uniquely African expression of Christianity because of its emphasis on spiritual experience and its remarkable ability to adapt to any cultural background in the world – relevant, flexible and rapidly increasing Christian formation."[51]

The only instance in the Old Testament where there is explicit communication with the dead is in the incident of Saul's use of a medium to bring back the prophet Samuel from the dead to communicate with him. This incident, however, is not paradigmatic of what other biblical prophets do. None of the Old Testament prophets engages in bridging the gap between the living and the dead. The venture as a whole did not receive a divine endorsement.

The neo-prophets do not necessarily follow the oracular pattern outline with reference to Old Testament prophets outlined above. However, it is clear that the neo-prophets have adopted several characteristics of the Old Testament prophets, commonly utilising the oracular types which work for them and can make their ministry successful. Some venture into the dimension of functioning as links between the living and the dead or ancestors, even though such has no foundation on prophetic practice as projected in the Old Testament. Therefore, it is incumbent upon the believing community to assess the practices of the neo-prophets in light of the prophetic tradition they claim to continue in.

The oracle forms of Old Testament prophets oscillated between two poles: judgment and salvation. The judgment oracles were accusatory, presuming rebellion on the part of the audience. Where there was rebellion the people could choose not to heed the warnings of the prophets; therefore, the prophets had to utter their oracles "whether they hear or refuse to hear" (Ezek 2:5, 7). The pre-exilic prophets of the eighth and seventh centuries BCE may be viewed as the prophets of doom; their prophecies found fulfilment in Judah in the sixth century BCE. However, after the fall of Judah, the prophetic oracles to a great extent shifted towards oracles of salvation. This, however, is not to imply that oracles of salvation or doom are to be confined to either pre-fall or post-fall Judah. Important to note is that the dimensions of judgment and salvation were characteristic of Old Testament prophets. However, within the neo-prophetic movement, one would not be off the mark to claim that the prophets tend to prefer oracles of salvation in the service of their audience.

The oracles of the Old Testament prophets, while they do focus on individual needs, were much broader in scope. Theirs was not simply an interest in peoples' needs; they were also concerned with national interests and international interests, and they also directed their messages to foreign nations. The neo-prophetic movement tends to focus on individuals' needs and not so much on addressing systematic structures of political and economic oppression and exploitation. These remain unchanged to the disadvantage of the people who remain in the realm of damnation and poverty. The prophetic spirit in the neo-prophetic movement should not be confused with the prophetic spirit of the Black Theology of Liberation. The prophetic spirit in the neo-prophetic movement tends to serve the interests of the followers, and therefore, they tend to focus on personal salvation. To a large extent the neo-prophetic movement promotes the pursuit of self-interests, as Frey argues:

> An ethic of self-interest is incapable of formulating a case against violating its own rules if the violation is motivated by self-interest. The ethic's notion of freedom is essentially without content, leaving each person "free" to be a slave for the desires of self. Finally, the economic ethic poses the paradox that freedom emerges as the highest value in a system that is essentially a deterministic web of material incentives.[52]

Where issues of national and international interest are addressed by the neo-prophets, it is mainly predictions about high-profile people or some or other event that may occur. If the prophet is able to predict events on a global scale, the image of the prophet is enhanced, and in our context, in which the world has become a global village, people are often willing to travel across countries and continents in order to have an encounter with that prophet.

Our society requires *rûaḥ*-filled prophets who are concerned about the common good, the marginalised, poor and suffering. The recent challenge of COVID-19 which all the nations of the world are facing, should serve as a wake-up call as those who stand to suffer the most are the ordinary people whose livelihoods are being shattered through the lockdown. In our South African context, due to the lockdown, those have lost their jobs now have to rely on the Unemployment Insurance Fund (UIF), as the other category of the unemployed become beneficiaries of government grants. The cushioning of the working class and the poor through the insurance fund, grants, donations, and food parcels point to the fact that the working class and the poor have had to carry the brunt of the worsening situation. Furthermore, the so-called new normal of social distancing and isolation should be watched carefully as it may just be the establishment of an exclusionary order entrenching ethnicism and racism. Like the prophets of old, contemporary prophetic voices have to speak against the injustices that are being perpetuated in this situation even under the guise of saving lives.

The purpose of this study is not to condemn the neo-prophetic movement. There is however a need to exercise caution, especially for those within the Christian circle who are drawn to the movement. Wherever there are prophets, false prophets will also be found. Therefore, it stands to reason that not all who claim to be prophets in the current context are operating under the *rûaḥ* of YHWH; instead, there are those working under their own spirits. The prophets of old, when they were found to be false prophets, technically had to be executed (Deut 18:9–22). However, where there are executions of prophets, even those who are not false prophets also become victims. The genuine prophets often find themselves as victims of persecution, slander, and demonisation, especially when their oracles are not accepted due to it being messages of judgment.

4.5 Conclusion

Returning to the question raised at the beginning of the paper: "Whence have all the prophets come?" In short, the prophets who are predominant in South Africa's public domain emerge from the neo-prophetic movement which is an offshoot of the Pentecostal-Charismatic Movement. The neo-prophets, love them or hate them, are here, and they are many, and reaching out to many – their focus is on the plight of the individual, not the community. Unlike the Black Theology of Liberation, which through its prophetic voice strived for the demise of colonialism and apartheid in South Africa, the neo-prophetic movement tend to represent an ethic of self-interest as those who pursue it seek prophecies for themselves with regard to their health, their spiritual and emotional wellbeing, and prosperity. The followers flock to these prophets in the hope of receiving an oracle that may just change their life situation.

The neo-prophets use various oracular forms which are drawn from and resemble the oracle forms utilised by the Old Testament prophets. However, the neo-prophets adapt the oracular forms in line with their own prophetic practices. The prophets of the Old Testament and their prophetic activity serve as a paradigm for their prophetic practise. The use of oracular forms, however, does not guarantee legitimate prophecy. Therefore, it is incumbent upon the hearers to determine if the oracles pronounced are legitimate or not.

Notes

1 Johannes G. Strydom, "Where Have All the Prophets Gone?" The New South Africa and the Silence of the Prophets," *Old Testament Essays* 10, no. 3 (1997): 491–511.
2 Johannes G. Strydom, "Being a Prophet in the New South Africa: Can We Learn from the Old Testament Prophets?" *Old Testament Essays* 13, no. 1 (2000): 103–18.
3 This criticism has been echoed by Simangalo Kumalo, "Prophetic Christianity and Church-State Relations After Ten Years of Democracy," *Missionalia* 33, no. 1 (2005): 99–110; John De Gruchy, "*Kairos* Moments and Prophetic Witness: Towards a Prophetic Ecclesiology," *HTS Teologiese Studies / Theological Studies* 72, no. 4 (2016): 1–7, a3414, https://dx.doi.org/10.4102/hts.v72i4.3414.
4 The concept of "black prophets" or "black theologians" is used in this regard to refer to those theologians who in their theological engagement have propagated the Black Theology of Liberation in South Africa since the late 1960s.
5 Kumalo, "Prophetic," 105–6.
6 Kelebogile T. Resane, "Ichabod – the Glory Has Departed: The Metaphor Showing the Church's Prophetic Failure in South Africa," *Pharos Journal of Theology* 97, no. 1 (2016): 1–12; C. Johan, "Where Have All the Prophets Gone? Perspectives on Political Preaching," *Stellenbosch Theological Journal* 1, no. 2

(2015): 367–83; Mbengu D. Nyiawung, "The Prophetic Witness of the Church as an Appropriate Mode of Public Discourse in African Societies," *HTS Teologiese Studies / Theological Studies* 66, no. 1 (2010): Art. #791, 1–8, https://doi.org/10.4102/hts.v66i1.791; Mookgo S. Kgatle, "The Prophetic Voice of the South African Council of Churches: A Weak Voice in Post-1994 South Africa," *HTS Teologiese Studies / Theological Studies*, no. 1 (2018): a5153, https://doi.org/10.4102/hts.v74i1.5153.

7 See among others, Jesse N. K. Mugambi, *From Liberation to Reconstruction: African Theology After the Cold War* (Nairobi: Acton English Press, 1995); Charles Villa-Vicencio, "Keeping the Revolution Human: Religion and Reconstruction," *Journal for the Study of Religion* 6, no. 2 (1993): 49–68.

8 Ramathate T. H. Dolamo, "Does Black Theology Have a Role to Play in the Democratic South Africa?" *Acta Theologica Supplement* 24 (2016): 43–61; Abraham O. Adebo and Godfrey Harold, "The Relevance of Black Theology in Post-Apartheid South Africa," *South African Baptist Journal of Theology* 22 (2013): 181–98; Timothy van Aarde, "Black Theology in South Africa – A Theology of Human Dignity and Black Identity," *HTS Teologiese Studies / Theological Studies* 72, no. 1: a3176, 1–9, http://dx.do.org/10.4102/hts..v72i1.3176; Cheryl Sanders, "Wanted Dead or Alive: A Black Theology of Renewal," *Pneuma* 36, no. 3 (2014): 406–16, https://doi.org/10.1163/15700747-03603044; Rothney S. Tshaka and Mpeane K. Makofane, "The Continued Relevance of Black Liberation Theology for Democratic South Africa Today," *Scriptura* 105 (2010): 532–46; Francisca H. Chimhanda, "Black Theology of South Africa and the Liberation Paradigm," *Scriptura* 105 (2010): 434–45; Jennifer Slater, "Black Theology: Funeral Arrangements or a Quantum Leap Towards Resuscitation," *Scriptura* 105 (2010): 446–58.

9 James H. Cone, *The Cross and the Lynching Tree* (Maryknoll, NY: Orbis Books, 2011).

10 Ibid., xvi–xv.

11 Ibid., 155.

12 De Gruchy, "*Kairos* Moments," 5.

13 Ibid.

14 See Dion Forster, "A State Church? A Consideration of the Methodist Church of Southern Africa in the Light of Dietrich Bonhoeffer's Theological Position Paper on State and Church," *Stellenbosch Theological Journal* 2, no. 1 (2016): 61–88, 68, http://dx.doi.org/10.17570/stj.2016.v2n1.a04.

15 On 12 September 2014, about 85 South Africans were among the 116 people who died when the guest house of the Synagogue Church of All Nations collapsed. See the reflection of this unfortunate event by Hulisani Ramantswana, "From the Blood of Abel to the Blood of Zechariah to the Blood of Victims Who Died at SCOAN: A Critical Reflection," in *Themes and Trends from Our Pots and Our Calabashes: Navigating African Biblical Hermeneutics*, eds. Madipoane Masenya and Kenneth N. Ngwa (Cambridge: Cambridge Scholars Press, 2018), 103–20.

16 Stig Hjarvard and Mia Lövheim, eds., *Mediatization and Religion: Nordic Perspectives* (Göteborg: Nordicom, 2012); Stig Hjarvard, "The Mediatisation of Religion: Theorising Religion, Media and Social Change," *Culture and Religion* 12, no. 2 (2011): 119–35; Stewart M. Hoover, *Mass Media Religion: The Social Sources of the Electronic Church* (Newbury Park, CA: Sage, 1988); Oliver Krüger, "The 'Logic' of Mediatization Theory in Religion: A Critical Consideration of a New Paradigm," *Marburg Journal of Religion* 20, no. 1 (2018): 1–28; Oliver Krüger, "The Internet as Distributor and Mirror of Religious and Ritual Knowledge," *Asian Journal of Social Science* 32, no. 2 (2004): 183–97; Liv I. Lied, "Religious Change and Popular Culture. With a Nod to the Mediatization

of Religion Debate," in *Mediatization and Religion: Nordic Perspectives*, eds. Stig Hjarvard and Mia Lövheim (Göteborg: Nordicom, 2012), 183–201.

17 Cephas N. Omenyo and Wonderful A. Arthur, "The Bible Says! Neo-Prophetic Hermeneutics in Africa," *Studies in World Christianity* 19, no. 1 (2013): 50–70, https://doi.org/10.3366/ swc.2013.0038.

18 Hakeem Collins, *Born to Prophesy* (Lake Mary, FL: Charisma Media Company, 2013).

19 Ibid., xviii.

20 Robert P. Menzies, *Pentecost: This Story Is Our Story* (Springfield, MO: Gospel Publishing House, 2016).

21 Marius Nel, *An African Pentecostal Hermeneutics: A Distinctive Contribution to Hermeneutics* (Eugene: Wipf & Stock, 2018), 138–39.

22 Alph Lukau, *The Rise of the Prophetic Voice* (Bloomington: Balboa Press, 2019), 3.

23 Ibid.

24 Amos's claim that he is "neither a prophet nor the son of a prophet" also points to the existence of families of prophets. For more on families of prophets see, Yechezkel Kaufman, *The Religion of Israel from Its Beginnings to the Babylonian Exile*, trans. and abridged Moshe Greenberg (New York: Schocken Books, 1972), 227–28; Martin Buber, *Moses: The Revelation and the Covenant* (New York: Harper & Brothers, 1958), 162–71.

25 We note here the following examples of circles of prophets: First, during the time of Samuel, the anointed Saul joins a band of prophets and start prophesying, resulting in the saying "Is Saul among the prophets?" (1 Sam 10:11); Samuel also presided over a group of prophets (1 Sam 19:18–24). Second, in the Northern Kingdom of Israel, during the time of King Ahab, when his wife Jezebel went on killing spree against the prophets, about one hundred were hidden in two caves (1 Kgs 18:4–5). For more on schools of prophets, see Ira M. Price, "The Schools of the Sons of the Prophets," *The Old Testament Student* 8, no. 7 (1889): 244–49.

26 In the succession from Elijah to Elisha, Elisha (a son) received a double portion of the spirit of the Elijah (a father). This form of succession became the paradigm for charismatic succession (Num 11; 27:15–23; Deut 34:9; see Joseph Blenkinsopp, *A History of Prophecy in Israel* [Revised and enlarged; Louisville, KY: Westminster, 1996], 63).

27 On prophecy and ecstasy see, Robert R. Wilson, "Prophecy and Ecstasy: A Re-Examination," *Journal of Biblical Literature* 98, no. 3 (1979): 321–37.

28 Susan Ackerman, "Why Is Miriam also Among the Prophets (and is Zipporah among the priests?)," *Journal of Biblical Literature* 121, no. 1 (2002): 47–80, 50–51; H. G. M. Williamson, "Prophecy and the Prophets in Ancient Israel," in *Prophecy and the Prophets in Ancient Israel*, ed. John Day (New York: T&T Clark, 2010), 65–80.

29 See Num 24:2; 1 Sam 10:10; 11:6; 19:20, 23; 2 Chron 15:1; 24:20.

30 Instances in which the "s/Spirit of God" is used with reference to prophetic possession: Ezek 11:5, 24; 37:1; Mic 2:7; 3:8; Zech 7:12.

31 James L. Crenshaw, *Prophetic Conflict: Its Effect Upon Israelite Religion* (Berlin: Walter de Gruyter, 1971).

32 Ibid., 3.

33 See Augustine Deke, "The Politics of Prophets and Profits in African Christianity," *Politics* 12, no. 1 (2015): 11–24; Marthinus. L. Daneel, "African Independent Church Pneumatology and the Salvation of All Creation," *International Review of Mission* 82 (1993): 143–66, https://doi.org/10.1111/j.1758-16631.1993. tb02659.x.

34 Simbarashe Pondani, "'Prophets of Doom': The Phenomenon of Healing and Power Dynamics in Neo-Pentecostal African Churches" (Master's thesis: Stellenbosch University, Stellenbosch, 2019).

35 For Westermann, the prophetic judgment speech developed from announcements of judgment against the individual, which features prominently in the historical books, to announcements of judgment against Israel and to the foreign nations (see Claus Westermann, *Basic Forms of Prophetic Speech* [Philadelphia: Westminster Press, 1967]).

36 Gene M. Tucker, "Prophetic Speech," in *Interpreting the Prophets*, eds. James Luther Mays and Paul J. Achtemeier (Philadelphia: Fortress Press, 1987), 27–40, 38–39.

37 Westermann, *Basic Forms*, 171, 176.

38 Marvin Sweeney, *Isaiah 1–39 with an Introduction to Prophetic Literature* (The Forms of the Old Testament; Grand Rapids, MI: Eerdmans, 1996), 533.

39 Westermann regarded the woe oracles as a subcategory of the judgment oracles (Westermann, *Basic Forms*, 190–94).

40 Klaus Koch, *The Growth of Biblical Tradition*, trans. S. Cupitt (New York: Scribner's, 1969), 206–15.

41 Sweeney, *Isaiah 1–39*, 25.

42 I am here indebted to Tremper Longman, III, *The Baker Illustrated Bible Dictionary* (Grand Rapids, MI: Baker Book House, 2013), 1248.

43 Marvin A. Sweeney, *The Prophetic Literature* (Interpreting Biblical Texts Series; Nashville: Abingdon Press, 2005), 41.

44 Ibid.

45 The giving of a sign also occurs in instances where there is no human intermediary involved; rather, the intermediary is angelic (Exod 3–4; Jdg 6) or there is no mention of an intermediary (Gen 9; 17; Exod 8; 12:8; 13:9; 31:13–18; Num 16:38; 17:10; Deut 1:1–6; 11:18; 2 Chron 32:24).

46 Some, however, tend to view the instruction in Deuteronomy 13:1–6 as putting restrictions on the prophetic institution. See Hans M. Barstad, "The Understanding of the Prophets in Deuteronomy," *Scandinavian Journal of the Old Testament* 8 (1994): 242–46; Jeffrey Stackert, "Mosaic Prophecy and the Deuteronomic Source of the Torah," in *Deuteronomy in the Pentateuch, Hexateuch, and the Deuteronomistic History*, eds. Konrad Schmid and Raymond Person (Tübingen: Mohr Siebeck, 2012), 47–63, 58–59; Jeffrey Stackert, *A Prophet Like Moses: Prophecy, Law, and Israelite Religion* (Oxford: Oxford University Press, 2014), 135–57.

47 Kgatle classifies this form of oracle as "forensic prophecy" and relates it to divinatory practices. In this form of oracle, the prophet is able to tell minute details such as street addresses, cell phone numbers, and so on (Mookgo S. Kgatle, "Reimagining the Practice of Pentecostal Prophecy in Southern Africa: A Critical Engagement," *HTS Teologiese Studies / Theological Studies* 75, no. 4 [2019]: a51834, https://doi.org/10.4102/hts.v75i4.5133). See also Cephas N. Omenyo, "Man of God prophesy unto Me: The Prophetic Phenomenon in African Christianity," *Studies in World Christianity* 17, no. 1 (2011): 42.

48 Allan Anderson, *Moya: The Holy Spirit in African Context* (Pretoria: University of South Africa, 1991), 53–54.

49 Omenyo, "Man of God Prophesy unto Me," 41.

50 In the confrontation between YHWH's prophet Moses (and Aaron) and the Egyptian magicians, the story is shaped so that the credit goes to Moses and so affirms him as a prophet of YHWH and projects YHWH as more powerful than the Egyptian gods (Exod 9:11; 12:12).

51 See, Allan Anderson, *Zion and Pentecost: The Spirituality and Experience of Pentecostal and Zionist/Apostolic Churches in South Africa* (Pretoria: University of South Africa Press, 2000), 26.
52 Donald E. Frey, "The Good Samaritan as Bad Economist: Self-Interest in Economics and Theology," *Cross Currents* 46, no. 3 (1996): 293–302, 301–2.

References

Adebo, Abraham O., and Godfrey Harold. "The Relevance of Black Theology in Post- Apartheid South Africa." *South African Baptist Journal of Theology* 22 (2013): 181–98.

Ackerman, Susan. "Why Is Miriam Also Among the Prophets (And Is Zipporah among the Priests?)." *Journal of Biblical Literature* 121, no. 1 (2002): 47–80.

Anderson, Allan. *Moya: The Holy Spirit in African Context.* Pretoria: University of South Africa, 1991.

———. *Zion and Pentecost: The Spirituality and Experience of Pentecostal and Zionist/Apostolic Churches in South Africa.* Pretoria: University of South Africa Press, 2000.

Barstad, Hans M. "The Understanding of the Prophets in Deuteronomy." *Scandinavian Journal of the Old Testament* 8 (1994): 242–46.

Blenkinsopp, Joseph. *A History of Prophecy in Israel.* Revised and enlarged. Louisville, KY: Westminster, 1996.

Buber, Martin. *Moses: The Revelation and the Covenant.* New York: Harper & Brothers, 1958.

Celliers, Johan. "Where Have All the Prophets Gone? Perspectives on Political Preaching." *Stellenbosch Theological Journal* 1, no. 2 (2015): 367–83.

Chimhanda, Francisca H. "Black Theology of South Africa and the Liberation Paradigm." *Scriptura* 105 (2010): 434–45.

Collins, Hakeem. *Born to Prophesy.* Lake Mary, FL: Charisma Media Company, 2013.

Cone, James H. *The Cross and the Lynching Tree.* Maryknoll, NY: Orbis Books, 2011.

Crenshaw, James. *Prophetic Conflict: Its Effect Upon Israelite Religion.* Berlin: Walter de Gruyter, 1971.

Daneel, Marthinus L. "African Independent Church Pneumatology and the Salvation of All Creation." *International Review of Mission* 82 (1993): 143–66. https://doi.org/10.1111/j.1758-16631.1993.tb02659.x.

De Gruchy, W. John. "*Kairos* Moments and Prophetic Witness: Towards a Prophetic Ecclesiology." *HTS Teologiese Studies / Theological Studies* 72, no. 4 (2016): 1–7, a3414. https://dx.doi.org/10.4102/hts.v72i4.3414.

Deke, Augustine "The Politics of Prophets and Profits in African Christianity." *Politics* 12, no. 1 (2015): 11–24.

Dolamo, Ramathate T. H. "Does Black Theology Have a Role to Play in the Democratic South Africa?" *Acta Theologica Supplement* 24 (2016): 43–61.

Forster, Dion. "A State Church? A Consideration of the Methodist Church of Southern Africa in the Light of Dietrich Bonhoeffer's Theological Position Paper on State and Church." *Stellenbosch Theological Journal* 2, no. 1 (2016): 61–68.

Frey, Donald. "The Good Samaritan as Bad Economist: Self-Interest in Economics and Theology." *Cross Currents* 46, no. 3 (1996): 293–302.

Hjarvard, Stig. "The Mediatisation of Religion: Theorising Religion, Media and Social Change." *Culture and Religion* 12, no. 2 (2011): 119–35.

Hjarvard, Stig, and Mia Lövheim, eds. *Mediatization and Religion: Nordic Perspectives.* Göteborg: Nordicom, 2012.

Hoover, Stewart M. *Mass Media Religion: The Social Sources of the Electronic Church.* Newbury Park, CA: Sage, 1988.

Kaufman, Yechezkel. *The Religion of Israel from Its Beginnings to the Babylonian Exile.* Translated and abridged by Moshe Greenberg. New York: Schocken Books, 1972.

Kgatle, Mookgo. "Reimaging the Practice of Pentecostal Prophecy in Southern Africa: A Critical Engagement." *HTS Teologiese Studies / Theological Studies* 75, no. 4 (2019): a51834. https://doi.org/10.4102/hts.v75i4.5133.

———. "The Prophetic Voice of the South African Council of Churches: A Weak Voice in Post-1994 South Africa." *HTS Teologiese Studies / Theological Studies* 4, no. 1 (2018): a5153. https://doi.org/10.4102/hts.v74i1.5153.

Koch, Klaus. *The Growth of Biblical Tradition.* Translated by S. Cupitt. New York: Scribner's, 1969.

Krüger, Oliver. "The Internet as Distributor and Mirror of Religious and Ritual Knowledge." *Asian Journal of Social Science* 32, no. 2 (2004): 183–97.

———. "The 'Logic' of Mediatization Theory in Religion: A Critical Consideration of a New Paradigm." *Marburg Journal of Religion* 20, no. 1 (2018): 1–28.

Kumalo, Simangalo. "Prophetic Christianity and Church-State Relations After Ten Years of Democracy." *Missionalia* 33, no. 1 (2005): 99–110.

Lied, Liv. "Religious Change and Popular Culture: With a Nod to the Mediatization of Religion Debate." In *Mediatization and Religion: Nordic Perspectives*, edited by Stig Hjarvard and Mia Lövheim, 183–201. Göteborg: Nordicom, 2012.

Lukau, Alph. *The Rise of the Prophetic Voice.* Bloomington: Balboa Press, 2019.

Menzies, Robert P. *Pentecost: This Story Is Our Story.* Springfield, MO: Gospel Publishing House, 2016.

Mugambi, Jesse N. K. *From Liberation to Reconstruction: African Theology After the Cold War.* Nairobi: Acton English Press, 1995.

Nel, Marius. *An African Pentecostal Hermeneutics: A Distinctive Contribution to Hermeneutics.* Eugene: Wipf & Stock, 2018.

Nyiawung, Mbengu D. "The Prophetic Witness of the Church as an Appropriate Mode of Public Discourse in African Societies." *HTS Teologiese Studies / Theological Studies* 66, no. 1 (2010): #791, 8 pages. https://doi.org/10.4102/hts.v66i1.791.

Omenyo, Cephas N. "Man of God Prophesy unto Me: The Prophetic Phenomenon in African Christianity." *Studies in World Christianity* 17, no. 1 (2011): 30–49. doi:10.3366/swc.2011.0004.

Omenyo, Cephas N., and Wonderful A. Arthur. "The Bible Says! Neo-Prophetic Hermeneutics in Africa." *Studies in World Christianity* 19, no. 1 (2013): 50–70. https://doi.org/10.3366/ swc.2013.0038.

Price, Ira M. "The Schools of the Sons of the Prophets." *The Old Testament Student* 8, no. 7 (1889): 244–49.

Ramantswana, Hulisani. "From the Blood of Abel to the Blood of Zechariah to the Blood of Victims Who Died at SCOAN: A Critical Reflection." In *Themes and Trends from Our Pots and Our Calabashes: Navigating African Biblical*

Hermeneutics, edited by Madipoane Masenya (Ngwan'a Mphahjele) and Kenneth N. Ngwa, 103–20. Cambridge: Cambridge Scholars Press, 2018.

Resane, Kelebogile T. "Ichabod – the Glory Has Departed: The Metaphor Showing the Church's Prophetic Failure in South Africa." *Pharos Journal of Theology* 97, no. 1 (2016): 1–12.

Sanders, Cheryl. "Wanted Dead or Alive: A Black Theology of Renewal." *Pneuma* 36, no. 3 (2014): 406–16. https://doi.org/10.1163/15700747-03603044.

Slater, Jennifer. "Black Theology: Funeral Arrangements or a Quantum Leap Towards Resuscitation." *Scriptura* 105 (2010): 446–58.

Stackert, Jeffrey. "Mosaic Prophecy and the Deuteronomic Source of the Torah." In *Deuteronomy in the Pentateuch, Hexateuch, and the Deuteronomistic History*, edited by Konrad Schmid and Raymond Person, 47–63. Tübingen: Mohr Siebeck, 2012.

Strydom, Johannes. "Where Have All the Prophets Gone? The New South Africa and the Silence of the Prophets." *Old Testament Essays* 10, no. 3 (1997): 491–511.

———. "Being a Prophet in the New South Africa: Can We Learn from the Old Testament Prophets?" *Old Testament Essays* 13, no. 1 (2000): 103–18.

Sweeney, Marvin. *Isaiah 1–39 with an Introduction to Prophetic Literature*. Vol. 16 of *The Forms of the Old Testament*. Grand Rapids, MI: Eerdmans, 1996.

———. *The Prophetic Literature*. Interpreting Biblical Texts Series. Nashville: Abingdon Press, 2005.

Tshaka, Rothney, and Mpeane K. Makofane. "The Continued Relevance of Black Liberation Theology for Democratic South Africa Today." *Scriptura* 105 (2010): 434–45.

Tucker, Gene M. "Prophetic Speech." In *Interpreting the Prophets*, edited by James Luther Mays and Paul J. Achtemeier. Philadelphia: Fortress Press, 1987.

Van Aarde, Timothy. "Black Theology in South Africa – a Theology of Human Dignity and Black Identity." *HTS Teologiese Studies / Theological Studies* 72, no. 1 (2016): a3176, 1–9. http://dx.do.org/10.4102/hts..v72i1.3176.

Villa-Vicencio, Charles. "Keeping the Revolution Human: Religion and Reconstruction." *Journal for the Study of Religion* 6, no. 2 (1993): 249–68.

Westermann, Claus. *Basic Forms of Prophetic Speech*. Philadelphia: Westminster Press, 1967.

Williamson, Hugh. "Prophecy and the Prophets in Ancient Israel." In *Prophecy and the Prophets in Ancient Israel*, edited by John Day. New York: T&T Clark, 2010, LBHOTS 531.

Wilson, Robert R. "Prophecy and Ecstasy: A Re-Examination." *Journal of Biblical Literature* 98, no. 3 (1979): 321–37.

———. *Prophecy and Society in Ancient Israel*. Philadelphia: Fortress Press, 1980.

5 "Simon the Sorcerer offered them money" (Acts 8:19)

Some Pentecostals have gone commercial instead of evangelical

Kelebogile T. Resane

5.1 Introduction

Almost half of Acts Chapter 8 focuses on the apostles' ministry to the individual known as Simon Magus or Simon the Sorcerer, who endeavoured to buy from the apostles the power of conferring the gifts of the Holy Spirit. This encounter resulted in the coining of a new word in the English language, namely "simony". All English dictionaries, ancient and modern, concur that "simony" refers to buying or selling something spiritual or closely connected with the spiritual. It is generally an act of selling church offices and roles or sacred things. It involves improper motives for wanting to be connected with a church office or role, namely financial returns.[1] The title, "magus" is rendered in the Greek text as *mageuō* from *magos*, which means a seer, prophet, false prophet or sorcerer, and it occurs only here in the New Testament.[2]

5.2 The context: identity of Simon the Sorcerer

Simon the Sorcerer was either a Jew or a Samaritan. He was an expert in the art of magic, which had made him famous. Some old Bible versions, such as Murdock's translation allude to the fact that Simon studied philosophy in Alexandria in Egypt and then went to live in Samaria.[3] When he realised that his fame was declining, he fell into sin and became the founder of the sect known as the Simonians. By the time of his encounter with the apostles, he no longer acknowledged Christ as the Son of God and he pretended to be a deity. He paid no heed to the Mosaic Law, although as an enemy of Christianity, he availed himself of some of its doctrines as a way of enhancing and advancing some of its doctrines. He astonished or amazed (*existanōn*) the people by confounding their judgements, which means that he captured their reasoning capacity. In the later verb used (*existēmi*), this means that he displaced people: He mesmerised them to such an extent that they fell under his control because they believed that he was vested with the power of God. The people thus became gullible in the presence of this impostor. In fact, they even supposed that he was the Great God,[4] since this power was considered a spark of God himself. He claimed to impersonate God.[5] Confronted with the gospel, he claimed to believe, but his belief was based more on miracles that he had witnessed than on his conviction that Christ was the means to redeem people from sin. When many of his followers converted to Christianity, he decided not to oppose them so that his trade would not be jeopardised. He could, however, see that the miracles performed by Philip were genuine, as opposed to his own, which were fraudulent.

Simon was thus a precursor of some modern Pentecostal preachers whose interest is in preaching purely for monetary gain. Indeed, Simon was not a real Christian, as is apparent from the whole narrative, especially in verses 18 and 21–23. Since Philip did not pretend to know the heart, Simon was accepted as a Christian because of his profession of faith in Christ. Barnes correctly asserts that this is the only evidence that ministers of the gospel have (i.e. the profession of faith by those to whom they preach) and, consequently, they end up being deceived like Philip was deceived by Simon. The reasons why Simon professed belief in Christ appear to have been the following:

a)   He gained the impression that Christianity was true; the miracles performed by Philip convinced him of this.
b)   Many other people were becoming Christians at that time and he simply followed the crowd. This is a common phenomenon in many revival meetings conducted by commerce-driven Pentecostal evangelists.
c)   He was willing to make use of Christianity to advance his own power, prestige and popularity, which is also a common characteristic among commercial gospel preachers.[6]

Essentially, Simon was amazed that Philip could perform so many miracles – even surpassing his (Simon's) own. The external expressions took precedence over the internal realities of faith in the Lord Jesus Christ. Miracles in this narrative in Acts were confirmation of the power of *kerygma*, not the power of the preacher, and neither were they for commercial gain.

5.3 Commercial gain: The motives and desires of Simon the Sorcerer

The miracles that Simon witnessed the apostles performing challenged his influence among the Samaritans. He therefore felt that he needed some extra powers for which he was prepared to pay to enhance his displays of sorcery. He wanted to employ the tricks of legerdemain for financial gain. He was determined to receive this new power, but without any sense of appreciating the need for Christ as the Saviour of his sins. In order to enhance his influence, he proposed some financial transactions for the purpose of gaining control over the people he led. Simon's motive was not only to pay to gain greater influence, but also to use money to gain control over people for commercial gain; his aim was to expand his commercial base. This idea was absurd, namely that "that which God himself gave as a sovereign could be purchased. It was impious to think of attempting to buy with worthless gold that which was of so inestimable value".[7] Consequently, Simon subtly continued to follow Philip with the aim of discovering the secret of Philip's power and *prosēnegken chrēmata* (offered the apostles money in exchange for receiving their powers). In other words, he was willing to pay money so that he could perform more tricks and thus gain more money. "He regarded spiritual functions as a marketable commodity."[8] Subsequently, when the evil practice of obtaining positions in the church by paying a price or offering a bribe developed, the sin gained the name of "simony" as a result of this incident.[9]

The intention of Simon the Sorcerer was not to obtain the gift of the Holy Spirit for himself, but to obtain the power to bestow the Holy Spirit on other people. He had the sinful desire to gain spiritual power for the wrong reasons and to gain that power by the wrong method.

5.4 Simon the Sorcerer and the Pentecostal preacher

The aim of this paper is to highlight the growing commercialisation of the gospel by some modern Pentecostal preachers. The word "Pentecostal" in this paper includes all within the Pentecostal movement, such as classical, Charismatic and neo-Charismatic branches of this form of Protestant Christianity. To pursue the argument, "commercialisation of the gospel" is defined as a way of understanding the broader context. It has become popular in theological discussions to speak of the "prosperity gospel". In this regard, commercialisation and commodification of the gospel cannot be detached from the prosperity gospel. The Lausanne Movement defines "prosperity gospel" as the teaching that believers have the right to the blessings of health and wealth, and that they can obtain these blessings through positive confessions of faith and the "sowing of seeds" through financial or material gifts[10]

McQuilkin refers to this as the unscrupulous methods of gaining funds through common deception, "bait and switch", psychological manipulation and/or asking for money in exchange for any item that may bring charm, luck or success of any sort.[11] Gitonga affirms this:

> Commercialization of the Gospel could be defined as presentation of the Biblical message either as a commodity for sale for material gain or as an object of investment for personal aggrandizement. The former refers to the sale of spiritual benefits, such as spiritual healing and offer of prayers for special needs. The latter refers to the donation of money or item(s) to the Church with an expectation that God will repay much more in return.[12]

The modern commercialist preachers are covetous men and women who use religion for personal gain. Their kerygmatic activities are the rhetorics of self-glorification in their own prosperity and in the prosperity of those close to them. Their covetous inclinations cause them to resort to lying, stealing, even murdering,[13] placing unconventional demands on the devotees, fraudulent tactics and deceptive transactions in order to get what they want. It is unfortunate that the use of objects and elements for mediating the supernatural is what is gaining prominence in sections of African Christianity.[14]

Commercialisation of theology or religion has become a reality that leaves Christianity with numerous tainted images that question its credibility and sanctity.[15] The past two decades have seen the South African church landscape undergoing a dramatic change. The proliferation of the neo-Pentecostal and neo-prophetic movement has evoked a feeling of either awe or passive disregard in many people. Apart from the claim of miracles being performed – though these are widely refuted as prefabricated – there is also a purely financial appeal that is promoted diversely in the following forms:

> Selling of artefacts or objects of points of contact, such as oil, water, handkerchiefs, prayer towels, etc. It is becoming common for the commercialist preachers to pour libations on the ground as a way of enhancing church growth, while bottles of oil, sand, water and other such substances are given to believers as tools of bringing the much-sought-after blessing. In other places, some of this oil has been sold as church merchandise, alongside hand bangles, handkerchiefs and similar objects.

Appealing to followers to "plant a seed" by contributing a particular amount, which will double or produce 100% returns in profit. The central theme of commercialisation of the gospel is to urge members to sow financial seeds continually so that they can reap bigger and bigger rewards. Praise and worship gatherings are often dedicated to nothing more than collecting offerings, and believers are almost instructed that this is the way to achieve wealth.

Followers are asked to buy a particular artefact, such as a wedding ring, so that they can receive a blessing in the form of a marriage partner. This is often punctuated by impressive testimonies from selected or volunteering church members, almost always bragging about how much they paid for their suits, shoes and jewellery, or how they travelled first class because of "God's blessing". It is an elaborate scam meant to railroad unsuspecting followers into parting with the little hard-earned cash at their disposal. It is simply a gospel of illegal shortcuts, where people are gathered and promised instant results and overnight success, including securing of husbands for desperate unmarried and ageing ladies.

Followers are asked to pay for the seats in auditoria. The closer a person sits to the "man of God" (papa, apostle, prophet or pastor), the more money they should pay and the higher the blessings they will receive. Sometimes these rows of seats are designated as golden, diamond, silver, copper, etc. The followers of the preachers merchandising God's blessing are always reminded that their promised windfall will not materialise unless they continue to give money to the church. These religious demagogues are not soteriological in their mission, but rather see dollar signs in any auditorium full of people.

The existence of doctrinal distortions, pulpit abuse, falsehood and the commercialisation of the gospel has become a hallmark of commercialist preachers. A "cash for Christ" approach earmarks their churches – the more cash you pay, the greater your chances of seeing a bigger miracle take place in your life. This gospel of greed is a disturbing trend that is gaining momentum. Capitalist desperados are masquerading as church planters and special envoys of Christ. In his book, *Foxes in the Vineyard, Insights into the Nigerian Pentecostal Revival*, Sean Akinrele quotes Bishop Mike Okonkwo, former president of the Pentecostal Fellowship of Nigeria (PFN):

> The PFN leadership has discovered that money has sadly become the yardstick for success in the Church, especially the Pentecostals. . . . Prosperity messages have therefore taken centre stage of most preaching at the expense of full gospel messages. This has degenerated to the extent that people now come to church primarily to get rich outside the richness in their souls. Pastors, too, have cashed in on the gullibility of unsuspecting members as symbolism in oil, mantle, honey, palm-leaves, sprinkling of blood, and other mediums are now evolved to build the faith of the people unto materialism.[16]

The commercialist preachers are part of the mainline Pentecostal and Charismatic Movement. They go by titles such as "evangelists", "prophets" and "apostles", often proudly declaring that God is revisiting his people in a fresher way. It is quite common to hear some of them deriding traditional Christian communities as "backslidden" and/or "outdated." A slick version of commercialisation of the gospel originated in the United States and spread from there. Without trivialising the extent of damage caused by commercialisation of the gospel, the reality is that African Christians have now taken this money-focused gospel to new and extremely dangerous levels. Despite the self-enrichment of these men and women of God, commercialisation of the gospel is severely damaging the African social fabric, as well as undermining the nobility and integrity of Christianity itself. It fuels greed and focuses on getting as opposed to giving. It is a selfish, materialistic faith with a thin veneer of Christianity. When these promises fail to materialise, as is always the case, the follower is simply blamed for not giving enough money in offerings or for lacking in faith.

The greatest temptation facing these churches today is materialism – a longing to enjoy the "good life." One result is the lavish style of conspicuous consumption that dominates many of these preachers. These preachers pose the greatest threat to Pentecostal communities. They aspire to ride in the best vehicles, live in the best homes, wear the finest minks and exclusive clothing, and to have large bank accounts. These churches are no longer confined to the storefronts, tents or shacks, but are boasting about building cathedrals or state-of-the-art auditoria.

These modern commercialist preachers thrive in South Africa, as it is a nation that worships health, wealth and happiness. The democratic era opened the country to the euphoria of "the sky is the limit". South Africa is not the only country that has witnessed the commercialisation of the gospel. For the past three decades or so, millions of believers around the world had been trapped into the "health and wealth gospel" through television and printed media. Thousands have flocked to seminars, conventions and telecasts to learn how to apply God's principles of success for prosperous living. The "health and wealth gospel" has become big business.[17] Christian communities and the non-Christian public have been outraged by media coverage of preachers who appear to be selling God for generous financial gain. This application of Simon the Sorcerer's attitude has elevated financial gain above the Bible, leading to the formation of personality cults more than any focus on the Saviour, Jesus Christ.

The question to be directed to these preachers is: Does the Bible teach that Christians will receive large financial returns if they sow their financial seeds in faith? This question is prompted by the charismatic preachers' teaching or reference to 2 Corinthians 9:10–11 to justify their seed-faith scheme:

> Now he who supplies seed to the sower and bread for food will also supply and I increase your store of seed and will enlarge the harvest of your righteousness. You will be enriched in every way so that you can be generous on every occasion, and through us your generosity will result in thanksgiving to God.

The closer examination of this text is that God enriches or blesses us in order to bless or enrich others, not to hoard material possessions for ourselves.

5.5 Brief history of commercialisation of the gospel

The United States of America is historically known as the birthplace of the prosperity gospel, theology and preaching. It is associated with preachers such as Essek William Kenyon (1867–1948), known as "the morning star" who promoted the role and principles of positive confession, faith and healing. The well-known characters who popularised and commercialised the gospel include the likes of Kenneth Hagin, Kenneth Copeland, John Osteen, Joel Osteen, Creflo Dollar and Robert Morris. Kenneth Hagin is the main character involved in this theology, which is why he is termed the "father" of the movement. His Word-Faith theology comprised two principal components: the first was divine healing and the second was the concept that God desired to bless believers materially. It is this second aspect of the Word-Faith theology that eventually developed into the prosperity gospel.

One of the proponents of the prosperity gospel was Oral Roberts. He was the one who introduced a commercialisation component into the gospel. He taught that the prerequisite for harnessing God-given authority is payment of a certain amount to a ministry. He claimed:

> God has given us the authority over sickness, disease, storms, finances and successes. But to exercise this authority, you give me a check, and I will in turn agree with you what decree is appropriate.[18]

Allen was another prosperity preacher who turned the healing ministry into a fundraising mechanism. He viewed prosperity, not as part of God's blessing to all believers, but as a charismatic gift given to him to bestow upon his followers.[19] He once announced that he received a new anointing and a new power to lay hands on the believers who gave $100 in support of his outreach and to bestow upon each of them the power to gain wealth.[20]

South Africa, too, has a plethora of prosperity gospel preachers who intertwine and popularize their gospel with commercialisation gimmicks. The pioneer of the gospel of prosperity in South Africa is Raymond McCauley of Rhema Bible Church. He earned his place in history, however, not just because he was the first South African to articulate the message, but because of how he took this theology to the elite multiracial masses. His message made an appeal to the South African fragmented society of the eighties, which was sharply divided because of racial segregation. His message was clear: Christians ought to have access to material wealth and live life to the full. McCauley believes that God created men and women for a better life than many are currently experiencing and that He never intended anyone to go through life imprisoned by their own superstitions. As far as he is concerned, God opens the door of success to every believer who will dare to step out and go after the good life. No one in God's family was ever destined to exist in sickness, fear, ignorance, poverty, loneliness or mediocrity. God's abundant goodness will be enjoyed and utilised by those who discipline themselves and become decisive, bold, adventurous, believing, daring (willing to take risks) and determined. Today, thousands of pastors across South Africa proclaim the same message as McCauley. These pastors preach in cities, towns, suburbs, townships and villages.

Among these and many other preachers of similar persuasion it is easy to see that their message focuses primarily on the establishment and enjoyment of the kingdom here on earth before that of heaven. Most of their preaching is void of socioeconomic or political activism. Materialism not gained by faith as a blessing from God and political involvement are the worldly pursuits that should not taint God's children, lest they miss the mark, which is the goal of getting to heaven.

5.6 Why gospel commercialists gained ground in South Africa?

South Africa is a country that has been engulfed in a cloud of darkness. This darkness came about because of colonial and segregationist ideologies that left many people in distress and poverty, as well as making them feel rejected and excluded on the African continent. Out of desperation to unshackle themselves from these dark clouds, South Africans started to view Christ from a need-providing perspective and as an immediate provider, comforter and miracle-worker who has the capacity to enrich them in the face of hardship, rejection and devastation. The socioeconomic problems of South Africa, as is the case all over the African continent, drive Africans to look to Jesus Christ for immediate solutions to their challenges.[21]

The commercialist theologians or preachers rely heavily on the interpretation of the Christian scriptures. They use the familiar theological language, which makes their message even more dangerous. They use scriptures to teach that believers can have whatever material goods they want, such as luxury homes and cars, and live a prosperous life. Their preaching promises believers that if they fulfil God's purpose in giving, God will open the floodgates of abundance into their lives; as long you believe, your seed will grow into multiple blessings from God. The Old and the New Testament passages are interpreted to suit the aim of achieving prosperity theology. The main tenet of prosperity theology is that God wants the believer to be materially wealthy and healthy. According to Temitope, these theologians always search for those verses in the Bible that could be interpreted to suit this purpose.[22] It does not matter whether that interpretation corresponds with what the author intended or matches its contemporary interpretation, following the authentic hermeneutic principles, as long as it suits the purpose of gaining the desired goal. The prosperity theologians shrewdly take advantage of the situation of the believers in their community or society. What really makes commodification and commercialisation of the gospel thrive in Africa is its emphasis on three Ps (power, protection and prosperity). These are exactly the reasons why Africans consult witchdoctors. The strategy works well and the formula has gained much ground on African soil. The third P sometimes represents not just prosperity, but also prestige.

In the typical African culture, a witchdoctor is consulted for various, one of them being to gain power. This may be power to prevail over enemies, power to control others, or power to repel bad omens or overcome life-challenging circumstances. The gospel commercialists emphasise this power, with the result that many Christians abandon their conservative Christian traditions and run to a prosperity preacher to gain this power.

Life is precious, so it should be protected. This is the second reason Africans flock to prosperity preachers: here they receive promises of protection by the blood of Jesus Christ. The followers are told of the curses that they were born with or that occur in their families. To break these curses, the followers are invited to believe in God by pledging an amount to the "man of God" or the "apostle" or the "prophet". Many people consult these preachers to obtain protection against their enemies' crafty tactics or protection of their possessions against natural disasters such as lightning strikes, floods, livestock miscarriages and even death.

The third reason for the prosperity gospel's gaining ground in Africa is the desire for prosperity. People want to succeed in all areas of life: employment, wealth, health, fertility, etc. Consequently, they consult a prosperity preacher to ensure success in life. Africans regard misfortunes as curses and evidence of showing disregard for their ancestors. Poverty, though rampant, is considered unacceptable. People whose lives are unsuccessful can be aligned and rectified by the prosperity preacher who leads the devotees into prayers of faith.

Temitope highlights the aforementioned three main factors that have caused the prosperity gospel to gain ground in Africa, but a few more are discussed below:

Ignorance: When a person is ignorant, it is very easy for them to be manipulated by someone who is informed. Many people have no understanding of the scriptures, even when they read them daily. The lack of critical and intellectual understanding of the scriptures make many very vulnerable to deception: they are easily convinced or do not even question whatever they are told in the name of God. This has made the task of prosperity theologians or preachers very easy.

Poverty: Many people live in abject poverty and in their desperation to achieve a better life, they are willing to do anything demanded of them, especially when such guidance comes from the church leadership. So it is easy to manipulate these people with the aid of the scriptures. They are asked to "sow seeds" – even with the little they have – so that they can "harvest plenty in return". Many scriptural verses are quoted out of context or are mishandled hermeneutically to support this idea.

Fear: Fear of financial loss and resulting poverty, well as the need to seek protection for their accumulated wealth, is the quest of the rich. As a result, it is easy to manipulate the rich into submission; seeking succor within the church, they are prepared to give any amount to secure it. So they become easy prey to prosperity theologians or preachers. It is easy to see that ignorance affects both the rich and the poor. They both lack or need something, but it is not what they think it is; it is knowledge. They are not familiar with the essence of the scriptures, neither do they understand the meaning and message of the gospel. Therefore, it is easy for these prosperity theologians or preachers to exploit their ignorance. Prosperity theologians have thus been able gain ground in their ministry of exploitation, rather than in the propagation of the gospel and the soteriology proclamation.

Claims of encounters with the supernatural: Most, if not all the commercialists, like many cultists, claim to have had a supernatural encounter with God. This is always in the area of healing or being enriched after living in poverty. In some cases, these preachers claim to have encountered miracle workers. Such encounters apparently do not leave the breakaway ministers untouched leading to what may be deemed the commercialization and commodification of the gift(s) of healing and miracles characterized by the purchase of certain spiritual items, such as holy oil, water, handkerchiefs, pens and pencils, et cetera.[23]

Young and inexperienced pastors: One of the greatest threats to the Pentecostal faith today is from its leadership, which is increasingly infiltrated by shameless swindlers. This is threatening the nobility and integrity of the Christian faith, as many who fall under their "spell" become victims and abandon or nullify the authenticity of the Christian faith. The aim of these commercialists is to advance the financial standing of their leader and his or her family. One of the main reasons for commercialists is the poor training of pastors or the total absence thereof. It has become a norm that many South African prosperity preachers authenticate themselves by making pilgrimages to Nigeria. They make a few visits or they frequent Nigeria and, thereafter, plant new churches where commodification and commercialisation of the gospel become the means and the ends of their ministry. The naivety of these preachers, which is exacerbated by a lack of theological training and their misunderstanding or ignorance of servant-leadership, results in their assuming the status of a movie star. They fall into the "star" trap and get caught up in the "man/woman of God" syndrome. The "man of God" syndrome is aptly described by Adeleye in the book, *Preachers of a Different Gospel* (2011), where he mentions that "men of God" have become "stars and celebrities".[24] Preaching has become a skilful marketing art for fundraising and commercial gain.

5.7 Simon the Sorcerer's tactics amounted to spiritual abuse

The association between religion and wealth (money) is a controversial topic for African Pentecostal and Charismatic Christianity. There has been much debate about how the wealthiest pastors have accumulated their wealth, since the majority of them have lavish lifestyles. Knowing how these men and women of God accumulate their wealth will enable us to make an accurate assessment whenever this topic comes up.[25] Spiritual abuse, or the abuse of the Holy Spirit, is closely associated with commercialisation of the gospel. "Spiritual abuse" refers to the mistreatment of a person who needs help, support or greater spiritual empowerment, with the result that is weakens, undermines or decreases that person's spiritual empowerment.[26] Often, financial deals or transactions are employed as a means of obtaining or attaining some form of spiritual empowerment; this may be dubbed by commercialist preachers as "spiritual breakthroughs" or "release from spiritual bondage". Typically, these preachers use Bible passages about generosity to justify controlling the victim's money.

There are two biblical concepts that appeal to these preachers and their listeners, namely revelation and anointing. Mainstream theology understands revelation as a doctrine where the *logos* (Christ) and *biblos* (Bible = Written Word) are the full revelation of God. However, the neo-Pentecostal leaders believe that such revelation is continuing and it is always called "the word of knowledge" or "prophecy". In most instances, these so-called prophetic utterances are personal and subjective. Therefore, they are difficult – if not impossible – to substantiate or judge according to the complete revelation of God, as contained in the bible. O'Donovan[27] claims that if these new revelations are true, then they are "different kind of revelation from the revelations in the Bible, which are for all men of all cultures".

The other point of appeal used by commercialist preachers is known as "anointing". Few of these preachers can define or analyse this concept; it is all substantiated by charisma, so-called inspiration and the eloquence of the preacher. Provided the preacher touches or goes beyond the cognitive level of the hearers, the response will always be that "he's moving under or by anointing". While Simon the Sorcerer wanted to use money to buy God-given power, commercialist preachers use biblical concepts to convince people to give them money. Moreover, they subtly accumulate wealth from people to cover up their money-mongering activities. Their accumulated wealth is not gained with the aim of bestowing power on others; it is purely for selfish gain.

Very little has been documented about the richest pastors in South Africa, which has caused this issue to be controversial. Commercialist preachers, even here in South Africa, continue to assure the public that their wealth is not from the congregants, nor from the clients who come to them for private consultations. They claim that their wealth is the result of their hard work, since they are also entrepreneurs. For instance, Prophet Paseka Motsoeneng (Mboro) has been accused of exploiting religion to get rich, but he claims that he accumulates wealth through a construction company and funeral parlour that he owns. Prophet Shepherd Bushiri is an accomplished entrepreneur who has invested in various fields of activity, among them real estate, gold mining, an electronics company and a telecommunications company. He also owns several farms in the country. In addition, he owns the Bushiri University of Agriculture, which is situated in South Sudan. Pastor Alph Lukau has an investment company that exerts much influence within the properties he owns. These properties make him one of the richest pastors on the continent.

5.8 Dealing with the doctrine correcting the viewpoint? of Simon the Sorcerer: return to the Pentecostal basics

Pentecostal theology and praxis are derived from the holiness movement, whose dogma was rooted in Wesleyanism, dispensationalism and evangelicalism in general. At the centre of it Pentecostal dogma is the doctrine of holiness, which emerged from the holiness movement that was associated with revivalist activities in the nineteenth century.[28] The early Pentecostal forebears were characterised by *kerygma* in terms of the two Ps, namely, purity and power. One of the modern Pentecostal teachers, Frank D Macchia, asserts the following:

Purity and power cannot be played off against one another or synchronized abstractly but viewed as attributes and works of the God revealed in Scripture, especially in Christ as redemptive love, who is present polyphonically in ever expansive and gifted relationships of love and faithfulness. It is divine love that is both pure and powerful.[29]

This refers to the desired purity of heart given to believers who are willing to submit to Christ to the fullest extent possible.[30] We should bear in mind that the Pentecostal movement was formed from among the people at the margins of mainstream society who felt oppressed, socially disinherited and economically disarmed, but who yearned to experience God. Pentecostals have always belonged to the marginalised members of society and are characterised by a radical para-modern counter-culture identity.[31] Things started to change towards the end of the twentieth century, when health and wealth became the primary focus for some Pentecostal preachers.

These two Ps, purity and power, were associated with the idea of sanctification as a second blessing that cleansed a seeker from inbred sin, thus preparing them for the reception of the Holy Spirit.[32] The historical development of the approach or view of holiness in Pentecostal dogmatology has assumed many forms. For instance, those emerging from the Wesleyan tradition incorporated into their vision of the spiritual life the motifs of both sanctification/perfection and spirit baptism.[33] Adherents of the holiness movement retained the place of sanctification as a "second blessing" that cleanses the seekers from their original sin. Those from reformed backgrounds, such as the Baptists in particular, are of the opinion that Christian experience involves two steps, namely, conversion and baptism with the Holy Spirit.[34]

The Wesleyan doctrine of sanctification influenced the Pentecostal view of holiness, especially because the Wesleyans did not formulate this doctrine by means of a system of logical deduction from textual propositions. "Their convictions on the possibilities of perfection in love in this life and a faith experience of heart cleansing subsequent to justification grow out of their attempt to see Scripture holistically."[35] Out of these deductive explorations, the Wesleyans and Pentecostals concur that the sanctified are to demonstrate the holiness and love that build a saintly character and to align this character with the character of God. The holy God wants to commune with holy people.

As mentioned above, one of the distinctive features of Pentecostalism is the emphasis on piety or holiness. The principle of moral thought with the most theological weight focuses solely on piety or holiness. Pentecostals tend to lean heavily on the Pauline theology in terms of morality. The moral thought emanates from the Pauline exhortations, such as that the task of the minister of Christ is to "present everyone perfect in Christ" (Colossians 1:28). Kärkkäinen expresses and summarises Pauline moral instruction, which – in addition to having charismatic, prophetic and eschatological dimensions – a moral transformation by means of the spirit.[36] It is the task of the Holy Spirit to renounce the flesh. Even though the new has come and the old has passed away, there is a constant struggle, even warfare, between spirit and flesh. Therefore, the believer is expected to take a personal responsibility to live their life in the power of the spirit.

The Holy Spirit's immediate inspiration is also key to Pentecostal ethics. Pentecostals tend to believe that a spirit-filled person will have the Holy Spirit as his or her internal moral compass for making sound moral and ethical decisions. This can rightly be judged as subjective, hence one reason for the numerous ethical scandals that have plagued Pentecostalism. Regardless of this doctrinal outlook, sanctification, which influences the Pentecostal doctrine of holiness, sets apart the Pentecostal *kerygma* and instils the fear of God in those who have been baptised with the Holy Spirit. Pentecostal systematic theologian ES Williams concurs that sanctification enables us to live above the sin, self-will and spiritual anarchy of the world and to live for God instead.[37] If this was well understood by modern-day commercialists, they would shun the spiritual anarchy (such as commercialisation of the gospel) in this world.

The Pentecostal understanding of holiness is associated with some forms of asceticism and, in some cases, also with certain extreme legalistic and teetotal practices. Eschatological emphasis, especially the second coming of Christ, did more to alter Pentecostal principles of moral thought and action than any theological instruction. It is believed that people should live righteously, lest the *parousia* catches them off guard, unprepared or engaged in sinful activities. This piety has always guided Pentecostal moral theology up to the present time. Pentecostals' belief in holiness continues to make them suspicious of anything that smacks of worldliness. For example, their abhorrence of alcohol consumption has always been associated with worldliness. We still encounter testimonies of people's being healed from alcohol and drug abuse (morphine and other opiates) and generally being delivered from morally vacuous behaviour, such as too much obscene dancing and other forms of immoral amusement. However, the doctrine of holiness, especially its meaning and application, continues to be under the radar. The divergent views and proliferations are rampant, hence: "Holiness doctrines present a greater problem of reinterpretation, and recent years have seen a variety of theological methods applied to the task."[38]

Despite all divergencies of holiness interpretations, the return to this doctrine instils a fear of God, respect and appreciation of human dignity and, of course, the piety for righteousness for the sake of the gospel of the forgiveness of sins. If the modern gospel commercialists could pursue this holiness, they would not be vying for ungodly financial transactions intended for self-enrichment. This involves not only financial ethics. Pentecostalism has been corroded by the spirit of Simon the Sorcerer. The Pentecostal church historians Shaull and Cesar decry this anomaly that corruption, sexual deviations, swindling, false miracles and exploitation of the poor are some accusations levelled against Pentecostal leaders.[39] Money is a driving force and it is used as both the means and the end to fake the power of the gospel.

One of the fundamental doctrines in Pentecostal theology is eschatological hope. Generally, Pentecostal eschatology is premillennial and apocalyptic. Belief in the physical, personal, literal second coming of Jesus ranks as one of Pentecostals' most important tenets of faith.[40] It is the most important feature of Pentecostal spirituality and it is a stimulus to Christian service, holiness and, in particular, evangelism. Steven J. Land expresses it as an "expectancy of the coming fullness of righteousness, peace, and joy that feeds the activism".[41] This *parousia* will be personal, sudden, glorious and unexpected. As a stimulus, this hope encourages the believers to walk morally and ethically, lest they be caught off guard. Pentecostal forebears lived and preached from an eschatological vantage point. They focused their spirituality on pathos, with a passionate yearning and sighing for the kingdom of God to come. Macchia alludes to the fact that Pentecostals view themselves as a missionary fellowship living from the outpouring of the Holy Spirit and anticipating the ultimate fulfilment of the divine goals for history.[42] This encourages them to connect personal sanctification with the eschatological restoration of God's kingdom. The central dictum was never predictions regarding dates or seasons of the second coming of Christ. The pertinent question has always been: "Are you ready for Jesus' return?" The stimulus effect of this question has always been deduced from the texts, such as "Occupy till I come" (Luke 19:13); "When the Son of Man comes, will he find faith on the earth?" (Luke 18:8); "Watch and pray so that you will not fall into temptation" (Matthew 26:41); and many others.

Archer paints a picture of Pentecostal preachers who, in their itinerant ministries, "challenged Christians to be prepared for the second coming of Jesus, which they believed would take place very soon".[43] This eschatological expectation is seen as a healing and a help towards the triumph of faith. In the present dispensation, Pentecostal believers are exhorted to wait patiently with this glorious hope in mind, with the understanding that this second coming may happen unexpectedly. Cox describes this eschatological hope as a *primal hope*, which is Pentecostalism's millennial outlook that a radical new age is about to dawn.[44] This is a Pentecostal theology of immediacy, which has seen the kingdom that is coming, but has also lived in the kingdom that is now.[45] Therefore, Pentecostal Christianity is Christianity on standby expecting something to happen. In the words of Nelson: "Many missionaries traveled from their Pentecostal experience to remote parts of the world sensing the missionary zeal to fulfill the Great Commission before Jesus' return."[46]

As can be expected, all Pentecostal practices are under the influence of the apocalyptic vision, which gives them urgency and focus. This is a focus that needs to be restored in the commercialist preachers so that they can implement it in their own lives, as the restoration of the Holy Spirit is imminent. Some serious self-examination by these preachers can contribute towards a return to the fundamentals, especially the fact that the Pentecostal mission here on earth is the restoration of the fallen humanity to the original state of fellowship with the holy God. It is disheartening to observe that indeed "a theology of success and power is expounded at the expense of a theology of the cross".[47]

Apart from the doctrine of holiness and of hope, Pentecostals of the past were known for their humility, as Archer alludes to the fact that Pentecostals were the oppressed, marginalised, poor working classes of society.[48] Yet they remained humble and continued to serve by imparting the message of hope in humility.

They moved from town to town walking, hopping delivery wagons, jumping freight trains, or bumming rides. They travelled throughout the land often warning sinners from courthouse steps, city parks, dance halls, gambling houses and red-light districts about the coming wrath of God.[49] Commercialist preachers consumed by the spirit of Simon the Sorcerer should learn to walk in humility by declaring the great commission, which involves the making of disciples in keeping with God's purpose. Humility compels us to accept that "ecclesial life is diaconal and missional",[50] as opposed to seeking self-enrichment, where wealth is amassed at the expense of the naïve and poor masses. Frank Bartleman, an eyewitness to the Azusa Street revival, in the closing remarks of his memoirs, states:

> The early church put God first, self last. We have self first, God last. This was the secret of the early church's power. The church is a backslider. But we are coming around the circle. She is to be fully restored . . . Humility, not infallibility, becomes fallen creatures. Water seeks the low places . . . The deepest repentance and humility, our own frailty and weakness, must be realized before we can know God's strength.[51]

One typical South African example of humble Pentecostal preachers is Nicholas H Bhengu of the Assemblies of God. According to Dan Lephoko's unpublished MA thesis at the University of Pretoria (2005: 64) Bhengu asserted that his hands were clean before God and men: "I have desired no high life, luxury, pomp, greatness, wealth, name, fame, or vain glory, I have taken no money for myself apart from what I take for the work of God for (sic) poor countries." He warned, however, that "some will see an opportunity to get rich". Bhengu further despaired: "The church leaders and the church itself are both capitalistic and scorn at all social concern for the people." (Undated circular). The same sentiment is expressed by Bhengu's wife, Nokwethemba, who testified to the simple lifestyle led by her late husband:

He would not spend the church's money on himself. All the money had to go toward mission and evangelism to bring people back to God. He lived in the township among the people in a four-roomed matchbox house. He warned his ministers not to live beyond their means (Telephonic interview: N. Bhengu 2003.10.27; 2005:23).

It is commonly believed among Christians and non-Christians alike that the desire among many evangelists, Christian workers to preach is motivated by greed for money they can make. At revival meetings evangelists give out envelopes to people with the promise that if they gave to the evangelist, God will give them more money and they can get rich and prosper in all spheres of their lives. This Prosperity Doctrine is also preached and promoted in many of the Charismatic Churches commonly known as Ministries.[52] Bhengu was a man who committed himself to using money to promote God's work rather than to enrich himself. What a legacy he left and what an example of humility he set! This is what the contemporary commercialist Pentecostal preachers should be seeking to emulate. Theology of the cross was at the centre of many Pentecostal preachers' message, but unfortunately that is a missing theology among these Charismatics today, so attempts must be made to inculcate this theology in any pastoral training and ministerial formation. It is to be acknowledged and accepted that the cross is not only to be interpreted as a source of victory, but also as a symbol of shame, humiliation and suffering.[53] Humility in God's service leads to honour – honour that cannot be achieved through power, business acumen, eloquence, money or ideal organisational structures and strategies. "Rather we find that God regularly is found among the least, the cast-off, and the weak. He uses the humble and those who seek Him."[54]

Conclusion

Commercialisation of the gospel is not a new thing, and it has increased with the evolution of technology, since "the publicity through diverse media, especially television, internet and radio attracts naïve subscribers at the exorbitant prices".[55] Ever since the time of Simon the Sorcerer, there have been many attempts to turn the spiritual into the commercial, to traffic the things of God and, especially, to purchase ecclesiastical office – deliberations known as "simony".[56] Simon the Sorcerer had the misguided idea that a person could obtain the power of God through some financial transaction. In today's world, the acts and the power of God to heal, bless, deliver, etc are all up for sale. The central idea of this paper is well summarised by Marshall:

> The possession of any kind of spiritual authority is a solemn responsibility rather than a privilege, and its possessor must constantly be aware of the temptation to domineer over those for whose spiritual welfare he is responsible; he must also beware of the danger of using his position

for his own ends, whether as a means of making money or bolstering his own ego.[57]

These preachers, who unfortunately subscribe to the Pentecostal faith, continue to deceive multitudes, both poor and eminent citizens, who seem to be as gullible as the masses described in the Book of Acts, and claim that "this man is the divine power known as the Great Power" (8:10). Like Simon the Sorcerer, the commercialist preachers believe – as do all Pentecostals – are converts and, of course, in a customary way they submitted to the rite of baptism. Their language is appealing as it sounds theologically accurate, biblically grounded and, of course, mentally and emotionally convincing. The majority of them are secessionists from either a classical Pentecostal denomination, a mainline denomination or another charismatic grouping, since many "Christians from mainline Christianity abandon their *catechesis* and *paradosis* to pursue these manifestations".[58] The call is for the modern Pentecostal preachers who have turned commercial to return to their Pentecostal forebears' pursuit of the doctrine of holiness, eschatological hope and humility, which characterised the Pentecostal preachers of the twentieth century.

Notes

1   Albert Barnes, *Notes on the New Testament: Explanatory and Practical. Acts* (Grand Rapids, MI: Baker Book House, 1979), 142.
2   Archibald T Robertson, *Word Pictures in the New Testament, Vol III: The Acts of the Apostles*, vol. III (Nashville: Broadman Press, 1930), 104.
3   James Murdock, *The New Testament: Translated from the Syriac Peshito Version* (New York: Broadway, 1852) (Mosheim I. pp 113–14). James Murdock lived before the 1900s. Unlike today, it was a time when literally all academic and ecclesiastical authorities believed in the inspiration of the Holy Bible, and the 'Syriac' Aramaic New Testament was especially held in high esteem. Murdock was an honest, Bible-believing Christian, and his translation is evidence that conviction. Like all his peers at the time, Murdock held the Peshitta in high esteem.
4   Barnes, *Notes*, 140.
5   Robertson, *Word Pictures*, 104.
6   Barnes, *Notes*, 140.
7   Ibid.
8   Robertson, *Word Pictures*, 107.
9   Howard Marshall, *The Acts of the Apostles: An Introduction and Commentary* (Leicester: Inter-Varsity Press, 1998), 158.
10 Lausanne Movement, accessed January 21, 2020, http://conversation.lausanne.org/en/home/prosperity-gospel.
11 Robertson McQuilkin. *An Introduction to Biblical Ethics* (Columbia, SC: Columbia Bible College and Seminary, Class Notes for Biblical Ethics, 1988), 358–62.
12 Nahashon Gitonga, "Commercialization of the Gospel in Africa with Particular Reference to Kenya: A Critique," *Kenya Methodist University* 2, no. 2 (2011): 320, accessed August 17, 2019, http://41.89.26.5/cgi-bin/koha/opac-detail.pl?biblionumber=146929.

13 Warren Wendel Wiersbe, *The Integrity Crisis: A Blemished Church Struggles with Accountability, Morality, and Lifestyle of its Leaders and Laity* (Nashville: Oliver-Nelson Books, 1991), 36.

14 Simon Kouessan Degbe, "African Pentecostal/Charismatic Iconography: A Study of their Significance and Relevance," *International Journal of Pentecostal Missiology* 6, no. 1 (2019): 64.

15 Kelebogile Resane, "Commercialisation of Theological Education as a Challenge in the Neo-Pentecostal Charismatic Churches," *HTS Teologiese Studies / Theological Studies* 73, no. 3 (2017): a4548, 3, https://doi. org/10.4102/hts. v73i3.4548.

16 Sean Akinrele, *Foxes in the Vineyard: Insights into the Nigerian Pentecostal Revival* (Lagos: Lerinyo Media, 2013), 112–13. This book seeks to answer these questions and more. The author, with a great burden and clear teaching mandate, delves into the past to challenge the pathetic reality of the Pentecostal church today. He challenges its wrong impressions about God, Jesus and the Spirit of God, the reality of self-idolatry, autocracy, illicit power acquisition and unscriptural indulgence's threatening to destroy the labour of old saints.

17 Michael Moriarty, *The New Charismatic: A Concerned Voice Responds to Dangerous New Trends* (Grand Rapids, MI: Zondervan Publishing House, 1992), 297.

18 Michael Horton, *The Agony of Deceit* (Chicago: Moody Press, 1990), 126–28.

19 Nico Horn, *From Rags to Riches* (Pretoria: University of South Africa, 1989), 34–35.

20 Ibid., 34.

21 Philip Jenkins, *The New Faces of Christianity: Believing the Bible in the Global South* (New York: Oxford University Press, 2006), 89–93.

22 Ogunlusi Clement Temitope, "Prosperity Gospel Preaching and Its Implications on National Developments," *International Journal of Humanities and Cultural Studies* 5, no. 1 (June 2018): 313–330, 317. ISSN 2356-5926, www.ijhcs.com/ index.php/ijhcs/index.

23 Madipoane Masenya and Malesela Masenya, "Church Breakaways as a Prototype of Commercialization and Commodification of Religion in the Pentecostal Church Movement in South Africa: Considering Curricula Offerings for Pastors," *Stellenbosch Theological Journal* 4, no. 2 (2018): 640.

24 Femi Adeleye, *The Preachers of a Different Gospel: A Pilgrim's Reflections on Contemporary Trends in Christianity* (Grand Rapids, MI: Zondervan Publishing House, 2011). The central message of this book is: Name it and claim it! Just have faith! Give and you will get! Catchphrases like these have convinced many Christians that trusting in God will bring health and wealth. But the gospel does not promise prosperity without pain or salvation without sanctification. Femi Adeleye draws on his wide-ranging experience as he examines the appeal and peril of this new gospel of prosperity that has made deep inroads in Africa, as well as in the West.

25 This information, including references to the pastors mentioned in this section, is derived from accessed February 28, 2020, https://briefly.co.za/32661-top-5-richest-pastors-south-africa-expensive-possessions.html.

26 David Johnson and Jeff Van Vonderen, *The Subtle Power of Spiritual Abuse: Recognizing and Escaping Spiritual Manipulation and False Spiritual Authority Within the Church* (Minneapolis: Bethany House Publishers, 1991), 20.

27 Wilber O'Donovan Jr, *Biblical Christianity in African Perspective* (Carlisle: Paternoster Press, 1996), 27.

28 Daniel Castelo, *Revisioning Pentecostal Ethics: The Epicletic Community* (Cleveland: CPT Press, 2012), 83.

29 Frank Macchia, *Baptized in the Spirit: A Global Pentecostal Theology* (Grand Rapids, MI: Zondervan Publishing House, 2006), 41.

30 Steven Land, *Pentecostal Spirituality: A Passion for the Kingdom* (Cleveland: CPT Press, 2010), 141.

31 Kenneth Archer, *A Pentecostal Hermeneutic: Spirit, Scripture and Community* (Cleveland: CPT Press, 2009), 23–24.

32 Vinson Synan, *The Holiness-Pentecostal Tradition: Charismatic Movements in the Twentieth Century* (Grand Rapids, MI: Eerdmans, 1997), 149.

33 Castelo, *Revisioning*, 83.

34 Synan, *The Holiness*, 149.

35 Melvin Dieter, "The Wesleyan Perspective," in *Five Views on Sanctification*, eds. Melvin Dieter, Anthony Hoekema, Stanley Horton, Robertson McQuilkin, John Walvoord, and Stanley Gundry (Grand Rapids, MI: Zondervan Publishing House, 1987), 30.

36 Veli-Matti Kärkkäinen, *The Holy Spirit in Ecumenical, International, and Contextual Perspective* (Grand Rapids, MI: Baker Book House, 2006), 33.

37 Edwin Williams, *Systematic Theology*, 2:264, in John Wyckoff, "The Doctrine of Sanctification as Taught by the Assemblies of God" (M.A. thesis, Bethany Nazarene College, Oklahoma, 1972), 68.

38 Donald Dayton, "The Holiness and Pentecostal Churches: Emerging from Cultural Isolation," *Christian Century*, 1979, 786.

39 Richard Shaull and Waldo Cesar, *Pentecostalism and the Future of the Christian Churches* (Grand Rapids, MI: Eerdmans, 2000), 62.

40 Keith Warrington, *Pentecostal Theology: A Theology of Encounter* (London: T&T Clark, 2008), 309.

41 Land, *Pentecostal Spirituality*, 224.

42 Frank Macchia, "The Church of the Latter Rain: The Church and Eschatology in Pentecostal Perspective," in *Toward a Pentecostal Ecclesiology: The Church and the Fivefold Gospel*, ed. John Christopher Thomas (Cleveland: CPT Press, 2010), 249.

43 Archer, *A Pentecostal*, 26.

44 Harvey Cox, *Fire from Heaven: The Rise of Pentecostal Spirituality and the Reshaping of Religion in the Twenty-first Century* (London: Cassell, 1996), 201.

45 Grant McClung, Jr, *Azusa Street and Beyond: Pentecostal Missions and Church Growth in the Twentieth Century* (South Plainfield, NJ: Bridge Publishing, 1986), 48.

46 Jeffery Nelson, "Pentecostal Missions: Past 100 and Beyond," *International Journal of Pentecostal Missiology* 6, no. 1 (2019): 21.

47 Allan Anderson, *An Introduction to Pentecostalism* (Cambridge: Cambridge University Press, 2006), 198.

48 Archer, *A Pentecostal*, 28.

49 Ibid., 26.

50 Amos Yong and Jonathan A Anderson, *Renewing Christian Theology: Systematics for a Global Christianity* (Waco, TX: Baylor University Press, 2014), 324.

51 Frank Bartleman, *Azusa Street: An Eyewitness Account (The Centennial Edition 1906–2006)* (Gainesville: Bridge Publishing, 1980), 183.

52 Daniel Simon Billy Lephoko, "The Mission of Nicholas B.H. Bhengu in a Divided and Polarised Society: An Analysis of the Life, Work and Contribution to Mission in Southern Africa of an Important 20th Century Pioneer" (MA [Theol] thesis, University of Pretoria, Pretoria, 2005), 64–120.

53 David Ngong, "Protesting the Cross: African Pentecostal Soteriology and Pastoral Care," *Journal of Theology for Southern Africa* 150 (2014): 6.

54 Jennifer Schaefer, "And a Little Child Shall Lead Them: Implications of the Changing Face of Mission," *International Journal of Pentecostal Missiology* 6, no. 1 (2019): 76.

55 Resane, "Commercialisation," 2.

56 John Stott, *The Message of Acts* (Leicester: Inter-Varsity Press, 1991), 151.

57 Marshall, *The Acts*, 158.

58 Kelebogile T. Resane, "Miracles in the Neo-Charismatic Movement: Historical and Theological Critique," *Verbum et Ecclesia* 38, no. 1 (2017): 1–8.

References

Adeleye, Femi B. *The Preachers of a Different Gospel: A Pilgrim's Reflections on Contemporary Trends in Christianity* (Hippo Series). Grand Rapids, MI: Zondervan Publishing House, 2011.

Akinrele, Sean. *Foxes in the Vineyard: Insights into the Nigerian Pentecostal Revival.* Lagos: Lerinyo Media, 2013.

Anderson, Allan. *An Introduction to Pentecostalism.* Cambridge: Cambridge University Press, 2006.

Archer, Kenneth. J. *A Pentecostal Hermeneutic: Spirit, Scripture and Community.* Cleveland: CPT Press, 2009.

Barnes, Albert. *Notes on the New Testament: Explanatory and Practical. Acts.* Grand Rapids, MI: Baker Book House, 1979.

Bartleman, Frank. *Azusa Street: An Eyewitness Account (The Centennial Edition 1906–2006).* Gainesville: Bridge Publishing, 1980.

Castelo, Daniel. *Revisioning Pentecostal Ethics: The Epicletic Community.* Cleveland: CPT Press, 2012.

Cox, Harvey. *Fire from Heaven: The Rise of Pentecostal Spirituality and the Reshaping of Religion in the Twenty-first Century.* London: Cassell, 1996.

Dayton, Donald W. "The Holiness and Pentecostal Churches: Emerging from Cultural Isolation." *Christian Century*, August 15–22, 1979, 786. Accessed February 1, 2020. www.christiancentury.org.

Degbe, Simon Kouessan. "African Pentecostal/Charismatic Iconography: A Study of their Significance and Relevance." *International Journal of Pentecostal Missiology* 6, no. 1 (2019): 54–74.

Dieter, Melvin E. "The Wesleyan Perspective." In *Commercialization of the Gospel in Africa with Particular Reference to Kenya: A Critique*, edited by Melvin E. Dieter, Anthony A. Hoekema and Nahashon Gitonga, vol. 2. Kenya Methodist University, 2011. Accessed August 17, 2016. www.kemu.ac.ke/new/index.php/ijpp/volumes- issues/131research/ijpp/volume-2/v2-issue2/320-commercialization-of-the-gospel-in-africa.

Horn, J. Nico. *From Rags to Riches.* Pretoria: University of South Africa, 1989.

Horton, Stanley M. *The Agony of Deceit.* Chicago: Moody Press, 1990.

Horton, Stanley M., J. Robertson McQuilkin, and John F. Walvoord. *Five Views on Sanctification.* Grand Rapids, MI: Zondervan Publishing House, 1987, 11–57.

Jenkins, Philip. *The New Faces of Christianity: Believing the Bible in the Global South.* New York: Oxford University Press, 2006.

Johnson, David, and Jeff Van Vonderen. *The Subtle Power of Spiritual Abuse: Recognizing and Escaping Spiritual Manipulation and False Spiritual Authority Within the Church.* Minneapolis: Bethany House Publishers, 1991.

Kärkkäinen, Veli-Matti. *Pneumatology: The Holy Spirit in Ecumenical, International, and Contextual Perspective.* Grand Rapids, MI: Baker Book House, 2006.

Land, Steven J. *Pentecostal Spirituality: A Passion for the Kingdom.* Cleveland: CPT Press, 2010.

Lephoko, Daniel Simon Billy. "The Mission of Nicholas B.H. Bhengu in a Divided and Polarised Society: An Analysis of the Life, Work and Contribution to Mission in Southern Africa of an Important 20th Century Pioneer." MA (Theol) thesis, Department of Science of Religion and Missiology, University of Pretoria, Pretoria, 2005.

Macchia, Frank D. *Baptized in the Spirit: A Global Pentecostal Theology.* Grand Rapids, MI: Zondervan Publishing House, 2006.

———. "The Church of the Latter Rain: The Church and Eschatology in Pentecostal Perspective." In *Toward a Pentecostal Ecclesiology: The Church and the Fivefold Gospel*, edited by J. Christopher Thomas, 248–58. Cleveland: CPT Press, 2010.

Marshall, I. Howard. *The Acts of the Apostles: An Introduction and Commentary.* Leicester: Inter-Varsity Press, 1998.

Masenya, Madipoane, and Malesela Masenya. "Church Breakaways as a Prototype of Commercialization and Commodification of Religion in the Pentecostal Church Movement in South Africa: Considering Curricula Offerings for Pastors." *Stellenbosch Theological Journal* 4, no. 2 (2018): 633–54. http://dx.doi.org/10.17570/stj.2018.v4n2.a29 Online ISSN 2413-9467 | Print ISSN 2413-9459. 2018 © Pieter de Waal Neethling Trust.

McClung, Jr L. Grant. *Azusa Street and Beyond: Pentecostal Missions and Church Growth in the Twentieth Century.* South Plainfield, NJ: Bridge Publishing, 1986.

McQuilkin, Robertson. *An Introduction to Biblical Ethics.* Columbia, SC: Columbia Bible College and Seminary (Class Notes for Biblical Ethics), 1988.

Moriarty, Michael G. *The New Charismatic: A Concerned Voice Responds to Dangerous New Trends.* Grand Rapids, MI: Zondervan Publishing House, 1992.

Murdock, James. *The New Testament: Translated from the Syriac Peshito Version.* New York: Stanford and Swords, 1852.

Nelson, Jeffrey. "Pentecostal Missions: Past 100 and Beyond." *International Journal of Pentecostal Missiology* 6, no. 1 (2019): 20–41.

Ngong, David T. "Protesting the Cross: African Pentecostal Soteriology and Pastoral Care." *Journal of Theology for Southern Africa* 150 (2014): 5–19.

O'Donovan, Wilbur. *Biblical Christianity in African Perspective.* Carlisle: Paternoster Press, 1996.

Kelebogile, Thomas Resane. "Commercialisation of Theological Education as a Challenge in the Neo-Pentecostal Charismatic Churches." *HTS Teologiese Studies / Theological Studies* 73, no. 3 (2017): a4548. https://doi. org/10.4102/hts.v73i3.4548.

———. "Miracles in the neo-Charismatic Movement: Historical and Theological Critique." *Verbum et Ecclesia* 38, no. 1 (2017): a1736. https://doi.org/10.4102/ve. v38i1.1736.

Robertson, Archibald T. *Word Pictures in the New Testament*, Vol III: The Acts of the Apostles. Nashville: Broadman Press, 1930.

Schaefer, Jennifer. "And a Little Child Shall Lead Them: Implications of the Changing Face of Mission." *International Journal of Pentecostal Missiology* 6, no. 1 (2019): 75–101.

Shaull, Richard, and Waldo Cesar. *Pentecostalism and the Future of the Christian Churches*. Grand Rapids, MI: Eerdmans, 2000.

Stott, John R. W. *The Message of Acts*. Leicester: Inter-Varsity Press, 1991.

Synan, H. Vinson. *The Holiness-Pentecostal Tradition: Charismatic Movements in the Twentieth Century*. Grand Rapids, MI: Eerdmans, 1997.

Temitope, Ogunlusi Clement. "Prosperity Gospel Preaching and Its Implications on National Developments." *International Journal of Humanities and Cultural Studies* 5 (June 1, 2018): 313–30. ISSN 2356-5926. Accessed January 16, 2020. www.ijhcs.com/index.php/ijhcs/index.

Warrington, Keith. *Pentecostal Theology: A Theology of Encounter*. London: T&T Clark, 2008.

Wiersbe, Warren Wendel. *The Integrity Crisis: A Blemished Church Struggles with Accountability, Morality, and Lifestyle of its Leaders and Laity*. Nashville: Oliver-Nelson Books, 1991.

Williams, Edwin S. *Systematic Theology* (2:264); in John W. Wyckoff, "The Doctrine of Sanctification as Taught by the Assemblies of God." M.A. thesis, Bethany Nazarene College, Oklahoma, 1972.

Yong, Amos, and Jonathan A. Anderson. *Renewing Christian Theology: Systematics for a Global Christianity*. Waco, TX: Baylor University Press, 2014.

6 Mission as discernment of spirits in the advent of the abuse of prophecy within Newer Pentecostal Charismatic Christianity in South Africa

Themba Shingange

6.1 Introduction

The alarming shift in the position of discernment of spirits in relation to prophecy within Pentecostal Charismatic Christianity (PCC) has left a lot to be desired. This shift actually signals the advent of the abuse of prophecy within the NPCC which has become evident in controversial religious practices which have shocked both Christians and society at large. It is not surprising that some of these sometimes outrageous religious practices received a lot of attention on different media platforms. The Commission for the Promotion and Protection of the Rights of Cultural, Religious and Linguistic Communities (otherwise known as the CRL Rights Commission) released its report on these practices named "The Hearings on the Commercialisation of Religion and Abuse of People's Belief Systems".[1] Moreover, these controversial religious practices and the abuse of prophecy have been the subject of many recent scholarly projects. Notably, these practices are depicted as common within the NPCC in South Africa.

The term "abuse of prophecy" is used in this chapter in the context of these controversial religious practices. These practices have generally left South African society bewildered regarding this particular expression of the Christian faith; in this chapter we have accepted this general negative reaction as premise. We also assume the decline of the discernment of spirits in relation to prophecy to be a huge challenge. The author is of the opinion that the contemporary adherents of the NPCC have a huge task in addressing these challenges in the light of it possibly being a sign of the times. These negative developments almost compel the NPCC to define an appropriate response in the form of a mission endeavour, hence the biblical metaphor of standing at the crossroads and reading and interpreting these phenomena as signs of the times when attempting to address its challenges. The point of departure here is to use some epistemological sources for a critical examination of the current position of the discernment of spirits in the context of the abuse of prophecy within the NPCC. Finally, the chapter points towards the redefinition of mission as the discernment of spirits constructed to transform the current negative realties.

6.2 The position of discernment of spirits in the Bible

Discernment of spirits is one of the Biblical imperatives used to guard against the abuse of prophecy. There are a number of examples from biblical times showing discernment of spirits. Amongst others, the story narrated in Acts 16:16–19 is critical in the understanding of the significant role of discernment of spirits. The story is about a female slave who had a spirit by which she was able to predict the future. Through these predictions she was making money for herself and her owners. She started to follow Paul and Silas daily when they went to a place of prayer. She shouted, "These men are servants of Most High God who are telling you the way to be saved". She kept on insisting until finally Paul became so bothered that he rebuked the spirit. However, her owners were not pleased since their means of making money was now gone. The owners then reported Paul and Silas to the authorities.

This story is an excellent example of the significance of the discernment of spirits. Although what the slave girl said was true, Paul, through the discernment of spirits, knew that her utterances were not coming from God. The event also clearly shows how "prophecy" can be abused to make money.

Christians therefore need to prayerfully ask and trust God for the gift of the discernment of spirits. The discernment of spirits is essential so that Christians don't accept every prophetic word as if it necessarily comes from God. In the case of the NPCC it has in fact become critical to exercise the discernment of spirits because there is clearly such a need to separate a manifestation from the Spirit of God from that of other spirits. Today, much the same as the owners of the female slave, some pastors abuse prophecy for their own financial gain. Sadly this abuse often happens at the expense of gullible congregants. Whenever this happens, one can assume that discernment of spirits has been neglected. One needs to be careful, though, not to assume that this reality is prevalent throughout the entire PCC as other Christians within the PCC continue to embrace and use discernment of spirits whenever they are dealing with prophecy. It is therefore important to be precise when identifying the area within the PCC where the abuse of prophecy is rife.

6.3 The advent of the NPCC in South Africa

A distinction needs to be made here between the general PCC and the NPCC in South Africa. The PPC refers to the old, well-established churches belonging to what is sometimes referred to as classical Pentecostalism.[2] The NPCC refers to some new forms of the PCC recently gaining currency within

Africa. The PCC embraces prophecy and emphasises the need for the baptism with the Holy Spirit as signified by speaking in tongues. The largest groups amongst them include the Apostolic Faith Mission (AFM), Assemblies of God (AOG) and Full Gospel.[3] Charismatic Christianity emphasises the use of spiritual gifts and ministries. It also embraces prophecy just like its Pentecostal counterparts. Amongst the Charismatic Churches are the famous Rhema Ministries in Randburg, Grace Bible Church in Soweto and Divine Bible Church in Mabopane South Africa.[4]

The terms Pentecostal and Charismatic are used together here because the two traditions are closely related. Both of them are also directly affected by the phenomenon under discussion. Additionally, it should also be borne in mind that the NPCC in South Africa originated primarily from the background of the PCC. Kgatle and Mofokeng point out:

> The African Independent neo-Pentecostal ministries emerged from the revivals conducted in the 1970s and 1980s by several denominational Pentecostal evangelists such as Nicholas Bhengu of the Assemblies of God, Richard Ngidi and Reinhard Bonnke from the Apostolic Faith Mission
>
> (AFM).[5]

The PCC can therefore not easily detach itself from the abuse of prophecy and the controversial religious practices happening within the NPCC. In fact, the PCC has a responsibility to challenge and correct the abuse of prophecy happening within the NPCC as many of the founders of the NPCC actually broke away from the PCC. Some broke away because they didn't want to be accountable to or submit to the PCC as their overseeing body. Whereas the PCC never promoted the abuse of prophecy, the contemporary generation of the NPCC is lamentably presenting a very different narrative. Amongst this group, there are a number of newly formed churches. Some familiar names include the Rabonni Centre Ministries, Incredible Happenings Church and End Time Disciples Ministry[6] among many more. In the NPCC, the abuse of prophecy is rife, and, there is a great need for further reflection around the discernment of spirits.

6.4 The abuse of prophecy within the NPCC in South Africa

The abuse of prophecy has literally been a challenge for ages. In the Old Testament, for example, the whole of Ezekiel 13 is devoted to denouncing the false prophets,[7] In the New Testament believers were warned in I John 4:1 not to believe every spirit, but to try every spirit in order to discern whether it was from God or not. John went further to warn the believers of many false prophets who had gone out into the world. The same challenge continues to this day as is clearly evident in the NPCC, for example, where it manifests in peculiar and controversial religious practices. Pretorius uses the terms cults and new religious movements (NRM)[8] in trying to explain the existence of the new phenomenon. The term NRM, however, does not adequately represent the peculiar dynamics of the new phenomenon. The term broadly encompasses new religious movements and doesn't specifically focus on the current realities within the NPCC.

Lauterbach[9] and Heuser[10] on the other hand use the term "prosperity gospel" to try and define similar practices. However, even though the prosperity gospel is commonly associated with some new global Pentecostal practices and have some commonalities with these new developments within the NPCC, these new developments point to something very different operating. Conversely, scholars such as Kgatle,[11] Resane[12] Masenya[13] simply use the term neo-Pentecostalism to identify the area where controversial religious practices are rife. However, on the other hand, Chetty grappled with whether to use the term neo-Pentecostalism or post-Pentecostalism.[14] That being the case all the same, the author, prefers to apply the term NPCC[15]. The reason for that preference is that NPCC specifically points to the newness, geographical position and the specific Christian traditions where the alarming shift in the position of discernment of spirits and the abuse of prophecy are manifesting.

The abuse of prophecy in the NPCC is often related to the title "Prophet". In most cases the title of prophet is used within the NPCC for spiritual leaders; even for self-appointed prophets. In some cases these prophets are even referred to as "Daddy",[16] "Woman/ Man of God", "Major one" and so forth. These titles are often used to indicate the authority these leaders have over their followers. In reality, the common thread amongst all of them is the abuse of prophecy and the iconic idolisation of spiritual leaders. The modus operandi[17] in these particular churches often entails flamboyant pastors who abuse prophecy to solicit their followers into giving them money and material possessions. While abusing prophecy they often make promises of miracles, healing and wealth to their followers. Some of the other abuses also include enforcing inhumane and degrading actions upon the followers, for example, a pastor encouraging his congregants to eat snakes and rats as a means of accessing God's blessing. Other common controversial practices associated with the abuse of prophecy will be discussed later in this chapter.

Generally the followers of these prophets believe that all their prophetic utterances are true and that they therefore have to unquestioningly accept it. This blind following points to the high level of influence and power that these spiritual leaders yield. Anderson and Otwang indeed describe these leaders as powerful and charismatic, attracting many followers to the Pentecostal-type indigenous churches.[18] However, it is worrying to notice the abuse of prophecy and the gullibility of the followers who treat these spiritual leaders as "celebrity prophets", hence they cannot easily access them.

According to Resane, for followers to have access to these spiritual leaders they have to first pay them a fixed amount of money.[19] The CRL Rights

Commission therefore came to the conclusion that "there is prima facie evidence of commercialisation of religion in South Africa".[20] The abuse of prophecy within the NPCC epitomises the commercialisation of the gospel (to be discussed at length in section 6.7 of this chapter). The next section looks at other controversial religious practices which can shed some further light on the nature of the abuse of prophecy happening within the NPCC.

6.5 Other controversial religious practices within the NPCC in South Africa

Many scholars lament the advent of controversial religious practices within the NPCC. These practices are undoubtedly propelled by the abuse of prophecy and the lack of discernment of spirits. Banda refers to these practices as "the commercialisation of religion",[21] Kgatle calls them "unusual practices",[22] Henrico refers to them as "malevolent practices"[23] and Dube sees them as "a conundrum of religious mafia".[24] These scholars are amongst those who have aptly discussed these controversial religious practices as an increasing threat to the mission of the PCC. These practices are peculiar to the NPCC and are different from the common accepted religious practices within classical Pentecostalism.

The same practices are often preceded by some form of disguised prophetic utterances which Kgatle speaks of as "forensic prophecy" which he sees as divination".[25] This kind of prophecy is often given to specific congregants in the middle of the sermon. It is often very convincing to the individual receiving the prophecy because it would contain personal details like their name, name of their spouse, profession, address, banking details, car registration number and personal problems[26] When hearing their personal details uttered by these pastors, most followers are convinced that the messages are undoubtedly from God. Consequently they do whatever the pastor demands from them after the prophecy without questioning a thing. This leads to the next discussion about the ugly reality of the abuse of prophecy.

6.6 The reality of the abuse of prophecy within the NPCC in South Africa

The abuse of prophecy is very real within the NPCC in South Africa. In most cases prophecies are followed by shocking incidents. In this regard Dube points out:

> On the news in South Africa and Zimbabwe, often one hears a lot about the controversial things the modern – day flamboyant Prophets are doing or have been doing. Stories of Prophets spraying "Doom" insecticides on their followers in church services, asking congregants to eat rats, grass, drink petrol, touching female congregants inappropriately in deliverance sessions, abusing and raping congregants and

profiteering amongst other abounds. All these have become common-place. In essence, the "Prophets" have become untouchable.[27]

This kind of abuse of prophecy has a distinctive identity as an African phenomenon. These realities are not only happening exclusively in South Africa, they also take place in other African countries. Anderson, for example, observed the same reality in Ghana where people from all walks of life are consumers who buy religious products in neo-Prophetic Pentecostal/Charismatic Churches.[28] Asamoah-Gyadu also observed, "The neo-Pentecostal churches have no problem with icons of modernity – fashionable clothing, luxury cars, organising special programmes in five star hotels, travelling first or business class, appearing in expensive jewellery".[29] Although there is nothing wrong with icons of modernity, the manner in which these pastors abuse prophecy to solicit their followers into giving them money to buy these luxuries is obnoxious.

It is disturbing that in South Africa some of these practices even entail life-endangering actions. Dube, for example, writes about a fatal shootout between the police and the Mancoba brothers who were part of the Seven Angels Ministry. These brothers are said to have attacked a local police station, killing some police officers and a retired army officer.[30] Dube points out that such ministries epitomise constitutional delinquencies, disregard education and children's rights, show extortionist tendencies, and are gender insensitive with a mentality of the pastor being some sort of superhero.[31] These practices often present inhumane elements and tend to infringe on the rights of communities. In the light of all this, one could say that this narrative portrayed by the NPCC projects a distorted picture of Christianity. Although the new democratic dispensation in South Africa has brought a lot of positive socio-political transformation, including a new level of freedom of religion and expression, it has sadly often been abused as is the case here. In fact, it has provided fertile ground for the abuse of prophecy to thrive as has been shown in the findings of the CRL Rights Commission.

The research process of the CRL Rights Commission involved about 85 religious leaders representing various religions in South Africa. Amongst its findings were some serious, but not deliberate, organisational and administrative deficiencies, deliberate exploitation of the poor, the use of personal bank accounts as an institution's account, subjecting members to control by extremists/fundamentalists who for instance forbid children from attending schools.[32] The findings further revealed cases of congregants who had to pay an amount of money before they could receive a blessing or prayers from their faith leaders.[33]

Subsequently, the chairperson of the CRL Rights Commission Ms Thoko Mkhwanazi-Xaluva lamented, "the recent news, reports and articles in the media about preachers have left a large portion of society questioning whether religion has become a commercial institution or commodity to enrich a few".[34] Her lament emanated from the abuse of religion and the public outcry about these practices,[35] and is definitely applicable to the abuse of prophecy within the NPCC. Moreover, the abuses fit into the commercialisation of the gospel as presented in the next section.

6.7 The commercialisation of the gospel in South Africa

The assertion about the commercialisation of the gospel in South Africa emanates from the spiritual abuses already discussed in this chapter. However, it should also be noted, there are also positive ways in which churches in general raise and use money for good causes. This was made clear in a report, "An Investigative Study of the Commercialisation of Religion in the Republic of South Africa: 2016 Gauteng Pilot Study"[36] by one of the respondents who maintained:

> When people use the term "commercialisation", there are very positive aspects to it that include for example that the church like any commercial venture, is just being well-funded and that there is very good oversight of how money is generated, managed and distributed to the community. The negative part is often for instance that in some churches, you might have a very high level of revenue and the leaders in the church are becoming very affluent but the money is not utilised to support development impact projects to uplift the community.[37]

The truth is that there is a clear link between the abuse of prophecy and the commercialisation of the gospel. Anderson notes with dismay that the commercialisation of religion has regrettably caused "the selling and purchasing of religious products and services between neo-Pentecostal Charismatic Churches and desperate religious consumers".[38] What is becoming increasingly clear is the disturbing abuse of prophecy in order to support the commercial icons of religion. The author has also observed practices indicating the commercialisation of religion within his immediate community. He observed amongst others the selling of religious artefacts such as bracelets, rings, calendars, holy water and oil to mention but a few. The money raised from these business activities went to individual pastors. Although there is nothing wrong per se with selling such religious items, it becomes a problem when prophecy is wrongfully used to make empty promises in order to compel the followers to buy these religious items.

Giving offerings and tithes are biblical and part of the Christian faith and practice. These need to be properly collected and administered in order to support the work of God such as helping the poor and supporting community-based development projects. In contrast, the tendencies of using prophetic utterances to lure followers into giving tithes which are then used to buy spiritual leaders expensive cars, clothes and other symbols of material wealth should be challenged at all cost. Dube, Nkoane and Hlalele are correct when pointing out that the commercialisation of religion has regrettably caused it to be used as a tool to amass wealth from church members through certain religious narratives.[39] Within the NPCC such religious narratives are used to present so-called prophetic messages. The role and responsibility of the PCC is to radically challenge such malpractices. That can happen amongst others when the PCC starts emphasising that healing and blessings come from God not by the mere purchase of religious product, The PCC should therefore, stand at the crossroads of the historical past and the current reality. The following section discusses this further.

6.8 Standing at the crossroads

The inevitable questions are, why and where did things start to go wrong? What needs to be done in order to correct the current disturbing situation? There can be a myriad of responses to these questions. Dube, Nkoane and Hlalele argue that religious illiteracy has led many adherents of neo-Pentecostalism to rely solely on their religious leaders – something which has caused them to uncritically accept everything these leaders say and do since they regard them as superheroes.[40] It has also been found that most Christians within the NPCC generally fail to challenge their leaders even if they do notice diversions from the common Christian faith and practices.[41] Kgatle's opinion is that certain theological, psychological and socio-economic factors[42] mark the point where things went wrong. These authors are all probably right within the context of the abuse of prophecy as presented in this chapter.

However, the author maintains, the negative shift in the position of discernment of spirits within the NPCC has immensely contributed to the challenges it is facing today. There is a need to stand at the crossroads and look for the right direction in order to correct the errors of the present. The biblical metaphor of standing at the crossroads is used here to delineate the corrective action that Christians should take. As the prophet Jeremiah summoned the people of Israel in Jeremiah 6:16 to go and stand at the crossroads, observe, and ask for the good path in order to walk in it, Christians are called to a similar action. The call to action here signifies an act of introspection whereby Christians firstly need to acknowledge the decline in the use of discernment of spirits. They also need to look in retrospect at the past generations of the APCC in order to find the right path again.

Such a move could possibly return the discernment of spirits in relation to prophecy to its rightful position. The metaphor of standing at the crossroads provides a relevant point of departure which can potentially transform the current status quo. By looking at the past one can therefore hope to find relevant solutions, but one should also just remember to not assume that the past was always correct. What is clear, however, is that the discernment of spirits as used by past generations of Pentecostal Christians should be restored in order to challenge the current abuses of prophecy.

The saying, "direction is best asked from those who are already ahead in the same journey" is very relevant here.[43] However, this does not suggest that classical Pentecostalism plays a superior role over the NPCC. It simply means that the new can always learn from the old when it _moves_ forward. The manner in which the past generations handled discernment of spirits when dealing with prophecy can therefore help the PCC and the NPCC in their current context.

The biblical story of Paul and the female slave again comes to the fore. Christians will have to pray to God and ask for the restoration of the gift of discernment of spirits. The same gift of discernment of spirits can help Christians in challenging the abuse of prophecy. This challenge, however, will be made complete if Christians are able to understand the times as discussed in the next section.

6.9 Understanding the times

The metaphor of understanding the times comes from the biblical narrative of the sons of Issachar. They are portrayed in 1 Chronicles 12:31 as having had the ability to understand the times; therefore knowing what Israel had to do. For our purposes relating to the abuse of prophecy it means that we need to go stand at the crossroads (i.e. look at the past) and from that place seek to understand the times we are living in (i.e. view the present to gain understanding of why the position of the discernment of spirits has shifted/ declined). Understanding the times, like the sons of Issachar, can help the NPCC to move from standing at the crossroads into the appropriate direction. In fact, positive changes in Christianity have always required a special understanding of a particular time.

To do this was common in the past; the same is required here. As David Bosch observed, "In earlier ages the church has responded imaginatively to paradigm changes; we are challenged to do the same for our times and context".[44] Therefore, in responding to the challenge of the abuse of prophecy, the NPCC should first rise to the occasion, acknowledging the dangerous shift in the position of the discernment of spirits and then attempt to understand what had led to this shift. This action would represent in a very real way a seeking to understand the times. In this way the eventual correction of errors that had led to the normalisation of the abuse of prophecy can potentially take place.

This eventual correction will entail bringing current practices in line with the prescripts of past generations of Christian faith and practice.

Such action will be in line with Paul and Dietterich's argument, "the ability to read and interpret the signs of the times is a core competency required of clergy and other church leaders".[45] By reading and interpreting the signs, Christians will be able to correctly proclaim the life-transforming gospel of Jesus Christ in current times.[46] The same correct proclamation is urgently needed in order to curb the abuse of prophecy and the negative shift in the position of discernment of spirits within the NPCC. It is not too late for the NPCC to make an about-turn as discussed in the next section.

6.10 Mission as discernment of spirits

Mission in classical Pentecostalism is summarised in Kgatle's assertion, "movement that believes in salvation through confession".[47] However, mission as salvation does not close the doors to the other manifestation of mission within the NPCC. Therefore, an understanding of Christians' responses to current challenges facing society can also be seen as a mission activity. Similarly, the envisaged mission can finally be realised when the NPCC make that about-turn by restoring the discernment of spirits to its key position when dealing with prophecy within their congregations. This can happen through a deliberate study of the Bible and by prayerfully asking God to impart the gift of discernment of spirits to church members. Consequently, Christians can find themselves being empowered to challenge the abuse of prophecy within their spiritual spaces.

Such reformative action should be understood in the same spirit imbued in the words of Johann Wolfgang von Goethe, "If everyone sweep in front of their own door steps, the whole world will be clean".[48] In other words, translated into our context, Christians in the NPCC should take their destiny into their own hands and challenge the abuse of prophecy within their religious spaces. It should be borne in mind, however, that heeding the call might prove to be more complicated than one can imagine. The discernment of spirits can be complex in the African context owing to the similarities between prophecy within the NPCC and divination within the African Traditional Religion (ATR). In this regard Kgatle observes, "In African Christianity, with the growth of Pentecostalism, people are failing to differentiate between biblical prophecy and divination".[49]

In essence, such failure led Anderson, amongst other things, to conclude, "There is a strong relationship between ancestors and the Holy Spirit in the African worldview. Additionally, the challenge is further exacerbated by the position of ancestors within some spirit-type churches which is ambiguous".[50] Christians should therefore earnestly strive to discern between the Spirit of God and divination. In grappling with the ambiguity, Christians within both the NPCC and the PCC should start examining carefully the operations and manifestation of spirit/s within the prophetic messages uttered by their pastors. Such a process should entail, amongst others, the scrutinising, testing, and questioning the spirit/s behind every prophecy.

As a result, these Christians will be paving a way for a transformative mission which can as well change the current narrative of abuse of prophecy.[51] The mission regarding the discernment of spirits is both old and current. It is old because of its historical past where Christians held the discernment of spirits in high esteem in curbing the abuse of prophecy. Through the discernment of spirits, Christians were able to challenge the false teachings of their times. This happened throughout history as Christians embraced challenges in different ages similar to what Bosch calls paradigm changes in missions.[52] These challenges can therefore be seen as paradigm shifts in the signs of the times. Once again, they manifest today as Christians are confronted with an issue like the outrageous abuse of prophecy – an issue they could never even have dreamt of. The issue of the abuse of prophecy needs to be urgently challenged today as the NPCC, and even society, are grappling with its disturbing presence. Christian responses to the abuse of prophecy need to be relevant to the times whilst being in harmony with the essence of the Christian faith.[53]

In this sense the mission is also new because it is now being implemented once again in the context of the current times. To be precise, it is being implemented within South African Pentecostal Charismatic spaces. In this regard Christians should embrace the new mission with creative but responsible freedom. In doing this Christians will take the ministry of Jesus Christ and the early church forward, in a creative and imaginative way adapting it to their own times and context as Bosch had envisioned.[54] Creativity is essential for crafting new responses to address new challenges facing Christians in different times and spaces. By embracing mission as discernment of spirits, the NPCC will be responding in a relevant and pragmatic manner to their generation.

Amongst other things, that same mission is also ingrained in the very work of the Holy Spirit who "searches everything, even the depths of God" as the first letter of the Apostle Paul to the Corinthians (1 Cor 2:10) puts it. The imperative for Christians is thus to reject every false prophets and embrace those who are genuinely sent by God. In order to discern this aspect correctly, Christians will have to look for the centrality of Christ in all the prophetic utterances. The measuring rod therefore will be the scrutiny of every prophecy in the light of biblical scriptures in what Kevin Lenahan called the task of discernment that brings together practices of attentive listening to the scriptural word and acts of building up the conditions of social life.[55] Rather than being oblivious of reality, Christians should start to listen carefully and judge what is being said from the pulpit.

Furthermore, they should scrutinise every practice in order to check if it builds up the conditions of Christian life. The reality is that not every message uttered under the common saying "thus says the Lord"[56] is necessarily from God. "Mission as discernment of spirits," therefore, seeks to identify the correct message from God amongst many other sources of prophecy. This is similar to what Kritzinger said, "The Holy Spirit is searching, questioning, discerning, and moving believers to ask questions in order to discern and understand what is going on in the world".[57] It should, therefore, be the main aim for Christians to search for the biblical truths and then in the light of that question any current abusive practices.

Masenya echoed similar sentiments of "mission as discernment" even though she spoke in a different context. She spoke within the context of other limiting forces such as poverty, patriarchy, xenophobia, etc. However, her concerns are also true within the context of mission as discernment of spirits: "Can the church afford to be silent in the midst of this death dealing context? It dares not be!".[58] "Mission as discernment of spirits" therefore, is an impetus for Christians to raise their prophetic voices against the abuse of prophecy underpinned by the dangerous negative shift in the position of the discernment of spirits in the NPCC. Mission for the NPCC in this regard is therefore to restore the gift of the discernment of spirits to its rightful place.

6.11 Conclusion

This chapter highlighted the negative shift in the position of discernment of spirits in relation to prophecy within the PCC. It further explained that the reports about the controversial religious practices within the NPCC flooding the different media platforms signalled this alarming shift. We identified a need for the PCC to learn from the biblical metaphors of standing at the crossroads and looking for the good way and like the sons of Issachar, to correctly interpret the times. There needs to come clear understanding of where things started to go wrong. In addition, what needs to be done to correct the current disturbing situation? The negative shift in the position of the discernment of spirits was identified as the point where things started to go wrong. This identification would be part of understanding the times, an essential element of reform. Consequently, by learning from past generations and reinstating the discernment of spirits in its rightful place when dealing with prophecy, the PCC will be redefining its mission. During this process the PCC will be able to start correcting the abuse of prophecy and, by refusing to keep quiet whenever prophecy is abused, declare the mission of God anew to the current generation.

Notes

1 CRL Rights Commission, "Report of the Hearings on the Commercialisation of Religion and Abuse of People's Belief Systems (South Africa, 2017), 2–59.
2 Mookgo Kgatle, "The Unusual Practices Within Some Neo-Pentecostal Churches in South Africa: Reflections and Recommendations," *HTS Teologiese Studies / Theological Studies* 73, no. 3 (2017): 1–7, https//doi.org/10.4102/hts.v73i3.4656.
3 Allan Anderson, "New African Initiated Pentecostalism and Charismatics in South Africa," *Journal of Religion in Africa* 35, no. 4 (2004): 66–92.
4 Ibid., 12–18.
5 Mookgo Kgatle and Thabang Mofokeng, "Towards a Decolonial Hermeneutic of Experience in African Pentecostal Christianity: A South African Perspective," *HTS Teologiese Studies / Theological Studies* 75, no. 3 (2019): 1–9, https://doi.org/10.4102/hts.v75i4.5473.
6 Ibid., 3.

7 Mookgo Kgatle, "Reimagining the Practice of Pentecostal Prophecy in South Africa: A Critical Engagement," *HTS Teologiese Studies / Theological Studies* 75, no. 4 (2019): 1–7, https://doi.org/10.4102/hts.v75i4.5183.

8 Stephanus Pretorius, "Spiritual Abuse Under the Banner of the Right to Freedom of Religion in Religious Cults Be Addressed," *Acta Theologica* 31, no. 2 (2011): 231, http://dx.doi.org/10.4314/acta.v31i2.11.

9 Karen Lauterbach, "Fakery and Wealth in African Charismatic Christianity: Moving Beyond the Prosperity Gospel as Script," *Faith in African Lived Christianity: Bridging Anthropological and Theological Perspectives* (2019): 111. doi:10.1163/9789004412255_007.

10 Andreas Heuser, "Charting African Prosperity Gospel Economies," *HTS Teologiese Studies / Theological Studies* 72/1, no. 1 (2016): 1, a3823, http://dx.doi.org/10.4102/hts.v72i1.3823.

11 Kgatle, "The Unusual Practices," 1.

12 Kelebogile Resane, "Commercialisation of the Theological Education as a Challenge in the Neo-Pentecostal Charismatic Churches," *HTS Teologiese Studies / Theological Studies* 73, no. 3 (2017): 1, a4548, https//doi.org/10.4102/hts.v73.4548.

13 Madipoane Masenya, "The Bible and Prophecy in African-South African Pentecostal Churches," *Missionalia: Southern African Journal of Missiology* 33, no. 1 (2005): 35.

14 Irivin G. Chetty, "Origin and Development of the New Apostolic Reformation in South Africa: A Neo-Pentecostal Movement or a Post-Pentecostal Phenomenon?" *Alteration Special Edition* 11 (2013): 190–206.

15 Allan Anderson, "The New Pentecostal and Charismatic Churches: The Shape of Future Christianity in Africa?" *PNEUMA: The Journal of the Society for Pentecostal Studies* 24, no. 2 (2002): 167–68.

16 Calling male preachers "Daddy" is a common practice in most of the PCC in South Africa.

17 This term is understood to refer to a particular way of doing things.

18 Allan Anderson and Samuel Otwang, *Tumelo: The Faith of African Pentecostals in South Africa* (Pretoria: University of South Africa Press, 1993), 29.

19 Resane, "Commercialisation," 3.

20 CRL Rights Commission, *Report on the Hearings on the Commercialisation of Religion and Abuse of People's Beliefs Systems* (Pretoria: CRL Rights Commission, 2017), 31.

21 Collium Banda, "Redefining Religion? A Critical Christian Reflection on CRL Rights Commission's Proposal to Regulate Religion in South Africa," *Verbum et Ecclesia* 40 (2019): 1, a1948, https://doi.org/10.4102/ve.v40i.1948:4.

22 Kgatle, "The Unusual Practices," 1.

23 Radley Henrico, "Proselytising the Regulation of Religious Bodies in South Africa: Suppressing Freedom?" *PER/PELJ* (2019): 8, http://dx.doi.org/10.17159/1727-3781/2019/v22i0a5315.

24 Bekithemba Dube, "Conundrum of Religious Mafia and Legislation in South Africa: When Does Religion Become a National Threat? Reference to the Seven Angels Ministry," *Verbum et Ecclesia* 40, no. 1 (2019): 1, a1864, https://doi.org/10.4102/ve.v40i1.1864.

25 Kgatle, "Reimagining," 3.

26 Ibid.

27 Elijah Dube, "Desperation in an Attempt to Curb Modern-Day Prophets: Pentecostalisation and the Church in South Africa and Zimbabwe," *Conspectus: The Journal of the South African Theological Seminary* 27 (2019): 29, www.sat.edu.za/dube-desperation-curb-mordern-day-prophets.

28 George Anderson, "Commercialisation of Religion in Neo-Prophetic Pentecostal/Charismatic Churches in Ghana: Christian Ethical Analysis of Their Strategies," *Journal of Philosophy, Culture and Religion* 42 (2019): 1. doi:10.7176/JCPR:3.

29 Kwabena Asamoah-Gyadu, "Anointing Through the Screen: Neo-Pentecostalism and Televised Christianity in Ghana," *Studies in World Christianity* 11, no. 1 (2005): 13. doi:10.3366/swc.2005.11.19.

30 Dube, "Conundrum," 1–8.

31 Ibid., 2–8.

32 CRL Rights Commission, "Report of the Hearings," 19–20.

33 Ibid.

34 Ibid., 4.

35 Ibid., 6.

36 Paul Kiyingi Kibuuka, Carel J. Van Aardt and Tustin Deon Herold, "An Investigative Study of the Commercialisation of Religion in the Republic of South Africa: 2016 Gauteng Pilot Study" (CRL Rights Commission, UNISA, Pretoria, 2016), 1–164.

37 Ibid., 114–15.

38 Anderson, "Commercialisation," 1.

39 Bekithemba Dube, Milton Nkoane and Dipane Hlalele, "The Ambivalence of Freedom of Religion, and Unearthing the Unlearnt Lessons of Religious Freedom from Jonestown Incident: A Decoloniality Approach," *Journal for the Study of Religion* 30, no. 2 (2017): 337, http://dx.doi.org/10.17159/2413-3027/2017/v30n2a1.

40 Ibid., 343.

41 Dube, "Desperation," 29–30.

42 Kgatle, "The Unusual Practices," 5–7.

43 The IsiZulu saying is often used to advise someone that if they want to know something they are unsure about, they should ask someone who have experienced the same thing before them.

44 David Bosch, "Transforming Mission Paradigm Shifts," in *Theology of Mission* (Maryknoll, NY: Orbis Books, 1991), 188.

45 Paul and Inagrace Dietterich, "Reading the Signs of the Times," *Transformation* 2, no. 1 (The Center for Parish Development) Chicago, 1995: 1.

46 Ibid.

47 Kgatle, "The Unusual Practices," 2.

48 The saying is attributed to the German writer and poet Johann Wolgang von Goethe, www.forbes.com, quotes.

49 Kgatle, "Reimagining," 2.

50 Allan Anderson, *Moya: The Holy Spirit in an African Context* (Pretoria: The Institute for Theological Research, UNISA, 1991), 10.

51 The concept of transforming mission was well articulated by the renowned missiologist David Bosch in his work *Transforming Mission: Paradigm Shifts in Theology of Mission* (1991).

52 Ibid., 181–261.

53 Ibid., 188.

54 Ibid., 18.

55 Kevin Lenehan, "Saying the Right Word at the Right Hour: Dietrich Bonhoeffer Reading the Signs of the Times," *Vatican II: The Continuing Agenda* 19 (1997): 141–60, http://digitalcommons.sacredheart.edu/supress_bks/19.

56 The saying "thus say the Lord" was commonly used by Old Testament prophets to show that their prophetic utterances were coming directly from God. The same phrase is also used by contemporary Christians.

57 Klippies Kritzinger, "A Question of Mission: A Mission of Questions," *Missionalia: Southern African Journal of Missiology* 33, no. 1 (2005): 35.
58 Masenya, "The Bible," 41.

References

Anderson, Allan. "The New Pentecostal and Charismatic Churches: The Shape of Future Christianity in Africa?" *Pneuma: The Journal of the Society for Pentecostal Studies* 24, no. 2 (2002): 167–68.

———. *Moya the Holy Spirit in an African Context*. Pretoria: University of South Africa, 1991.

———. "New African Initiated Pentecostalism and Charismatics in South Africa," *Journal of Religion in Africa* 35, no. 4 (2004): 66–92.

Anderson, Allan, and Samuel Otwang. *Tumelo: The Faith of African Pentecostals in South Africa*. Pretoria: UNISA, 1993.

Anderson, George. "Commercialisation of Religion in Neo-Prophetic Pentecostal/Charismatic Churches in Ghana: Christian Ethical Analysis of Their Strategies." *Journal of Philosophy, Culture and Religion* 42 (2019): 1–8. doi:10.7176/JCPR.

Asamoah-Gyadu, Kwabena. "Anointing Through the Screen: Neo-Pentecostalism and Televised Christianity in Ghana." *Studies in World Christianity* 11, no. 1 (2005): 9–28. doi:10.3366/swc.2005.11.19.

Banda, Collium. "Redefining Religion? A Critical Christian Reflection on CRL Rights Commission's Proposal to Regulate Religion in South Africa." *Verbum et Ecclesia* 40 (2019): 1–11. https:// doi.org/10.4102/ve.v40i.1948.4.

Bosch, David. *Transforming Mission Paradigm Shifts in Theology of Mission*. Maryknoll, NY: Orbis Books, 1991.

Chetty, Irvin G. "Origin and Development of the New Apostolic Reformation in South Africa: A Neo-Pentecostal Movement or a post-Pentecostal Phenomenon?" *Alteration Special Edition* 11 (2013): 190–206.

Dube, Bekithemba. "Conundrum of Religious Mafia and Legislation in South Africa: When Does Religion Become a National Threat? Reference to the Seven Angels Ministry." *Verbum et Ecclesia* 40 (2019): 1–8. https://doi.org/10.4102/ve.v40i1.1864.

Dube, Bekithemba, M. Nkoane Milton, and Dipane Hlalele. "The Ambivalence of Freedom of Religion, and Unearthing the Unlearnt Lessons of Religious Freedom from Jonestown Incident: A Decoloniality Approach." *Journal for the Study of Religion* 30, no. 2 (2017): 343–37. http://dx.doi.org/10.17159/2413-3027/2017/v30n2a14.

Dube, Elijah Ngoweni. "Desperation in an Attempt to Curb Modern-Day Prophets: Pentecostalisation and the Church in South Africa and Zimbabwe." *Conspectus: The Journal of the South African Theological Seminary* 27 (2019): 29–30. www.sat.edu.za/dube-desperation-curb-mordern-day-prophets.

Henrico, Radley. "Proselytising the Regulation of Religious Bodies in South Africa: Suppressing Freedom?" *PER* (2019): 1–27. http://dx.doi.org/10.17159/1727-3781/2019/v22i0a5315.

Heuser, Andreas. "Charting African Prosperity Gospel Economies." *HTS Teologiese Studies / Theological Studies* 72, no. 1 (2016): 1–9. http://dx.doi.org/10.4102/hts.v72i1.3823.

Kibuuka, Paul Kiyingi, Carel. J. Van Aardt, and Deon Herold, Tustin, "An Investigative Study of the Commercialisation of Religion in the Republic of South Africa: 2016 Gauteng Pilot Study." CRL Rights Commission, UNISA, Pretoria, 2016.

Kgatle, Mookgo Solomon. "The Unusual Practices Within Some Neo-Pentecostal Churches in South Africa: Reflections and Recommendations." *HTS Teologiese Studies / Theological Studies* 73, no. 3 (2017): 1–8. https//doi.org/10.4102/hts. v73i3.4656.

———. "Reimagining the Practice of Pentecostal Prophecy in South Africa: A Critical Engagement." *HTS Teologiese Studies / Theological Studies* 75, no. 4 (2019): 1–7. https://doi.org/10.4102/hts.v75i4.5183.

Kgatle, Mookgo Solomon and Thabang R. Mofokeng. "Towards a Decolonial Hermeneutic of Experience in African Pentecostal Christianity: A South African Perspective." *HTS Teologiese Studies / Theological Studies* 75, no. 4 (2019): 1–9. https://doi.org/10.4102/hts.v75i4.5473.

Kritzinger, Klippies. "Section 5-Mission and Missiology in the 21st Century. A Question of Mission-a Mission of Questions." *Missionalia* 30, no. 1 (2002): 144–73.

Lauterbach, Karen. "Fakery and Wealth in African Charismatic Christianity: Moving Beyond the Prosperity Gospel as Script." *Faith in African lived Christianity: Bridging Anthropological and Theological Perspectives* (2019): 111–32. doi:10.1163/9789004412255_007.

Lenehan, Kevin. "Saying the Right Word at the Right Hour: Dietrich Bonhoeffer on Reading the Signs of the Times." *Vatican II: The Continuing Agenda* 19 (1997): 141–60. http://digitalcommons.sacredheart.edu/supress_bks/19.

Masenya, Madipoane. "The Bible and Prophecy in African-South African Pentecostal Churches." *Missionalia: Southern African Journal of Missiology* 33, no. 1 (2005): 35–41.

Paul and Dietrich Inagrace T. "Reading the Signs of the Times." *Transformation* 2, no. 1 (2005): 1.

Pretorius, Stephanus Petrus. "Spiritual Abuse Under the Banner of the Right to Freedom of Religion in Religious Cults Can Be Addressed." *Acta theologica* 31, no. 2 (2011): 219–40. http://dx.doi.org/10.4314/acta.v31i2.11.

Resane, Kelebogile. "Commercialisation of the Theological Education as a Challenge in the Neo-Pentecostal Charismatic Churches." *HTS Teologiese Studies / Theological Studies* 73, no. 3 (2017): 1–7. https//doi.org/10.4102/hts.v73.4548.

SA CRL Rights Commission, *Report of the Hearings on the Commercialisation of Religion and Abuse of People's Belief Systems.* South Africa (2017): 2–59.

Wolgang von Goethe, Johann. www.forbes.com> quotes.

7 Rethinking the Seven Angels Ministry's praxis of pneumatology as seen through the lens of decoloniality

Bekithemba Dube

7.1 Introduction

This chapter focuses on the Seven Angels Ministry that rose to prominence in 2018 for some shocking reasons that are discussed below. The Seven Angels in this instance are not biblical divine beings but seven brothers living in Ngcobo who, at some point, started to regard themselves as angels. Through critical analysis this chapter aims to show how the use of the pneuma has been problematic in many post-colonial countries like South Africa. Under the guise of following the Spirit of God many neo-Pentecostal churches including cult movements have opened gateways for religious abuse, criminality and mafia-like tendencies. This chapter poses the critical question, who possesses that Spirit and was its previous reference and usage associated with criminality and religious abuse? In this regard this chapter briefly discusses the Seven Angels Ministry, their history, philosophy and beliefs, which its adherents regard as informed by the Spirit of the Lord. The chapter interrogates the Seven Angels Ministry practices informed by a decoloniality lens, especially its motifs such as coloniality of being, power and knowledge. It seeks to uncover and expose religious delinquency as practiced by the Seven Angels Ministry under the banner "thus says the Spirit of the Lord".

Problematising the use of pneuma in post-colonial African discourses is critical in the sense that once the phrase "thus says the Spirit of Lord" is used, some religious followers immediately shun critical thinking, community safety and human rights. This approach tends to endanger both perpetrators and adherents; hence, the need for a radical rethink in how the term "Spirit of the Lord" is used. The chapter concludes with suggesting how the religious mafia and criminality under the guise of "Spirit of the Lord" can be mitigated. In the following section the Seven Angels Ministry in general are discussed.

7.2 The Seven Angels Ministry

Little is known about the origins of the hugely controversial Seven Angels Ministry., First established in Umzimkhulu, KwaZulu Natal, the Seven

Angels Ministry was founded in 1986 by Siphiwo Mancoba, a father of seven boys who, from a young age, have referred to themselves as the Seven Angels.[1] The Ministry initially adopted the name Angel Ministry which is an acronym for All Nations God's Evangelical Lamp Ministry.[2] Shortly after the death of its founder in April 2015, Mancoba's seven sons refused to succeed him as leaders of his church and chose instead to form the Seven Angels Ministry in defiance of being led by their mother who was positioned to take over leadership after the death of Siphiwo. Currently the ministry is situated in Ngcobo, a small village in the Eastern Cape, one of South Africa's nine provinces. The ministry's leaders are known as "angels".[3] One of the Mancoba brothers echoed this during the hearing on abuse of religion by the CRL Rights Commission (2016) when he noted "As you see us here, we are angels. We come from heaven. . . . Firstly, I am not a pastor. I am an angel from heaven, sitting at the right hand of the Lord". It is quite extraordinary that they are claiming to be from heaven, angels sitting at the right hand of God, and not pastors as the leaders in most Christian churches are usually called. Their claim to be angels could be associated with the Seven Angels in the book of Revelation, indicating that they are invoking the Bible for their mandate. The Seven Angels Ministry clearly regards themselves as a legitimate ministry.[4] They see themselves as incarnate beings with a divine mandate from the Spirit of God[5] who have come to earth to look for Lucifer.[6] Whilst many would see the Seven Angels Ministry as an illegitimate cult, they see themselves as legitimate and mandated directly from heaven – something which many Pentecostal churches claim. It is therefore relevant (albeit contentious) to discuss the Seven Angels Ministry and its use of "the Spirit of God" within the wider Pentecostal category.

7.3 Religious mafia

I have used the term "religious mafia" on many platforms and was subsequently accused by some readers and critics as being too emotional about what is currently happening in the field of religion in many post-colonial countries. While I may argue that the term should be interpreted within the context in which it is used, I am glad that one of the books distributed by Amazon entitled *Church mafia: Captured by secret powers: an untold African narrative*, written by Makhado Sinthumule Ramabulala and published in 2019,[7] highlights how various religious practices can be referred to as mafia-like. The term "religious mafia" is thought-provoking and signalling the need for religious malpractices to be taken seriously as they have the potential to disintegrate into crime under the guise of religious obedience. My use of the term is drawn from the activities of criminals that are known for using drugs and dangerous weapons to commit various crimes.[8] In our context it should be understood as a term referring to the abuse of religion by religious leaders and organisations to accomplish their personal agendas, while destroying social cohesion. In fact, there are religious movements in

South Africa that have been in the media in recent years for various reasons related to drug abuse, money laundering, and human trafficking to name but a few. Cognisant of this, I have argued that the existence of something akin to the mafia within some religious movements is obvious, with the Seven Angels Ministry being an example of this phenomenon as will be shown in the chapter. The term "religious mafia" must be understood as describing various forms of criminality, mind-controlling activities and suspect practices meant to covertly deceive gullible and unsuspecting congregants for political, religious and financial gain.

7.4 Pneumatology

The doctrine of pneumatology is one of the common subjects in the field of theology. It is generally understood as the study of the Holy Spirit in relation to the Godhead. This chapter does not intend to go into theologising about pneumatology and pursue debates around it; it simply uses the term in a general sense.

7.4.1 Mapping the problem

The main problem addressed by the chapter is the misuse of the pneuma by the Seven Angels Ministry to establish its criminal agenda. For our purposes we call this whole organisational setup an example of the "religious mafia".

The Seven Angels Ministry became well-known and notorious after five police officers and an unarmed soldier were killed by church members at the Ngcobo police station; the subsequent investigation uncovered a host of disturbing underhand activities that were done by this ministry under the pretext of "obedience of the Spirit of the Lord." These underhand activities were so traumatic that community members called for the ministry to be closed down. Banele Mancoba, the leader of the Seven Angels Ministry, firmly believed that all the actions of the ministry were executed in obedience to the "Spirit of God". One of the challenging issues with the Seven Angels Ministry was the abuse of women and children, at least as seen by outsiders. Melusi Gigaba, a former South African Minister of Home Affairs, commented on this issue:

> Of particular concern to me, is the exploitation of children and women whose rights have been blatantly disregarded by being denied their basic right; their sense of belonging; their birth right to identity.[9]

Under normal circumstances members of society should protect women and children, and Christians even more so as Christianity has always advocated a love for all people as commanded by Jesus in John 13:35. However, the Seven Angels Ministry under the pretext of listening to the Spirit of the Lord, denied women and children their basic rights, for example the basic right to education in the case of children. Denying children the right to education deprives them of a better future and inhibits the development of any society. In fact, any organisation that is future-oriented and focused on sustainable development will invest in children. However, with the Seven Angels Ministry and other likeminded religious organisations the opposite is true. Here education is generally regarded as evil, compromising one's obedience to the Spirit of the Lord. In this regard Jordaan and Mabuza claim that the church advocated for people not to work and for children not to go to school, insinuating that schools were under Satan's control.[10] There is a firm belief that the devil is operational at school and therefore forbidding the children to attend school is an act of obedience to God. With this in mind, the question of whose spirit is it that would deny children a basic right such as education becomes very relevant. I would argue that such ideologies and questionable actions are prevalent what can be referred to as a mafia religion and it should be widely problematised in order to reclaim the rights of, in this instance, children in the Seven Angels Ministry and other similar religious organisations.

Apart from denying women and children their rights, the Mancoba Seven Angels Ministry was all over the news early in 2020 when police arrested some of its members after they were informed that the church had, for a long time, been used as a hideout by the attackers of the Ngcobo Police Station.[11] In addition there were allegations that some member of the Seven Angels Ministry bombed an ATM which was 100 metres from the church. Upon investigation, the police discovered that the criminals were housed at the Seven Angels Ministry and the subsequent shootout between these criminals and the police led to the death of some of the leaders of the Seven Angels Ministry including three of the brothers – Xolisa (37), Philile (33) and Thandazile (38).[12] In the light of the Seven Angels Ministry's involvement in criminal activities, so much so that we could call them religious mafia acting in ways that are radically contrary to biblical beliefs, we need to seriously ask which spirit is leading them. At the time of writing this chapter the community had in fact petitioned for this ministry to be abolished. The Minister of Police, Bheki Cele, cited by SowetanLive, said:

> We will then take the petition to the relevant structures, like the municipality and the chiefs. In the not so distant future those structures that were harbouring the people who were out of order there, who call themselves angels, will be demolished.[13]

It is clear that in the court of public opinion, the community see the ministry as a criminal organisation. As such, it is important that the Seven Angels Ministry's theology and criminality be subjected to further scrutiny since it clearly and disturbingly destroys the beauty of religion in society. As it stands, the Seven Angels Ministry, although claiming to operate under the guidance of pneuma, does not present what is generally expected from adherents of the Christian faith. In the following section we discuss decoloniality as the theoretical framework of this study.

7.4.2 Theoretical framework: decoloniality

The chapter is couched in decoloniality theory. Decoloniality is a theory that allows me to problematise the abuse of pneumatology in postcolonial religious settings like in South Africa. In terms of its origins, the theory is contested. Scholars such as Wanderley and Barros[14] argue that the theory has its roots in Latin America and leading scholars such as Walter Mignolo, Maldonado-Torres, Quijon, Dussel. Mignolo and Walsh[15] are of the view that decoloniality has a history and praxis of more than 500 years. From its beginnings in the Americas, decoloniality has been a part of (trans) local struggles, movements, and actions to resist and refuse the legacies and ongoing power relations and patterns established by external and internal colonialism. It should be noted that decoloniality is not a static condition, an individual attribute, or a lineal point of arrival or enlightenment. Instead, decoloniality seeks to make visible, open up and advance radically distinct perspectives and positionalities in order to displace Western rationality as the only framework and possibility of existence, analysis and thought.[16] Without a doubt, decoloniality is also contextual, relational, and practice-based to address the lived realities of people experiencing oppression. In addition, it is intellectually, spiritually, emotionally and existentially entangled and interwoven to address coloniality.[17] As contextualised within the Global South, Ndlovu-Gatsheni[18] argues that decoloniality is "born out of a realisation that ours is an asymmetrical world order that is sustained not only by colonial matrices of power but also by pedagogies and epistemologies of equilibrium that continue to produce alienated Africans".

The struggle of decoloniality is against coloniality. Coloniality refers to long-standing patterns of power that emerged because of colonialism, defining culture, labour, intersubjective relations, and knowledge production well beyond the strict limits of colonial administrations. Thus, coloniality has outlived colonialism.[19] It continues to haunt people and manifests in different formats. As such a concerted effort is needed in order to combat it from different angles. Amongst others, it manifests itself through the abuse of pneuma for personal gain and renders the victims of abuse useless and powerless to confront their lived realities. In many cases, coloniality itself remains invisible yet its impact can be clearly seen in social injustice, abuse and exploitation of the weaker members of society. Thus I agree with Ndlovu-Gatsheni[20] who argues that the struggle of decoloniality is a "melee against invisible vampirism of imperialism technologies and colonial matrices of power (coloniality) that continue to exist in the minds, lives, languages, dreams, imaginations, and epistemologies of modern subjects in Africa and the entire global South".

7.4.3 *Challenging the use of the pneuma in South Africa*

The manipulation of the Spirit by some religious mafia movements in South Africa poses various challenges which can be personal, institutional and/or national. By using the Seven Angels Ministry as example, this chapter identifies various challenges regarding the abuse of pneuma. The Seven Angels Ministry can be regarded as religious mafia in the sense that they disregard social justice, respect for human rights and render the very term "religious" suspect because of their scandalous religious malpractices. While the challenges cited below may not be peculiar to the Seven Angels Ministry, the examples will be drawn from them as the specific focus of this chapter

7.5 Inciting civil disobedience

One of the things that the Seven Angels Ministry emphasised was their view that the South African constitution was evil and therefore not meant to be obeyed by those led by the Spirit. Such a stance presents serious challenges and religious scholars know that when a religious community promotes a view such as this, catastrophe is inevitable. When he gave his Ministry's view of the constitution, Banele Mancoba the leader of the Seven Angels Ministry said:

> There is an angel that left heaven by the name of Lucifer whom we have come to seek on earth. He has come and has breathed into the constitution of South Africa and its schools. He took schools and the constitution to himself . . . we also say that the people must not listen to the constitution because it is controlled by the devil.[21]

These sentiments by the leader of the Seven Angels Ministry are disturbing; it is an example of religion posing a national threat that cannot be ignored. The constitution of a country serves as the terms of reference for its citizens to live together in harmony and is usually guided by principles such as freedom, democracy, good citizenry and fair treatment of all. The South African constitution came into existence through wide consultations and all citizens were invited to contribute to its drafting including members of the Seven Angels Ministry who should have seized an opportunity to put across their ideas rather than standing aside and emerge later only to criticise the constitution. It is because of its constitution that a society can function orderly and manageable towards the common good for all its citizens. Furthermore, it can also be argued that the Bible is a Christian community's constitution in the same way that the Quran is undoubtedly the Islamic religion's constitution. In this regard Paul teaches in the New Testament that Christians should obey the laws of the land. It is therefore unlikely that a religious community like the Seven Angels Ministry can refute the Bible as their religious constitution under their professed loyalty to the Spirit of God.

The Seven Angels Ministry's criticism of the constitution, however, fails to mention that the South African constitution calls for amendment where it does not resonate well with the general populace.

This serves to reinforce my argument that this ministry represents a mafia religion, since the mafia is known for its arrogant disregard and even sabotage of the government for its own agenda. Such a "mafia" stance from a religious body is always disastrous. A good example of this is the Jim Jones religious community that became notorious in the 1970s in the US; it was basically an anti-government religious cult. Jim Jones in consolidating his religious empire isolated his followers from the outside media and subjected them to near constant haranguing. He used propaganda to blackmail the US government and his followers' families back home. The news media, according to Jones, sought to destroy his community.[22] Consequently, 918 people died from poison in a mass suicide which Jim Jones saw as a redemptive act and revolutionary suicide.[23]

In the case of the Seven Angels Ministry, five police members and an off-duty soldier were killed by followers and some leaders of the ministry, perhaps as a result of the notion or belief that the police and soldiers are the custodians of the constitution of South Africa. In conclusion, this chapter agrees with the observation by Enroth[24] that those in positions of spiritual power often become strong role models through their dogmatic teaching, bold confidence and arrogant assertiveness. However, this chapter doesn't necessarily call for the dissolvement of Seven Angels Ministry, in fact, they should exist as the constitution permits but then they should not fight the constitution which allows them to operate.

7.6 Violation of children's right to basic education

The second challenge raised in this chapter is the Seven Angels Ministry's violation of the right to basic education for children as provided by the South African Department of Basic Education, whether in a private or a public school. The South African constitution guarantees that everyone in South Africa has the right to basic education which requires active measures to constantly improve education in the country.[25] Therefore, under normal circumstances religious movements should be in the forefront in ensuring that education is propagated since in most countries formal education had been linked to mission churches. The adult members of the Seven Angels Ministry can choose not to pursue their own education; however, it becomes problematic when they deprive their children of basic education under the pretext of obeying the Spirit of God. This does not only diminish the future of the children, but also that of the community and the country at large; thus, in decoloniality, children's exclusion from education by powerful members of a religious organisation must be problematised, exposed and challenged.

Banele Mancoba, speaking on behalf of the Seven Angels Ministry, is cited by the South African Broadcasting Cooperation (SABC) saying:

> We are saying as Seven Angelic Ministries, firstly I am not a pastor; I am an angel from heaven, seated at the right of the Father. We say that children should not go to schools because the devil has intervened with the schools. We will continue to tell the learners to stop going to school and not to listen to the constitution because the devil has taken over the schools.[26]

Masweneng expands the belief of the Seven Angels Ministry by noting that:

> We are saying that education is wrong. Because Satan has taken over schools after Nelson Mandela allowed him to do so. We are saying children should not go to school as Satan has infiltrated schools. People must not listen to the constitution because it's driven by Satan. I consider the Constitution to be an evil spirit. We are saying that life must return to the Lord and Satan must go.[27]

The church continued to malign the constitution and discredit schools as dangerous and evil, preventing learners to attend school. In addition, the Ministry is alleged (issue is still before the South African courts) to have housed about 100 "sex slaves", the youngest of whom was 12 years old.[28] This paints an overall picture of religious leaders wielding catastrophic influence in their religious community. It is very disturbing that many church members agree with the church's stance that denies children the right to be educated, despite these church members themselves having had the privilege to go to school. Dube[29] refers to this as trajectories of mutual zombification, where the religious exploited and exploiters agree to buttress socially impunitive conditions benefitting the Ministry leaders. The problem here is that religious knowledge is believed to be the sole privilege of the Seven Angels Ministry leaders and as such, whatever they say and promote is believed to be from the Spirit of God.

Decoloniality problematises the use of religion for the purpose of exploitation and criminality. It is the coloniality of knowledge which poses epistemological questions that are linked to: (a) the politics of knowledge generation; (b) questions of who generates which knowledge and for what purpose; (c) the question of relevance and irrelevance of knowledge; and, (d) how some knowledge disempowers/empowers communities and peoples.[30] The teaching of the Seven Angels Ministry clearly disempowers not only the children but indirectly also the entire South African nation because, as the saying goes, educating a child is educating a nation. Informed by this ongoing process of depriving children of their education, Kaunda[31] warns that "as long as the African mind remains one of the spaces for oppressive religious structures there seems to be no possibility of academy and knowledge decolonization and consequently, no social transformation, no political progress and no economic development". In the following section the financial extortion taking place in the Seven Angels Ministry is discussed.

7.7 Financial extortion in the Seven Angels Ministry

One the characteristics of a religious mafia group is assuming a neo-liberal approach to financial issues whereby the religious group is a profit-making one and/or entrenches an agenda of illicit financial deals. The Seven Angels Ministry is no exception and one can argue that this ministry has definitely been mafiarised. Having said that, it doesn't mean that members shouldn't contribute towards the advancement of the ministry; it does however become a concern when leaders downplay their accountability regarding church members' contributions. In an attempt to expose this blunt refusal to show any accountability regarding members' contributions, the SABC cites the Seven Angels Ministry's view on finances:

> We operate by getting the money hard cash and using it for the needs. We cannot disclose publicly the offering of congregants and tell the details of who exactly give what to the church and what influenced them to make such offerings.[32]

Masweneng further sheds light on the Seven Angels Ministry's view on finances:

> Our mission is to return the world to Jehovah, God. We have not registered anything in this world. We do not have any of the documents, which were required of us. We do not have them [bank statements].[33]

The implication here is that those who make financial contributions (or offerings) to the ministry are not entitled to be updated on how the money is spent which possibly opens a gap for financial maladministration. Without financial accountability, the leaders can easily use the ministry's finance to furnish their lavish lifestyle while the members who make financial contributions drown in poverty. If the ministry leaders were not squandering financial contributions from their members, why then would they not want to disclose the financial records for all to see and so clear their names regarding possible financial maladministration? Although harshly put, the chapter agrees with Ngcukana[34] that most prophets "need money and are desperate. However, this goes unnoticed because most people in churches are brainwashed. They only live in their own world". In this regard Pheladi[35] sheds more light on how the leaders of the Seven Angels Ministry accumulated wealth. Many of the members were either teachers or working in local businesses. When they went to the church, they were told to give away their material possessions in order to serve without the "satanic" attachments, in other words money and belongings.

The Seven Angels leaders were able to convince hard-working people to hand over their money and even some other belongings for the promise of a better life beyond this one. This is one of the deceits that religious mafia groups use to extort money from people. Unfortunately, the deceived religious adherents cannot see the discrepancy between them having to wait for a better life in heaven one day whilst their religious leaders enjoy a lavish lifestyle with the resources they have given them in the hope of that better life. Pheladi[36] claimed that the Seven Angels Ministry even had some paid-off cars that actually belonged to some of the members, supporting my argument. One member, who was a teacher for eleven years, told us that she was instructed to withdraw all her pension money and bring it to the church. Some may well argue that church members are adults who must make their own decisions about life and their finances; yet, this notion doesn't take into account leaders deceitfully using "the Spirit of God" as a pretext forcing people to give their own resources to them. The Seven Angels Ministry, however, dispute the idea that they loot people's money through religion claiming, "We have people who come to us for help, we pray for them, and when they are healed they say here is R200 000 and we say 'thank you'".[37] This is very interesting since traditionally religious help is free, but here healing seem to be paid for.

The chapter agrees with Larsen[38] who argues that many religious leaders give their followers hope, and make them believe that positive change is possible, thus making it easy for them to entrust them with their own resources. There is widespread concern about this practice, in fact, even President Cyril Ramaphosa, said,

> We are concerned about this trend that is evolving in our country where pastors or religious leaders of questionable practices have surged to the fore and have started doing things that appear like they are taking advantage of our people.[39]

In a similar vein, Epondo[40] believes that some ministries are being run like insurance companies, owning sanctimonious spiritual powers and playing on the hopes and fears of their followers in exchange for generous tithes. He further suggests that this is happening because prophets are human beings too who need a good life. This chapter however does not want to imply that prophets or pastors should not be paid for their services, only that if or when they are paid, it should be done in a transparent manner, with accountability. There should be no suspicion of prophets or pastors squandering their followers' money. Furthermore, giving to any ministry should not be coerced and manipulated.[41] Jesus as our model taught that people must not be compelled or forced to give but should rather do so wholeheartedly.

Today, from the perspective of decoloniality, there is a need to heed Jesus's teaching in order for the church to remain relevant and to contribute to sustainable development. Furthermore, the money that church members give to ministries should contribute to transforming their lives and also be used in projects that generate money so that they are not continuously burdened by having to give money without ever receiving anything in return.

7.8 Rethinking the use of pneuma in South Africa: Resisting the mafiarisation of pneuma

The chapter does not only problematise the Seven Angels Ministry's view of the pneuma but also want to look at positive alternatives. This chapter therefore agrees with Bottoms, Shaver, Goodman and Qin[42] that, "[In] the long run, society should find ways to protect people [against] religion-related abuse, and help religion evolve in the direction of treating people better". In a similar way as Marcos argues,[43] this chapter does not only give a counter argument but also looks at ways to protect the South African religious space, including religious followers and their children, from the criminalisation of religion by ministries such as the Seven Angels Ministry. This is done in the understanding that decoloniality advocates for new paths that lead to new arrangements of thought, knowledge, theorising, and thinking within and toward the political, and to new constructions of life, living, and societal articulation that give significance, concretion, and substance to life.[44]

7.9 Restoring religious education

Many challenges that society faces related to the religious mafia flow from the fact that religion and religious education have basically been removed from the national curriculum. I am not implying that the presence of religious education in the curriculum will put an end to the religious mafia, but it can be one of the ways to mitigate the problem. In any case, the presence of religious education within the national curriculum will no doubt serve a positive function. Some leaners can use it constructively to address their own vulnerability such as abuse within religious spaces. However, religious education was removed from the South African national curriculum. This removal attests to the fact that religious education was seen as inadequate and maybe even irrelevant to deal with religious diversity in the postcolonial development of South Africa. However, while failure to integrate various religions into the curriculum could have been a challenge, removing religion education altogether was a great mistake.

The removal of religion from schools meant that religious leaders could step into the gap and facilitate religious knowledge from their own individual space. I submit, though some writers may disagree, that this marked the beginning of mafia religion emerging in South Africa. Some religious leaders exploited the lack of religious knowledge to push their own agenda which often involved criminality. Given this current arrangement, religious leaders become one of the few sources of religious knowledge transmission from "the divine" to the people, clearly opening up religion to huge abuse. Through this a coloniality of knowledge is created whereby a multiplicity of religious voices is neglected only for a few religious leaders to become powerful and exploit their community. These religious leaders cannot be questioned and become untouchable.[45] In the case of the Seven Angels Ministry, the leaders saw themselves as super humans and thus they referred to themselves as angels. This led to church members believing that whatever these leaders said were true and should not be questioned – to the extent that police officers and a soldier were murdered and an ATM machine bombed and robbed. During the police murder trial, one of the accused noted that "I believed Thandazile [one of the Mancoba brothers and a church leader] because he said he was the son of the Lord".[46]

In the light of all this, I would argue that religious education should be re-introduced in schools in order to start equipping society with religious knowledge from a neutral perspective. Furthermore, learners should be exposed to different religions which would also counter the abuse of religion by religious mafia groups. There is an urgent need for a curriculum that can deconstruct and demystify religion, preventing it from being highjacked by a few for their personal gain. This chapter therefore agrees with Wane and Todd[47] that there is a need for decolonial curricula that offer resistance to and revival in the wake of colonial structures, allowing schools and society to flourish by casting off the hegemony of deceitful religious leaders.

7.10 Monitoring of religious organisations

This chapter departs from the notion of the regulation of religion, which has been supported[48] but also disputed.[49] Instead it advocates the monitoring of religious praxis especially when it becomes clear that there could be a violation of human rights. Monitoring seems to be a balancing viewpoint between those advocating for and those resisting the regulation of religion. This monitoring is not a done deal, a condition to be reached, or a stage of critical enlightenment,[50] but rather entails a continual watching and even troubling of institutions that disregard the country's constitution such as the Seven Angels Ministry. Recognised religious leaders, lawyers and social justice oriented scholars should do the monitoring, ensuring that human rights are respected in the religious praxis. Such monitoring should involve the exposing of religious practices that are not consistent with generally accepted normal religious praxis and see to it that these get rectified.[51] As such, as argued from decoloniality, monitoring cannot be state-led. Monitoring should happen through people organizing themselves in their local histories, delinked from the colonial matrix.[52] In this way, this chapter hopes that when people work collectively (through scholars prone to social justice, human rights and religious leaders) religious abuse and oppression can be mitigated.[53]

I conclude this point agreeing with Alvesson and Willmott[54] that there is a need for collective effort to free "individuals and groups from suppressive social and ideological situations, particularly those that place socially unnecessary precincts upon development and enunciation of human consciousness". In the following section, I focus on decolonising the superhero mentality.

7.11 Decolonising the superhero mentality

Finally I want to highlight the need for decolonising the superhero mentality for both religious leaders and religious followers. I do admit that this would be difficult to do because spiritual issues are personal and thus to bring about any changes in the way people view a religious system would also be personal and difficult to accomplish. However, difficult though it may be, it is desirable and doable and academia may present a space where one can begin to tease out and challenge a religious mafia system.

Many of the problems with the praxis of religion in post-colonial South Africa stem from the fact that some religious leaders have occupied a superhuman, almost superhero space where their authority and mafia practices cannot be questioned, let alone exposed and challenged, ultimately creating serious problems of religion in society. Unfortunately as argued by McClure,[55] the "victims of spiritual abuse may continue to support the abusive leader because of their naïveté or loyalty to the leader".

Cognisant of this, South African society cannot afford to have a few individuals exercising mafia-like control over their followers because of their religious loyalty. Larsen[56] attempts to identify the root cause of this problem by saying oppressive religious hegemony emanates from black traditions. There is a tendency to give a religious leader the designation "Father" or "Daddy". This implies giving an individual absolute authority and consequently, his followers will owe him absolute obedience. Thus, Hooks[57] is probably right to argue that "unless the people of South Africa transform the way they perceive religion, we cannot make radical interventions that will fundamentally alter our situation". Decoloniality requires likeminded social justice scholars to challenge hegemonic epistemologies that marginalise, dehumanise and deny the legitimacy of some other epistemologies and dehumanise some peoples of the world.[58]

7.12 Conclusion

This chapter has problematised the misuse of the Spirit of the Lord by the Seven Angels Ministry. It has further discussed the rise to prominence of the Seven Angels Ministry and their criminal traits which could be described as mafia-like tendencies. These include, among others, spiritual leaders forbidding children to attend school, money laundering and actively opposing the South African constitution. The chapter used decoloniality as the lens through which to critique the religious mafia. The chapter further challenged the misuse of the pneuma with reference to the Seven Angels Ministry. The chapter concluded by arguing that religious education needs to be re-introduced in schools and that the superhero myth needs to be busted in religious mafia circles.

Notes

1 Sithandiwe Velaphi, Khaya Koko, and Tebogo Monama, "Engcobo Cult's Deadly Plan Exposed," *IOL News*, February 26, 2018, sec. Eastern Cape, www.iol.co.za/news/south-africa/eastern-cape/engcobo-cults-deadly-plan-exposed-13481060.

2 Derrick Spies, "Ngcobo Massacre: Seven Suspects Dead After Police Shootout," *News24*, February 24, 2018, www.news24.com/SouthAfrica/News/ngcobo-massacre-seven-suspects-dead-after-police-shootout-20180224.

3 Alexis Haden, "Seven Angels Cult: Seven Children Denied Education Rescued from Their Father," *The South African*, October 13, 2015, sec. News, www.thesouthafrican.com/news/seven-angels-cult-seven-children-rescued-oct-2018/.

4 Enerst Mabuza, "Extremist Church Was Identified by CRL in Its Report Last Year," *Sowetan Live*, February 26, 2018, www.sowetanlive.co.za/news/south-africa/2018-02-26-extremist-church-was-identified-by-crl-in-its-report-last-year/.

5 Ibid., 1.

6 Zanele Zama, "2016 Video Reveals Mancoba Church Leader Telling the CRL Commission He Is on a Mission to Find the Devil," *702 News*, www.702.co.za/articles/293755/watch-i-am-not-a-pastor-i-m-an-angel-from-heaven.

7 Makhado Sinthumule Ramabulana, *Church Mafia: Captured by Secret Powers: An Untold African Narrative* (Pretoria: Makhado Sinthumule Ramabulana, 2019).

8 Juan Carlos Garzón, *Mafia & Co: The Criminal Networks in Mexico, Brazil and Colombia* (Washington, DC: Woodrow Wilson International Center for Scholars, n.d.); L. Paoli, "Organised Crime in Italy: Mafia and Illegal Markets – Exceptions and Normality," in *Organised Crime in Europe: Concepts, Patterns and Control Policies in the European Union and beyond, Part 1*, eds. C. Fijnaut and L. Paoli (Dordrecht: Springer, 2004), 263–302.

9 Kgaugelo Masweneng, "Constitution and Schools Are Driven by Satan: Seven Angels Ministries," *TimesLive*, March 1, 2018, www.timeslive.co.za/news/south-africa/2018-03-01-constitution-and-schools-are-driven-by-satan-seven-angels-ministries/.

10 Nomahlubi Jordaan and Enerst Mabuza, "Seven Angels Ministry, Site of a Deadly Shoot-Out on Friday, Is 'Extremist'," *Business Day*, accessed March 20, 2018, www.businesslive.co.za/bd/national/2018/02/2018-seven-angels-ministry-site-of-a-deadly-shoot-out-on-friday-is-extremist.

11 Lubabalo Ngcukana, "'Seven Angels' Cult Members in Court for Police Station Massacre," *City Press*, November 5, 2018, sec. News, https://citypress.news24.com/News/seven-angels-cult-members-in-court-for-police-station-massacre-20181105.

12 Ibid., 1.

13 SowetanLive, "'Seven Angels' Church to Be Demolished," *SowetanLive*, April 23, 2018, www.sowetanlive.co.za/news/south-africa/2018-04-23-seven-angels-church–to-be-demolished/.

14 Sergio Wanderley and Amos Barros, "Decoloniality, Geopolitics of Knowledge and Historic Turn: Towards a Latin American Agenda," *Management & Organizational History* 14, no. 1 (2018): 79–97.

15 Walter Mignolo and Catherine Walsh, *On Decoloniality, Concepts, Praxis* (Durham: Duke University Press, 2018).

16 Ibid., 11.

17 Ibid.

18 Sabelo Jeremiah Ndlovu-Gatsheni, "Why Decoloniality in the 21st Century?" *The Thinker for Thought Leaders* 48, no. 10 (2013): 10–16.

19 Nelson Maldonado-Torres, "Thinking Through the Decolonial Turn: Post-Continental Interventions in Theory, Philosophy, and Critique – An Introduction," *Transmodernity: Journal of Peripheral Cultural Production of the Luso-Hispanic World* 1, Fall (January 1, 2011): 1–15.

20 Ndlovu-Gatsheni, "Why Decoloniality in the 21st Century?", 11.

21 SABC Digital News, *Angels Ministries, E Cape Swears to Defy Constitution*, 2016, www.youtube.com/watch?v=qxWPLgA-XrQ.

22 Paul VanDeCarr, "The Jonestown That Won't Fade Away. Twenty-Five Years Later: A Filmmaker Examines the Lasting Consequences," *Harvard Divinity Bulletin*, Fall (2003): 24–25.

23 David Chidester, *Salvation and Suicide. Jim Jones: The Peoples' Temple and Jonestown* (Bloomington: Indiana University Press, 2003).

24 Ronald Enroth, *Churches That Abuse* (Grand Rapids, MI: Zondervan Publishing House, 1992).

25 Chris McConnachie, Anna Skelton, and Cameron McConnachie, "The Constitution and the Right to a Basic Education," *Basic Education Rights Handbook: Education Rights in South Africa*, Section 27, 2017, 13–35, http://section27.org.za/basic-education-handbook/.

26 South African Broadcasting Cooperation (SABC) Digital News, *Seven Angels Ministries, E Cape Swears to Defy Constitution*, 2016, www.youtube.com/watch?v=qxWPLgA-XrQ.

27 Masweneng, "Constitution and Schools Are Driven by Satan."

28 Koko and Monama, "Engcobo Cult's Deadly Plan Exposed."

29 Bekithemba Dube, "Conundrum of Religious Mafia and Legislation in South Africa: When Does Religion Become a National Threat? Reference to the Seven Angels Ministry," *Verbum et Ecclesia* 40 (January 21, 2019), https://doi.org/10.4102/ve.v40i1.1864.

30 Claude Ake, *Social Science as Imperialism: The Theory of Political Development* (Ibadan: Ibadan University Press, 1982).

31 Chammah Kaunda, "The Denial of African Agency: A Decolonial Theological Turn," *Black Theology* 13, no. 1 (April 1, 2015): 73–92, https://doi.org/10.1179/1476994815Z.00000000048.

32 SABC Digital News, *Seven Angels Ministries, E Cape Swears to Defy Constitution*.

33 Masweneng, "Constitution and Schools Are Driven by Satan."

34 Ngcukana, ' "Seven Angels' Cult Members in Court for Police Station Massacre.'

35 Batlile Pheladi, "Hawks Probe Mancoba Seven Angels Ministries Church Bank Accounts," *Sowetan Live*, March 12, 2018, www.sowetanlive.co.za/sundayworld/news/2018-03-12-hawks-probe-mancoba-seven-angels-ministries-church-bank-accounts/.

36 Ibid., 31.

37 SABC News Online, "Ngcobo Murder Saga Brings Religious Sector Regulation in the Spotlight," *SABC News*, February 24, 2018, sec. Home, www.sabcnews.com/sabcnews/engcobo-murder-saga-brings-religious-sector-regulation-spotlight/.

38 Lars Edvart Larsen, *What Went Wrong with the People's Temple? A Closer Look at Jim Jones and the People's Temple* (Stavanger: School of Mission and Theology in Stavanger, 2010).

39 Kamva Somdyala, "Bogus Pastors: Ramaphosa Concerned by Questionable Surging to the Fore," *News24*, February 28, 2018, www.news24.com/South Africa/News/bogus-pastorsramaphosa-concerned-by-questionable-practices-surging-to-the-fore- 20190228.

40 Palesa Thinane Epondo, "'Con' Pastors Thrive as Africans Become Increasingly Desperate for Miracles," *Mail & Guardian*, July 23, 2015, sec. *Voices of Africa*, http://voicesofafrica.co.za/con-pastors-thrive-africans-be come-increasingly-desperate-miracles/.

41 Phaladi, "Hawks Probe Mancoba Seven Angels Ministries Church Bank Accounts."

42 Bette Bottoms, Michael Nielsen, Rebecca Murray, and Henrietta Filipas, "In the Name of God: A Profile of Religion-Related Child Abuse," *Journal of Social Issues* 51, no. 2 (1995): 85–111.

43 San Marcos, "Comunicado del CCRI-CG del EZLN. Y ROMPIMOS EL CERCO. « Enlace Zapatista," de Agosto del 2019, https://enlacezapatista.ezln.org.mx/2019/08/17/comunicado-del-ccri-cg-del-ezln-y-rompimos-el-cerco-sub-comandante-insurgente-moises/.

44 Mignolo and Walsh, *On Decoloniality, Concepts, Praxis.*

45 Bekithemba Dube, "'Go and Prophesy in Your Own Land': Foreign Prophets and Popularism in South Africa. Evoking the Need of Jonathanic Theology for Peaceful Resolution of Difference," *Religions* 11, no. 1 (January 2020): 42, https://doi.org/10.3390/rel11010042.

46 African News Agency Reporter, "Ngcobo Police Shooting: Suspects Reveal All in Bail Hearing," *IOL News*, March 8, 2018, sec. Eastern Cape, www.iol.co.za/news/south-africa/eastern-cape/ngcobo-police-shooting-suspects-reveal-all-in-bail-hearing-13663318.

47 Njoko Nathani Wane and Kimberley Todd, "Introduction: A Meeting of Decolonial Minds," in *Decolonial Pedagogy: Examining Sites of Resistance, Resurgence, and Renewal*, eds. Njoko Nathani Wane and Kimberly Todd (London: Palgrave Macmillan, 2018).

48 Dube, "Conundrum of Religious Mafia and Legislation in South Africa," 4.

49 Collium Banda, "Redefining Religion? A Critical Christian Reflection on CRL Rights Commission's Proposal to Regulate Religion in South Africa," *Verbum et Ecclesia* 40, no. 1 (2019): 1–11, https://doi. org/10.4102/ve.v40i1.1948.

50 Mignolo and Walsh, *On Decoloniality, Concepts, Praxis.*

51 Dube, "Conundrum of Religious Mafia and Legislation in South Africa."

52 Ibid., 5.

53 Ibid.

54 Mats Alvesson and Hugh Willmott, "On the Idea of Emancipation in Management and Organization Studies," *Academy of Management Review* 17, no. 3 (July 1, 1992): 432–64, https://doi.org/10.5465/amr.1992.4281977.

55 John McClure, *AAC Proposal by Holy Trinity Orthodox Church* (London: State College, 2014).

56 Mildred Larson, *Meaning-Based Translation: A Guide to Cross-Language Equivalence*, 2nd ed. (Lanham, MD: University Press of America, 1998).

57 bell hooks, *Black Looks: Race and Representation* (Boston, MA: South End Press, 1992).

58 Chikumbutso Herbert Manthulu and Yusef Waghid, *Education for Decoloniality and Decolonisation in Africa* (Cham: Palgrave Macmillan, 2019).

References

African News Agency Reporter. "Ngcobo Police Shooting: Suspects Reveal All in Bail Hearing." *IOL News*, March 8, 2018, sec. Eastern Cape. www.iol.co.za/news/south-africa/eastern-cape/ngcobo-police-shooting-suspects-reveal-all-in-bail-hearing-13663318.

Ake, Claude. *Social Science as Imperialism: The Theory of Political Development*. Ibadan: Ibadan University Press, 1982.

Alvesson, Mats, and Hugh Willmott. "On the Idea of Emancipation in Management and Organization Studies." *Academy of Management Review* 17, no. 3 (July 1, 1992): 432–64. https://doi.org/10.5465/amr.1992.4281977.

Banda, Collium. "Redefining Religion? A Critical Christian Reflection on CRL Rights Commission's Proposal to Regulate Religion in South Africa." *Verbum et Ecclesia* 40, no. 1 (2019): 1–11. https://doi. org/10.4102/ve.v40i1.1948.

Bottoms, Bette, Michael Nielsen, Rebecca Murray, and Henrietta Filipas. "In the Name of God: A Profile of Religion-Related Child Abuse." *Journal of Social Issues* 51, no. 2 (1995): 85–111.

Chidester, David. *Salvation and Suicide. Jim Jones: The Peoples' Temple and Jonestown*. Bloomington: Indiana University Press, 2003.

Dube, Bekithemba. "Conundrum of Religious Mafia and Legislation in South Africa: When Does Religion Become a National Threat? Reference to the Seven Angels Ministry." *Verbum et Ecclesia* 40 (January 21, 2019). https://doi.org/10.4102/ve.v40i1.1864.

———. '"Go and Prophesy in Your Own Land': Foreign Prophets and Popularism in South Africa. Evoking the Need of Jonathanic Theology for Peaceful Resolution of Difference." *Religions* 11, no. 1 (January 2020): 42. https://doi.org/10.3390/rel11010042.

Enroth, Ronald. *Churches That Abuse*. Grand Rapids, MI: Zondervan Publishing House, 1992.

Epondo, Palesa Thinane. "'Con' Pastors Thrive as Africans Become Increasingly Desperate for Miracles." *Mail & Guardian*, July 23, 2015, sec. Voices of Africa. http://voicesofafrica.co.za/con-pastors-thrive-africans-be   come-increasingly-desperate-miracles/.

Garzón, Juan Carlos. *Mafia & Co: The Criminal Networks in Mexico, Brazil and Colombia*. Washington, DC: Woodrow Wilson International Center for Scholars, n.d.

Haden, Alexis. "Seven Angels Cult: Seven Children Denied Education Rescued from Their Father." *The South African*, October 13, 2015, sec. News. www.thesouthafrican.com/news/seven-angels-cult-seven-children-rescued-oct-2018/.

Hooks, bell. *Black Looks: Race and Representation*. Boston, MA: South End Press, 1992.

Jordaan, Nomahlubi, and Enerst Mabuza. "Seven Angels Ministry, Site of a Deadly Shoot-Out on Friday, Is 'extremist'." *Business Day*. Accessed March 20, 2018. www.businesslive.co.za/bd/national/2018/02/2018-seven-angels-ministry-site-of-a-deadly-shoot-out-on-friday-is-extremist.

Kaunda, Chammah. "The Denial of African Agency: A Decolonial Theological Turn." *Black Theology* 13, no. 1 (April 1, 2015): 73–92. https://doi.org/10.1179/1476994815Z.00000000048.

Larsen, Lars Edvart. *What Went Wrong with the People's Temple? A Closer Look at Jim Jones and the People's Temple.* Stavanger: School of Mission and Theology in Stavanger, 2010.

Larson, Mildred. *Meaning-Based Translation: A Guide to Cross-Language Equivalence.* 2nd ed. Lanham, MD: University Press of America, 1998.

Mabuza, Enerst. "Extremist Church Was Identified by CRL in Its Report Last Year." *Sowetan Live,* February 26, 2018. www.sowetanlive.co.za/news/south-africa/2018-02-26-extremist-church-was-identified-by-crl-in-its-report-last-year/.

Maldonado-Torres, Nelson. "Thinking Through the Decolonial Turn: Post-Continental Interventions in Theory, Philosophy, and Critique – An Introduction." *Transmodernity: Journal of Peripheral Cultural Production of the Luso-Hispanic World* 1, Fall (January 1, 2011): 1–15.

Manthula, Chikumbutso Herbert, and Yusef Waghid. *Education for Decoloniality and Decolonisation in Africa.* Cham: Palgrave Macmillan, 2019.

Marcos, San. "Comunicado del CCRI-CG del EZLN. Y ROMPIMOS EL CERCO. Enlace Zapatista," de Agosto del 2019. https://enlacezapatista.ezln.org.mx/2019/08/17/comunicado-del-ccri-cg-del-ezln-y-rompimos-el-cerco-subcomandante-insurgente-moises/.

Masweneng, Kgaugelo. "Constitution and Schools Are Driven by Satan: Seven Angels Ministries." *TimesLive,* March 1, 2018. www.timeslive.co.za/news/south-africa/2018-03-01-constitution-and-schools-are-driven-by-satan-seven-angels-ministries/.

McClure, John. *AAC Proposal by Holy Trinity Orthodox Church.* London: State College, 2014.

McConnachie, Chris, Ann Skelton, and Comeron McConnachie. "The Constitution and the Right to a Basic Education." *Basic Education Rights Handbook – Education Rights in South Africa,* 13–35. Section 27, 2017. http://section27.org.za/basic-education-handbook/.

Mignolo, Walter. *Local Histories/Global Designs: Coloniality, Subaltern Knowledges, and Border Thinking.* Princeton University Press, 2000. www.jstor.org/stable/j.cttq94t0.

Mignolo, Walter, and Catherine Walsh. *On Decoloniality, Concepts, Praxis.* Durham: Duke University Press, 2018.

Ndlovu-Gatsheni, Sabelo Jeremiah. "Why Decoloniality in the 21st Century?" *The Thinker for Thought Leaders* 48, no. 10 (2013): 10–16.

Ngcukana, Lubabalo. " 'Seven Angels' Cult Members in Court for Police Station Massacre." *City Press,* November 5, 2018, sec. News. https://city-press.news24.com/News/seven-angels-cult-members-in-court-for-police-station-massacre-20181105.

Pheladi, Batlile. "Hawks Probe Mancoba Seven Angels Ministries Church Bank Accounts." *Sowetan Live,* March 12, 2018. www.sowetanlive.co.za/sundayworld/news/2018-03-12-hawks-probe-mancoba-seven-angels-ministries-church-bank-accounts/.

Ramabulana, Makhado Sinthumule. *Church Mafia: Captured by Secret Powers: An Untold African Narrative.* Pretoria: Makhado Sinthumule Ramabulana, 2019.

South Africa Broad Casting Cooperation Digital News (SABC). *Angels Ministries, E Cape Swears to Defy Constitution,* 2016. www.youtube.com/watch?v=qxWPLgA-XrQ.

South Africa Broad Casting Cooperation (SABC) News Online. "Ngcobo Murder Saga Brings Religious Sector Regulation in the Spotlight." *SABC News,* February

24, 2018, sec. Home. www.sabcnews.com/sabcnews/engcobo-murder-saga-brings-religious-sector-regulation-spotlight/.

Somdyala, Kamva. "Bogus Pastors: Ramaphosa Concerned by Questionable Surging to the Fore." *News24*, February 28, 2018. www.news24.com/SouthAfrica/News/bogus-pastorsramaphosa-concerned-by-questionable-practices-surging-to-the-fore- 20190228.

SowetanLive. "Seven Angels Church to Be Demolished." *SowetanLive*, April 23, 2018. www.sowetanlive.co.za/news/south-africa/2018-04-23-seven-angels-church-to-be-demolished/.

Spies, Derrick. "Ngcobo Massacre: Seven Suspects Dead After Police Shootout." *News24*, February 24, 2018. www.news24.com/SouthAfrica/News/ngcobo-massacre-seven-suspects-dead-after-police-shootout-20180224.

VanDeCarr, Paul. "The Jonestown That Won't Fade Away: Twenty-Five Years Later: A Filmmaker Examines the Lasting Consequences." *Harvard Divinity Bulletin*, Fall (2003): 24–25.

Velaphi, Sithandiwe, Khaya Koko, and Tebogo Monama. "Ngcobo Cult's Deadly Plan Exposed." *IOL News*, February 26, 2018, sec. Eastern Cape. www.iol.co.za/news/south-africa/eastern-cape/engcobo-cults-deadly-plan-exposed-13481060.

Wanderley, Sergio, and Amos Barros. "Decoloniality, Geopolitics of Knowledge and Historic Turn: Towards a Latin American Agenda." *Management & Organizational History* 14, no. 1 (2018): 79–97.

Wane, Njoki Nathani, and Kimberley Todd. "Introduction: A Meeting of Decolonial Minds." In *Decolonial Pedagogy: Examining Sites of Resistance, Resurgence, and Renewal*, edited by Njoki Nathani Wane and Kimberly Todd. London: Palgrave Macmillan, 2018.

Zama, Zanele. "Video Reveals Mancoba Church Leader Telling the CRL Commission He Is on a Mission to Find the Devil." *702 News*, 2016. www.702.co.za/articles/293755/watch-i-am-not-a-pastor-i-m-an-angel-from-heaven.

8 Pneumatology and Prophetic Pentecostal Charismatic Christianity during COVID-19 in South Africa

Maria Frahm-Arp

8.1 Introduction

From its early beginnings in the 1900s the larger Pentecostal movement has been able to hold "two seemingly incompatible impulses in tension"[1] namely, the supernatural including the belief in extraordinary miracles and spiritual powers, and the natural world with aspects such as physical well-being and material needs. In this process, the broader Pentecostal movement has developed a self-acknowledged "potential Trinitarian anaemia"[2] in which a theological understanding of the nature and the role of the Holy Spirit, in particular, is often unclear.[3] Within these circles there is an ongoing debate "about the spiritual gifts of the Holy Spirit such as baptism in the Spirit, the gift of prophecy, the gift of healing and other such spiritual gifts which play an important role in Pentecostal spirituality".[4] Within specifically African debates, the nature and work of the Holy Spirit are understood within the context of an oral theological tradition that has shaped African religious thought for centuries.[5] African Pentecostal theology is not "a reified enterprise, but simply human reflection on the relationship of God-in-Christ to human beings and to the world of nature through His love and the power of the Holy Spirit".[6] Cameroonian theologian Ngong notes, "African Pentecostal pneumatology is more concerned with what the Spirit does in the life of the believer than with reflection on the nature of the Spirit".[7] In line with this argument, this chapter does not engage in pneumatology in Pentecostalism generally but focuses specifically on how the nature and role of the Holy Spirit are conceptualised and understood in the oral theology of three prophets expressed in the context of the COVID-19[8] pandemic in South Africa.

During the first weeks of the pandemic, the key role of the Holy Spirit was expressed as giving prophets an understanding of why the pandemic was happening, what the future would hold, and to protect ordinary people from the virus. Healing and claiming wealth through "seed money", while still important, was not the primary focus of the prophets' messages. They implored their congregations to understand what God was doing through the crisis and pray for "victory" over the disease. This victory was conceptualised as people being protected and preserved from the crisis, not as praying or claiming that the pandemic would/was being miraculously lifted from South Africa or the world. Using Discourse Analysis (DA) this chapter shows that these prophets established a pneumatology which offered followers a way to make sense of and cope with COVID-19. None of these churches violated the government regulations; as a matter of fact they encouraged people to obey all lockdown protocols. While these churches still told people that for the prophecies given to individual people to be truly powerful they had to give the church money, they did not ask for payment when praying for the nation and the general preservation of all believers from COVID-19. These prophets each gave a clear message that through the power of the Holy Spirit and their anointing in the Holy Spirit, they knew the will of God. God, they said, was in control. They maintained that they had foretold this disaster and that because they clearly knew the will of God they could also foretell what was to come. This chapter examines the messages of the prophets; it does not examine how people understood this message or what effect it had on their lives. During this time of crisis, the pneumatology expressed by these prophets translated into a message that offered people a sense of hope and created a worldview that explained the crisis and chaos that people were living through.

8.2 The rise of Prophetic Pentecostal Charismatic Christianity in Africa

Prophets, prophecy and prophetic healings within the larger Pentecostal movement in Africa became popular throughout Sub-Saharan Africa during the late 1990s and early 2000s. Some scholars perceive this as a fourth wave[9] and others a fifth wave[10] within the movement. One of the earliest of these prophets was Prophet T.B. Joshua who established the Synagogue Church of All Nations (SCOAN) in Nigeria in the 1980s. His

> success and that of his church is found in the fact that they have taken the message of the prophets very seriously and that the modus operandi and modus vivendi of Joshua and SCOAN are reminiscent of the prophetic traditions of Elijah and Elisha in ancient Israel.[11]

In earlier work, I looked at a random sample size of 100 churches in the Gauteng area during 2016.[12] I argued that within the contemporary or fourth wave of Pentecostalism there were three clusters, Achievements, Empowerment and Miracle PCC but the study did not engage with mega-miracle style prophets. Prophets claiming to foretell the future, heal people of any disease, raise the dead and bring fabulous wealth to believers only began to gain popularity in South Africa in about 2014.[13] In light of this new development within the movement, I argue that in its contemporary form there are now four clusters of Pentecostal Charismatic Christianity.

Achievements, Empowerment, Miracle and Prophetic forms of Pentecostal Charismatic Churches which are in varying degrees influenced by the Evangelical movement.[14] The fourth new cluster is marked by the miraculous prophetic ministry of the leaders of mega-churches – I refer to these as Prophet Pentecostal Charismatic Christianity (PPCC). This cluster is far less influenced by the Evangelical movement.[15]

A key feature of PPCC is that these prophets regard themselves as contemporary versions of the Old Testament prophets. These "white collar prophets"[16] are largely young blacks who "are often semi-literate and have no theological education but who claim to be anointed by God and led by the Holy Spirit".[17] Sears describes Old Testament and contemporary Christian prophecy

> as having the following features: a message sent from the divine world; inspiration through ecstasy, dreams or inner illumination with the likelihood that the message is unsolicited and the likelihood that the message is exhortatory or admonitory. . . . and is defined according to its purpose as a divine mandate rather than simply an answer to human questions.[18]

Much like their Old Testament counterparts who were frequently called on by God to deliver a divine message that was unsolicited by an individual or community,[19] these prophets like Shepherd Bushiri and Lesego Daniel call out individuals in their congregations and declare their sins of, for example, infidelity, corruption and substance abuse in front of everyone. Again drawing on the Old Testament example of the prophet/seer who, filled with Spirit of God, can perform extra-ordinary miracles,[20] these prophets are believed by their followers to engender prophetic ecstasies through which people are overcome with emotions so powerful that they suspend all reason and self-control.[21] Fohrer understands ancient Israelite prophets to have been either seers foretelling the future to their nomadic communities through visions and dreams, or social reformers amongst settled communities imploring them to live by a divinely inspired moral code.[22] Brueggemann resists these neat categorisations and suggests rather that while prophets foretell future events "they are concerned about the future as it impinges upon the present".[23] For Brueggemann "the task of prophetic ministry is to nurture, nourish, and evoke a consciousness and perception alternative to the consciousness and perception of the dominant culture around us".[24] The problem with the contemporary PPCC prophets is not that their claim to prophesy is in the tradition of the Old Testament, but rather, as Dube shows, that they are theologically illiterate and to "satisfy their over-expectant followers, this modern brand of 'Prophets' twist and tweak Scripture to their taste" thus often departing from orthodox Christian theology.[25]

In this chapter, the nature of the prophetic ministries of three contemporary South African prophets is analysed. The chapter shows that in a time of international crisis their ministries still continued harmful practices such as maintaining hierarchies within the Christian community, a theology that perpetuates the belief that some Christians have more or better access to God and that miracles are most effective when people give all their money to the churches. But despite this they also offered a message of hope and meaning in a time of uncertainty and hopelessness.

Leaders of these churches are individuals who claim to be anointed by the Holy Spirit to perform miraculous acts of healing and quick fixes for the "radical insecurities"[26] of daily economic, social and political life faced by many in Sub-Saharan Africa. The prophets or "Men of God" as they themselves and their followers call them are so named because they supposedly have unlimited and divinely anointed access to God.[27] They have become extremely popular and large mega-churches with multiple branches across nations have sprung up all over Africa. Many of these churches were influenced by Nigerian[28] or Latin-American Pentecostal churches such as the Universal Church of the Kingdom of God[29] rather than by American Pentecostalism in contrast to the earlier waves of the movement in Africa.

Some scholars see these prophets as a positive development in African Pentecostalism. Quayesi-Amakye argues that in Ghana, while there are people who are critical of these prophets and believe they are only in it to make money out of innocent believers, these churches are growing in popularity all the time and offer hope to people as they minister to their physical and spiritual needs.[30] In Nigeria Amanze,[31] who studied Prophet T.B. Joshua and SCOAN in detail, maintains that God has called Joshua and other prophets like him in the same way Old Testament prophets were called by God in ancient Israel to bring healing to the sick and guidance to those in political leadership. Kayange[32] and Asamaoh-Gyadu[33] both find this new form of prophetic Pentecostalism in Africa problematic because of its focus on the individual to the detriment of the African spirit of community, and also because of the abusive practices of some of these prophets.

Scholars commenting particularly on PPCC in Zimbabwe and South Africa have been highly critical of these prophets. Writing about Zimbabwe, Togarasei,[34] Kgatle,[35] and Dube[36] argue that these prophets make themselves wealthy by offering false hope to ordinary people in a time of economic and political crisis while preaching a gospel that justifies their wealth as the product of their tremendous faith in God and the poverty of their followers as the consequence of their sin and lack of faith. Zimunya and Gwara understand these churches within a Marxist theoretical framework and argue that this brand of Christianity offers a "great tranquillizer, shifting people's attention from these problems to the promise of earthly riches and miracles".[37] In South Africa Conradie[38] and Dube[39] show how many of these prophets are abusive towards their congregations by asking people to do outrageous things like eat grass, drink petrol, accept intimate kisses from the prophets and hand over their life savings. All three of the prophets in this study, Shepherd Bushiri, Nana Poku and Lesego Daniel, have had public allegations of abuse made against them.

Another area of scholarly disagreement pertains to the relationship between African Independent Churches (AICs) and African Traditional Religions (ATRs), and these PPCC churches. Anderson,[40] Freston,[41] Kaunda,[42] Sundkler[43] and Daneel[44] regard the larger Pentecostal movement in all its phases and forms as different from "African Initiated Churches (AICs) which sought to subordinate the Bible to African cultures".[45] Authors like Zimunya and Gwara[46] argue that the PPCC churches "pay scant respect to African traditional culture" and insist on preaching in English thereby not embracing African culture or traditions. The second group of scholars like Asamoah-Gyadu,[47] Shoko and Chiwara,[48] Mwandayi,[49] and Quayesi-Amakye[50] argue that this most recent form of Pentecostalism is much closer to ATR than the earlier waves of Pentecostalism. The prophet leaders of these churches have much in common with the n'anga (traditional healer) in ATR, particularly given their status as a mediator between believers and the divine, their charismatic gifts, and their use of a holy object.[51] Quayesi-Amakye maintains that in Ghana, "in responding to the material/physical and social needs of adherents, Pentecostal prophets unintentionally tend to exploit the existing Akan religio-cultural worldview".[52] While the phenomenological experience of being overcome by spiritual forces and the role of the prophet or leader as a mediator between followers and the divine may appear similar between the AICs and the PPCC, the PPCC perspective of the ancestors and ancestral veneration as evil is too diametrically opposed for these two traditions to ever be seen as one movement.

Having shown that the understanding of PPCC is contested terrain I now proceed to outline the methodology used in this study and then examine the lived pneumatology being constructed "on the ground" in the context of COVID-19 by three churches with their headquarters in South Africa.

8.3 Methodology

Purposive sampling was used as the methodology to study the developing pneumatology being created and preached by prophets at the start of the COVID-19 crisis in South Africa. Subsequently three PPCC churches were chosen and two online church services of each that were streamed during the first three weeks of the lockdown in South Africa were analysed (25 March to the 14 April 2020). Throughout the study, the recordings that are referenced are not referred to by date, but rather by the day of the lockdown they occurred on, for example day 8 of the lockdown. The period of this study includes Easter Sunday which was on day 19of the lockdown, 12 April 2020. These specific churches were chosen because they met certain criteria that were representative of the most popular PPCC churches in South Africa at present. The churches all had to be mega-churches that had established TV shows aired either on a TV channel or on their social media platforms. They needed to be able to transition to an online church service setting during the lockdown. The sample had to include both churches that appealed to a middle-class, urban constituency, and churches that appealed to working and unemployed classes in peri-urban contexts. Within the sample, there also had to be trans-national churches that had a significant following outside of South Africa. The prophets within the sample had to include at least one South African and one foreign national.

The three churches chosen were Enlightened Christian Gathering (ECG),[53] Rabboni Centre Ministries[54] and Kingdom Prayer Ministry International (KPMI).[55] ECG was established by the Malawian Shepherd Bushiri in 2011 and currently has its headquarters in Pretoria. The church has branches throughout the world. On Easter Sunday over a hundred different prophets from ECG branches throughout the world Skyped into the online Easter service led by Bushiri from his home in South Africa. ECG is a multiracial church with many middle-class and aspiring middle-class urban members. Lesego Daniel, a South African, started Rabboni in 2002 in Ga-Rankuwa, a peri-urban area outside Pretoria. It only attracts black people and has a primarily South African congregation drawn from the working class and the unemployed. The Ghanaian Nana Poku's KPMI church was established in 2013 in Rustenburg, a relatively small town that has suffered an economic downturn as the mining industry in South Africa has been significantly reduced over the last ten years. Poku's church attracts a diverse following of largely working-class black people from countries all over Africa.

These three churches were intentionally chosen because they all epitomised PPCC. Each church had recently grown significantly in size and popularity due to the miracles performed by their prophets. All three churches streamed their church services via their Facebook pages, their TV channel or on YouTube. Each prophet preached a very clear message of divine healing, exorcism of evil spirits and fabulous wealth to the followers who had enough faith. Each of these prophets claimed to be able to heal any illness. The extra-ordinary nature of their miracles and the extreme lengths they expected their members to go to prove the strength of their faith had brought each of these prophets to the attention of the media. Allegations of endangering the lives of their followers or abusing their followers had been levelled against these prophets but this had not diminished the popularity of their churches.

This study examines the emerging pneumatology of PPCC churches during a world pandemic and asks if their message and practices reflected a pneumatology that was abusive of their followers. Abuse in this study is understood according to the definition of abuse established within gender-based violence, only with a wider application. The United Nations defines violence against women (VAW) as "any act of gender-based violence that results in physical, sexual or mental harm or suffering to women, including threats of such acts, coercion or arbitrary deprivation of liberty, whether occurring in public or in private life".[56] In similar terms, this study defines abusive behaviour as any act that results in physical, sexual, mental, spiritual or emotional harm or the deprivation of personal liberty, or any threats of such acts. To gather the data three online church services streamed on the Facebook pages of these three different PPCC churches were recorded and transcribed. The Facebook platform was chosen as this showed the comments of followers to the service in real-time. These services took place during the lockdown when people were not allowed to attend church services. Discourse Analysis (DA) of the transcribed online church services was chosen as the method of analysis because it examines how language shapes ideology and social constructs and in so doing influences how people understand their social situatedness.[57] Fairclough and Wodak understand language as "social practice" through which ideas and ideologies are constructed and perpetuated.[58] This chapter is particularly sensitive to the multiple meanings latent within words. Grammar and words are not understood as having fixed meanings but rather fluid meanings that are continually being shaped within different social contexts and institutions.[59]

The limits of this methodology are that we do not hear how followers reflect on the messages of the prophets outside the online church service or how their daily lives might have been shaped or influenced by the messages of the prophets. It also does not provide an opportunity to interview the prophets and hear how they reflect on the pandemic or the theology they are establishing to make sense of this crisis. The strength of DA is the intense focus on the wording used, grammatical constructs and verbal interactions allowing one to analyse in detail the ideas and in this case the theology (and particularly the pneumatology) being constructed through language. This is ideal for a study seeking to examine how a pneumatology is being shaped. The limitation of this analytical process is that it does not lend itself to reviewing large numbers of conversations or verbal interactions and therefore this study is only focused on three churches.

The use of DA is appropriate to this study because the theoretical lens through which these churches are being examined is one of oral theology. This theology argues that Christians are continually re-shaping and re-creating their lived theologies through the oration of theological ideas in the contexts of sermons, prayers, music and testimonies, particularly within the Pentecostal tradition.[60] Hartman contends that to understand contemporary African Pentecostal pneumatology three issues need to be considered in tandem.[61] The first is to understand that in this context divine revelation is understood as ongoing and that it interacts with African spiritual cosmologies. The second is that theology is not a written doctrine but is developed out of, and concerning human experience with a particular focus on healing and material security. The third is to appreciate that the Holy Spirit is the primary actor through which the divine interacts with people and the spirit world.

8.4 Ministering in a time of COVID-19

All three churches followed the same basic pattern for their online services and they held services almost daily. They began with praise and worship music, which was generally comparatively short when compared to the lengthy praise and worship sessions normally held by these churches when believers gather physically. The second part was usually a Bible study of some sort, which in the case of all three churches was done by women. At Rabboni the women who welcomed Prophet Daniel and gave sermons or reflections on the Bible were referred to as "prophetesses" and later on in the service they would also give prophecies. As a build-up to the highlight of the service these women, in the case of ECG and Rabboni, and one woman at KPMI, praised the prophet or "Man of God" that was about to come and bless the viewers with extraordinary prophecies. The prophets then began to speak, sometimes reading from the Bible and giving their understanding of what this scripture meant, at other times going straight into their prophetic ministry. The "Man of God" would then begin to prophesy and take calls from viewers. Poku went straight into taking calls and began most of them with "What can I do for you?"[62] With each call, he told people that they would only receive what they had asked for if they paid R200.00 into his bank account. Throughout every service, the banking details of KPMI ran as a ribbon at the bottom of the screen. Poku was particularly agitated because his church would not be able to continue to stream services live if people did not urgently contribute money. Daniel and Bushiri both asked people to tithe and contribute to the church but they did not demand payment with each prophecy. ECG only gave their banking details during the breaks in the service but Rabboni ran a ribbon with the church's contact details and bank account details throughout most of the show. In all three churches many people phoned in to give testimonies of how the prayers of the prophets had healed them or how the prophecies of the prophets spoke into their lives.

Some of these services went on for up to eight hours. The prophets did not prophecy throughout these eight hours. Rabboni and ECG both had very long services during which various prophetesses and one or two minor prophets explained Bible verses to people, prayed in tongues for people and gave prophecies to the viewers. At Rabboni, throughout each service, six women known as prophetesses sat in a semi-circle with a meter between them, according to social distancing regulations, and ministered to people while Prophet Daniel took a break. Many people phoned in and commented on Facebook how the prophecies of these prophetesses, and not just the prophecies of Daniel, had healed them or broken a spell of depression or anger that was hanging over them. All three church services had "commercial" breaks in which they often played clips from earlier services. ECG and Rabboni both used this to highlight various services from 2018 and 2019 when Bushiri and Daniel respectively had predicted that a major crisis was imminent. During all the services there were times when the "Man of God" and the prophetesses prayed with the viewers "in the Name of Jesus Christ" and the "power of the Holy Spirit" for their healing, increase in wealth, blessings from God and the delivery of the nation from COVID-19.

8.5 The Holy Spirit and Jesus

Jesus Christ was regarded as the immediate figure of the Trinity and was continuously referred to and invoked, while the Holy Spirit was a more elusive, ghost-like entity with enormous spiritual power. All three prophets said that people must declare faith in Jesus Christ as their personal Lord and Saviour and accept Him into their life before any miracles could be performed or before the power of the Holy Spirit could be invoked. The emphasis on being born again is very much in line with the broader Pentecostal Charismatic message in Africa where this individualist salvation also justifies a break with the past and traditional cultures which are understood as the locus of demonic powers that block people from realising personal wealth and success.[63]

Pentecostal theologians have traditionally understood the Holy Spirit as being subordinate to, or less than, Jesus Christ. Therefore, Kärkkäinen argues, in "African Pentecostal practices the Holy Spirit is spoken of and evoked as the way to connect the believers to Jesus Christ the Son of God".[64] Studebaker studying Pentecostalism generally maintains that one of the ironies that characterises some forms of Pentecostalism is that they emphasise the power of the Holy Spirit whilst making the Spirit subordinate to Jesus Christ.[65] "Christ achieves redemption, and his work is the objective basis of justification. The Spirit applies the work of Christ, and this work of the Spirit is the subjective sanctification of the believer".[66] The churches in this study understood the Holy Spirit as an elusive and powerful entity that could only be accessed through Jesus Christ who mediates between the people and the Holy Spirit. To invoke the Holy Spirit people had to pray through the power of the Name of Jesus Christ while the Holy Spirit was generally called on when prayers in the Name of Jesus Christ were not enough. Poku's prayers exemplified this when he prayed: "In the mighty Name of Jesus Christ I pray against dying prematurely, by the power of the Holy Spirit".[67] He also prayed, "May the Holy Spirit take away all your stress in the mighty Name of Jesus Christ".[68] In all three churches, however, the mediation between Jesus and the Holy Spirit on behalf of believers was not enough; a "Man of God" was first required to mediate between the people and Jesus Christ, who then in turn would mediate between the people and the Holy Spirit.

8.6 Accessing the Holy Spirit

The elusive and miraculous power of the Holy Spirit could therefore not be directly accessed by ordinary people but had to be channelled through an anointed "Man of God", various rituals or quasi-magical formulas and holy objects. The pandemic challenged or tested these different conduits of the Holy Spirit in various ways. The infilling or anointing of the prophets by the Holy Spirit was in many ways the cornerstone of all their pneumatologies. If this was in doubt, then their following would fall away. Much like Zimbabwean "Men of God" and sometimes "Women of God" these prophets were understood as being better able to commune with God; "these privileged individuals can become bridges that help others cross flooded rivers between their sinful lives and the holy lives demanded by God".[69] Both Bushiri and Daniel made little direct reference to the Holy Spirit but, as anointed prophets, they were understood to be filled with the Holy Spirit and could "stand in the way of any illness" and in Jesus' Name ward off evil.[70] This theology was clearly stated by one of the prophetesses when she claimed: "The prophet prophecies in the power of the Holy Spirit, not in his own power".[71] Filled with this Holy Spirit Daniel "commands" evil spirits, the coronavirus and various other disasters to be removed from people in the Name of Jesus Christ. Bushiri similarly spoke against "every attack of the devil" and told the devil and the coronavirus, "I command you to change direction!"[72] Poku said, "I speak as a Prophet of God. I take away any virus. By the power of the Holy Ghost I pray against this virus".[73] While Poku told people that as born-again believers the Holy Spirit was wherever they were and intervening on their behalf, their own access to the Spirit was limited. As a prophet Poku had extra-ordinary access to the power of Holy Spirit and he could therefore declare things like, "I speak as a prophet of God"[74] and "I feel the Holy Spirit now,"[75] unlike most people who could not feel the Holy Spirit and were oblivious to the presence of the Holy Spirit all around them. These prophets each stated repeatedly that they could manage, contain or even remove the virus, but they could not do this alone. They needed their followers to pray with them and believe in them and the power of the Holy Spirit to perform miracles. This pneumatology has an abusive element because believers cannot access the power of the Holy Spirit on their own; they are dependent on the prophets to intervene on their behalf.

In channelling the power of the Holy Spirit into people's lives, prophets often use quasi-magical formulas.[76] Bushiri's quasi-magical formula during his online services was the repetition of "we decree and declare," "we speak deliverance," "we speak protection," and "we speak against".[77] The "we" being referred to here is the prophet speaking in the Name of Jesus Christ and the power of the Holy Spirit. His formula was coupled with a ritual: he continuously encouraged people to move around and clap their hands when they prayed as this would break the spiritual bondages they might have been in. Daniel often used the formula "I declare" and so he would pray, "I declare healing on you" or "I declare that the Office of the President is victorious" in the time of COVID-19.[78] Poku's formula was, "I pray in the power of the Holy Spirit in the name of Jesus Christ".[79] Poku also gave people small rituals to perform to empower their prayers. A particular favourite was telling people to write down the amount of money they wanted in their bank account five times on a piece of paper, blow on it, send R200.00 to the prophet and then call him in order to receive this money.[80] During the lockdown when congregations could not physically meet, quasi-magical prayer formulas and rituals were clearly still possible. These formulas in themselves are not abusive, but when linked with payment that had to be made to the prophet, as Poku required, they become part of a commercialisation of God's blessings.

Linked to the holy formulas, and before lockdown, the prophets at all three churches offered believers anointed objects that they could buy as a way to channel the power of the Holy Spirit. Banda explains, "anointing is the process by which prophets sanctify an object through a prayer of blessing or touching it to impart on it God's miracle-working power."[81] Ordinary people are seen as not anointed by God and thus not able to control the Holy Spirit or access it easily; holy objects therefore become a means by which they can secure the miraculous powers of the Holy Spirit. During the lockdown the prophets didn't sell holy objects during the services or told people to put oil or water near their screens so that the prophets could pray over it to make it holy as Asamoah-Gyadu[82] found in Ghana. Bushiri however instructed people, "place your hands on the TV screen in this name of Jehovah you will experience breakthrough financial blessing, healing from corona".[83] Perhaps the experience of isolation during this epidemic might see a shift in pneumatology from one that makes people reliant on holy objects to one that shows them they can access the grace of God themselves without these tools; however there was no evidence to support such a development.

The second form of holy object used by these churches was "seed money" that people gave to the prophets. Conradie clearly states the theological problem of "seed money" when he shows how belief in "seed money" distorts the relationship between the work of the Father and the Spirit. This he says is best seen in the notion of " 'transactional giving' where the giver 'sows' seed money (by tithing and voluntary gifts) in expectation of reaping a rich harvest".[84] Tithing and paying money to the prophet for specific prophecies is understood as a way to unlock God's material blessing on his people.[85] The role and importance of voluntary giving were particularly evident in Poku's services. Most of his engagements with followers went something like this: "Hello, what is the problem, how can I help you?" The caller explains their problem, then the prophet says, "Now put R200.00 in the bank account then I will help you" and then he goes on to pray for the person or declare a prophecy. He ends the call with a reminder that the person must deposit the money otherwise they will not receive their desired blessing.[86] Other times he told people, "I need to do something for you. Put R200.00 into my account, and then call me".[87] As Asamoah-Gyadu[88] has observed the believer pays God, via the prophet, for his blessings much like a customer pays a shop in exchange for the goods they want. If God takes too long to reward the faithful, the believer can leverage their faithfulness to demand the manifestation of God's power by the Holy Spirit.[89] This payment for the blessings of God goes against the Pauline pneumatology clearly stated in the New Testament that the gifts of God are freely given to the people of God.

At Rabboni and ECG, followers were particularly worried that during lockdown they would not be able to tithe. Towards the end of their church services, Rabboni and ECG impressed upon people the need to continue to tithe because it was part of the Christian call and an important way in which to access God's blessings. Bushiri said, "We are still allowing people to give"[90] because tithing (their money made holy by the prophets who pray over it once it has been offered up) was a crucial way in which people were able to bridge the gap between their state of unholiness and God's great holiness. Daniel said repeatedly that he was praying for people who were worried about their finances. He said God would bless them with wealth and that they should claim these blessings by seeding money to the church via SnapScan or PayFast.[91] The prophets, by praying over the money people gave, profess to close the great gap between ordinary believers and God. Banda argues however that this gap has been theologically created by these prophets and that having done so they "undermine Christ's sufficiency in blessing African believers" and instead lead them to develop a reliance on the so-called holy objects for their healing and salvation rather than Christ.[92] This relationship to money is part of a larger "name it and claim it theology" in which believers "sow a seed" to the church and the prophet. But "rather than promoting the ethics of hard work and social engagement"[93] which earlier prosperity theology had done, they demand that followers give more and more money to their church. They maintain that wealth will come not through hard work but through faith.[94] The more money people give to the church, often at the expense of their families, the more the believer will ultimately be blessed. These practices have proven to be abusive as members give away family possessions and money meant for rent and food to the church.[95]

The third type of holy objects is the strange things people have been expected to ingest such as eating grass or drinking petrol at Rabboni's church or being sprayed with insecticide[96] – all to access the Holy Spirit or break the power of evil forces in their lives. During the four weeks of this research, none of the churches suggested any such measures.

8.7 The war of good and evil spirits and the role of the Holy Spirit during this crisis

A key feature of PPCC is the role played by the Holy Spirit and prophets to break the powers of evil, sin and witchcraft. Many of life's uncertainties, illnesses and failures are attributed to the work of evil spirits and the powers of African witchcraft. These forces of evil can infiltrate ordinary objects like houses, cars, clothes, and even people, communities and family members that have been consciously or unconsciously dedicated to Satan by neighbours, relatives or unknown members of the larger community. With enough faith and payment of money or use of other holy objects, ordinary Christians can overcome these challenges when prophets pray on their behalf and vanquish these evil forces through the power of the Holy Spirit.[97] Evil is never completely eradicated, largely because unbelievers continue to exist and continue to do evil and/or invoke the powers of ancestral witchcraft in Africa. Understood theologically, this is not a sign of failure but of God's patience.[98] In this battle between good and evil, the Holy Spirit is understood by the three churches in this study in an "anthropomorphic, quasi-material and quasi-literal way".[99]

In the PPCC in this study, exorcism performed by the "Men of God" using holy objects and praying in tongues was seen as a central part of the work of the prophet. Believers praying in tongues and being slain in the Spirit accompanied these exorcisms. In the time of lockdown face-to-face encounters of prophecy and exorcism were not possible. What these churches did do was to pray live with their followers during the online services. In these prayer sessions, the prophets and other elders on set prayed in tongues for people who phoned in with a request. People sent in SMSes or WhatsApp messages after the prayers saying that they felt healed but the experience of being slain in the Spirit was not mentioned.

Demonic powers and the work of the devil was a central issue of prayer and discussion during the first weeks of the epidemic. One person sent in a text which summarised what many people were saying, "Maybe the whole drama with this virus is a lie of the devil to scare people, to destroy the economy. I have peace and joy".[100] Many other people wondered if God had abandoned them and someone texted, "I am so grateful for prophetess Dube, she has taught us that Jesus is not sleeping in COVID-19".[101] Daniel prayed often, "I pray that every curse is broken".[102] Bushiri prayed, "I command every evil that is about to enter your house, it must not enter, it must not locate your house, your job, your business, your finances, your marriage".[103] "We speak against every attack of the devil."[104] Poku kept reminding people, "As soon as you give your life to God, Satan will not like it. He'll do everything to drag you back".[105] According to Poku, COVID-19 was not a physical illness but a spiritual one. "This sickness came for Christians to worship God, for our prayers to be strong."[106] Understanding and explaining COVID-19, why it was happening, where God was during this crisis and what would happen in the future became the most important aspects of each prophet's online services during the lockdown.

8.8 The Holy Spirit brings protection and understanding in these "end times"

The potential of a theology that understands the world as a spiritual battle between good and evil, with key leaders anointed by God to exercise divine power to intercede on behalf of their followers to win this war, is that every-thing including a real physical illness is explained in spiritual terms. A pneu-matology that disregarded the physical realities of a disease and told people to disregard health care guidelines would be harmful to followers and place them in danger. On the other hand, a spiritual message that brought mean-ing to a crisis and a sense of certainty to the profound uncertainty could be psychologically helpful. The three churches in this study did not violate or go against any of the government regulations and they impressed upon their followers to keep all social distancing regulations. While they all prayed for healing, none of them told people that the virus was removed from the world, that all infected people were healed, or that all believers would be spared. As Kobylinski points out, these churches "believe that supernatu-ral phenomena, such as the miracles and healings described in the Bible, occur just as frequently today if the faith of the church members is ardent enough".[107] It was therefore somewhat surprising that these prophets did not preach a message that they had removed the coronavirus and healed the world. In the first weeks of the COVID-19 crisis, each of the prophets saw their most important role as that of making sense of what people were experiencing, telling them what they should be doing to cope with or over-come the epidemic and, at a time when everything felt uncertain, giving their followers a sense of certainty about what the future would hold. When we examine their messaging about COVID-19 we see that these churches offered their congregations hope by proclaiming that God was in control and had a plan. When praying for the nation, unlike individual people, they did not ask for money concerning their prophecies and prayers and they cre-ated a discourse of the end times that brought a sense of order and purpose in a time of chaos.

Conradie argues that in PPCC churches "the will of the Father seems so arbitrary so that benefits and burdens are randomly distributed. The Spirit does not proceed from the Father; the Father's hand is turned by the Spirit".[108] This was not how the prophets in this study explained the will of the Father to their followers. They were very clear that the will of the Father was not arbitrary or difficult to understand. They maintained that their key role was to make clear God's will to His people, particularly in this time of crisis. The will of the Father according to Bushiri was to bring wealth to the poor and hope to the rejected.[109] He assured people that the Holy Spirit guided him to have divine wisdom and insight into the Bible and was giv-ing him new revelations all the time.[110] According to these revelations, the coronavirus was a sign of the end times. "We cannot pray to stop it because these end times are foretold in the Bible but we can pray to be preserved".[111] Daniel kept reminding everyone that God's will was to protect and heal them. He referred to this as "God locates you". In other words, nothing and no one is hidden from God the Father. According to him, "COVID-19 is how God is making us dependant on Him".[112] Poku maintained, "God is working in this time".[113] God had not abandoned people and God's will was to protect people. "If you have a sickness others have died from don't lose faith – God has a greater purpose for your life than for the others so you will not die".[114]

Bushiri and Daniel made much of the fact that they had foretold this disaster. Three clips of Bushiri prophesying a worldwide disaster were repeated during the "commercial breaks" in the EGC online church services. The first was a prophecy from February 2017 when he said, "[The] time has come where the Spirit of the Lord shall vindicate you. . . . Days of trouble are coming. . . . Men will look and say what is this? God will say, 'I am restoring my church'".[115] On 11 November 2018, he proclaimed, "The time is coming when people will not have the grace to worship God freely as a congregation." "Rising of prophets in your land . . . is God giving you the last chance".[116] His third prophecy was on 12 May 2019 when he said, "A time of confusion is coming. Churches that preach the Holy Spirit will grow . . . People will become more stubborn and not believe in God or His servants".[117] He explained to his congregation that he had seen a vision of a red sun rising in the East. According to him, the Bible explained that something coming from the East always meant a tragedy would happen. The red sun meant judgment was coming.[118] Through the repetition of these prophecies, ECG reminded followers that their "Man of God" was so powerful that he had foretold the coronavirus. KPMI did not show any footage of Poku having foretold a major international crisis. At Rabboni they repeatedly showed a clip of Daniel giving a prophecy on 12 January 2020 in which he said that students would not have a good year and he called everyone to pray for students because he foresaw that their studies would be interrupted. The rest of Daniel's prophecies were immediate. He prophesied, "People are worried about finances" and "I see money disappearing fast".[119] All three prophets saw this epidemic as being in God's control. In traditional Old Testament language, they explained that the epidemic was a call from God for people to repent, turn away from sin and unbelief, give their lives to God and believe in His salvation.

Possibly the most measured message of these prophets was telling people what to do to cope during the crisis. They did not preach an abusive or misleading message of vainglory in which they declared that they had healed the world of COVID-19 or that their followers as Christians would be miraculously protected from the virus through their prayers as prophets. Instead, they encouraged people to stay calm, not move around and pray for healing. Poku repeated, "People must not panic." "Don't move around. No matter the storms that rise up, you are a child of God. Stay calm".[120] On the 20th day of the lockdown when people were not taking the lockdown seriously enough in many parts of the country, Bushiri implored his followers to pray and fast for three days because this virus was more serious than they realised. From 14 to 16 May, ECG ran an intense campaign calling everyone to pray and fast for worldwide deliverance from the virus. They released various "prayer points" on social media throughout each day explaining how people should pray. At Rabboni, Daniel told his followers, "Our job in corona is to pray and declare God's victory".[121] Daniel spent a lot of time praying for the essential services, medical staff, police and army, the government and everyone in a position of authority. His prayers entailed asking God that the world be protected, that the medical teams would be victorious in the battle against COVID-19 and people in leadership would be given wisdom in how to deal with this disease and make the right decisions.[122] His prayers were sensible and measured and he told people to stay calm, assuring them that they had nothing to fear because as born-again believers, God already blessed them and they would be protected.

In the same way that the prophets had the power to foretell the crisis and already knew how their followers should handle it, they also foresaw what was yet to come. None of them was foreseeing a world of ease and blessings. Bushiri maintained, "This virus will leave scars that will be financial, job losses, fights in families like never before".[123]

> As a prophet I am seeing the results of the pandemic. You may not be sick, but we are going to be sick of the results, of poverty that is going to come after. The world will go through a financial recession, there will be financial problems across the world, people will suffer, and we are praying that you will be preserved from that. Preserved from any danger. Preserved from any trouble, in the mighty Name of Jesus Christ.[124]

Poku similarly foresaw a bleak future, saying, "Bad things are coming, people must change their mind, turn away from worldly things".[125] Daniel was pessimistic but maintained that the future would be difficult for everyone and he foresaw that unless people began to repent and turn to God the future would be worse than the current situation.[126]

8.9 Conclusion

This chapter has explained why three popular PPCC prophets, Bushiri, Daniel and Poku, are so powerful and why they have so much influence over the people that follow them. It has shown how the three churches that they lead, ECG, Rabboni and KPMI respectively, all adapted quickly and easily to online services and streaming them over YouTube, Facebook and their TV channels. In analysing six services in the first 21 days of lockdown this study showed how some forms of abusive practices such as charging people for prophecies and proclaiming a gospel in which there is a hierarchy amongst believers, with ordinary believers remaining dependant on anointed leaders to access the Holy Spirit and understand God's will, have continued. However, other abusive behaviours like asking people to ingest harmful things like petrol or poisonous snakes, intimately kissing female congregants and putting people's lives at risk in unsafe or overcrowded buildings were all stopped.

In a time of crisis and lockdown while these congregations could not meet physically, their leaders continued to re-shape and re-establish pneumatologies to make sense of and minister to their followers, particularly when previous disturbing practices such as selling holy objects, spraying people with insecticide to exorcise demons and demanding sexually intimate experiences with female followers were no longer possible. As these prophets moved away from these harmful practices they all established pneumatologies that focused on making sense of this crisis moment in history. They maintained the belief of a hierarchy of access to the Holy Spirit. Only born-again Christians who claim Jesus as their Lord and Saviour can benefit from the Holy Spirit's blessing in their lives and being delivered from demons. While in everyday practice Jesus is the most immediate and prominent figure of the Trinity, through an analysis of the preaching of these prophets it became clear that the Holy Spirit is the one called upon when great spiritual power is needed. Ordinary believers cannot readily access the power of the Holy Spirit who is understood as an elusive, ghost-like figure that can best be channelled through quasi-magical means like holy objects, prayer formulas and sacred rituals. The most important and influential person to access the Holy Spirit is an anointed prophet, who through his anointing is infused with the power of the Holy Spirit. This anointing or infusing gives the prophet special powers to foretell the future, explain to people the will of God, drive out demons, identify what ails people and spiritually remove obstacles or spirits that are blocking the blessings God wants to bestow on them.

In conclusion, at a time of crisis, these churches have seamlessly moved their understanding of the work of the prophets and the Holy Spirit away from fantastical and sensational claims and behaviour to a more measured message of hope, calm and clarity. They all offered certainty in an uncertain world as they claimed to have understood the will of God and what God was doing through the coronavirus. They offered clarity about what people should be doing such as praying, fasting, remaining calm, not moving around and obeying the government regulations. In this way, they offered people a message of empowerment in a time of helplessness. Finally, they offered people a message of hope. God has not abandoned His people; everyone can be forgiven and if everyone turns back to God this disease can be defeated.

Notes

1 Grant Wacker, "Early Pentecostals and the Study of Popular Religious Movements in Modern America," in *The Work of the Spirit: Pneumatology and Pentecostalism*, ed. M. Welker (Grand Rapids, MI: Eerdmans, 2006), 126–46, 133, 143.

2 Veli-Matti Kärkkäinen, "Pneumatologies in Systematic Theology," in *Studying Global Pentecostalism: Theories and Methods*, eds. A. Anderson, M. Bergunder,

A. Droogers, and C. Van der Laan (Oakland, CA: University of California Press, 2010), 223–44, 227.

3 Shane Clifton, "The Spirit and Doctrinal Development: A Functional Analysis of the Traditional Pentecostal Doctrine of the Baptism in the Holy Spirit," *Pneuma* 29, no. 1 (2007): 5–23; George Lindbeck, *The Nature of Doctrine: Religion and Theology in a Postliberal Age* (Louisville, KY: Westminster Press, 1984); Bernard Lonergan, *Method in Theology* (London: Darton, Longman & Todd, 1972); Clark Pinnock, "Church in the Power of the Holy Spirit: The Promise of Pentecostal Ecclesiology," *Journal of Pentecostal Theology* 14, no. 2 (2006): 147–65; Kevin J. Vanhoozer, *The Drama of Doctrine: A Canonical Linguistic Approach to Christian Theology* (Louisville, KY: Westminster John Knox, 2005).

4 Eugene Jugaru, "Two Distinct Perspectives on Pneumatology: Similarities and Differences Between the Romanian Pentecostal and Evangelical Theology," *Ecumenical Review Sibiu* 7, no. 2 (2015): 243–55, 243.

5 John Mbiti, *African Religions and Philosophy* (London: Heinemann, 1969).

6 Ogbu Kalu, *African Pentecostalism: An Introduction* (Oxford: Oxford University Press, 2008), 249.

7 David Ngong, "African Pentecostal Pneumatology," in *Pentecostal Theology in Africa*, ed. Clifton R. Clarke (Eugene, OR: Pickwick Publications, 2014), 84.

8 COVID-19 is a new form of the coronavirus which first appeared in Wuhan in Hubei province, China, towards the end of 2019. The disease quickly spread throughout the world and by March 2020 South Africa reported its first case. On 24 March 2020 South Africa went into lockdown with all citizens except essential services personnel required to stay at home.

9 Chammah, Kaunda, "The Making of Pentecostal Zambia: A Brief History of Pneumatic Spirituality," *Oral History Journal of South Africa* 4, no. 1 (2016): 15–45, 18; Mookgo S. Kgatle, "Reimagining the Practice of Pentecostal Prophecy in Southern Africa: A Critical Engagement," *HTS Teologiese Studies / Theological Studies* 75, no. 4 (2019): 51–83; Mookgo S. Kgatle, *The Fourth Pentecostal Wave in South Africa: A Critical Engagement* (Abingdon: Routledge, 2019). Kgatle argues that this is a wave of Pentecostalism started in Southern Africa by Uebert Angel, the spiritual father of Shepherd Bushiri. This wave of Pentecostalism has been heavily influenced by African traditional religious practices of divination.

10 Joseph Quayesi-Amakye, "Ghana's New Prophetism: Antecedents and Some Characteristic Features," *Australasian Pentecostal Studies* [online] 15 (2015), accessed April 2, 2020, http://aps-journal.com/aps/index.php/APS/article/view/125/122.

11 James Amanze, "The Role of Prophecy in the Growth and Expansion of the Synagogue Church of All Nations," *Scriptura* 112, no. 1 (2013): 1–14, accessed April 2, 2020, http://scriptura.journals.ac.za.

12 Maria Frahm-Arp, "Pentecostalism, Politics and Prosperity in South Africa," *Religions* 9, no. 10 (2018): 289–317.

13 Ibid.

14 Ibid., 290–92.

15 Maria Frahm-Arp, ' "Can't They See They Are Being Manipulated?': Miracle-Prophets and Secular South African Radio," in *Radio, Public Life and Citizen Deliberation in South Africa*, ed. Sarah Chiumbu (Routledge, forthcoming).

16 Fainos Mangena and Samson Mhizha, "The Rise of White Collar Prophecy in Zimbabwe: A Psycho-Ethical Statement," in *Prophets, Profits and the Bible in Zimbabwe*, eds. Ezra Chitando, Masiiwa Ragies Gunda, and Joachim Kügler (Bamberg: University of Bamberg Press, 2013), 133–53, 149.

17 Quayesi-Amakye, "Ghana's New Prophetism," 6.

18 Joshua Michael Sears, "False Prophets in Ancient Israelite Religion," *Studia Antiqua* 7, no. 1 (2009): 97–106, 98.
19 Roger Norman Whybray, "Prophets," in *The Oxford Companion to the Bible*, eds. Bruce M. Metzger and Michael D. Coogan (Oxford: Oxford University Press, 1993), 621.
20 Michael Ramsey, "The Authority of the Bible," in *Peake's Commentary on the Bible*, eds. M. Black and H. H. Rowley (Middlesex: Thomas Nelson & Sons, 1977), 2.
21 Frahm-Arp, ' "Can't They See They Are Being Manipulated?"; Quayesi-Amakye, "Ghana's New Prophetism," 9.
22 Fohrer Georg, *History of Israelite Religion* (London: SPCK, 1972), 224.
23 Brueggemann Walter, *The Prophetic Imagination* (Johannesburg: Fortress Press, 1978), 12.
24 Ibid.,13.
25 Elijah Dube, "Desperation in an Attempt to Curb Modern-Day Prophets: Pentecostalisation and the Church in South Africa and Zimbabwe," *Conspectus* 27, no. 1 (2018): 25–34, 28.
26 Achille Mbembe, "Religion, Politics and Theology: A Conversation with Achile Mbembe," *Boundary* 34, no. 2 (2007): 149–70.
27 Kaunda, "The Making of Pentecostal Zambia," 18.
28 Charity Manyeruke and Shakespear Hamauswa, "Prophets and Politics in Zimbabwe," in *Prophets, Profits and the Bible in Zimbabwe*, eds. Ezra Chitando, Masiiwa Ragies Gunda, and Joachim Kügler (Bamberg: University of Bamberg Press, 2013), 281–97, 291–2.
29 Mangena and Mhizha, "The Rise," 136.
30 Quayesi-Amakye, "Ghana's New Prophetism."
31 Amanze, "The Role of Prophecy," 3.
32 Grivas M. Kayange, "Rediscovering Individual-based Values in Ubuntu Virtue Ethics: Transforming Corporate Entities in Post-colonial Africa," *An African Path to a Global Future*, eds. Rianna Oelofsen and Kọ́lá Abímbọ́la (Washington, DC: Council for Research in Values and Philosophy [RVP], 2018).
33 Kwabena Asamoah-Gyadu, *Contemporary Pentecostal Christianity: Interpretations from an African Context* (Oxford: Regnum Books, 2013).
34 Lovemore Togarasei, "The Pentecostal Gospel of Prosperity in African Contexts of Poverty: An Appraisal," *Exchange* 40, no. 1 (2011): 336–50.
35 Mookgo S. Kgatle, "The Unusual Practices Within Some Neo-Pentecostal Churches in South Africa: Reflections and Recommendations," *HTS Teologiese Studies / Theological Studies* 73, no. 3 (2017): 46–56.
36 Dube, "Desperation," 25–34.
37 Clive T. Zimunya and Joyline Gwara, "Pentecostalism, Prophets and the Distressing Zimbabwean Milieu," in *Prophets, Profits and the Bible in Zimbabwe*, eds. Ezra Chitando, Masiiwa Ragies Gunda, and Joachim Kügler (Bamberg: University of Bamberg Press, 2013), 187–201, 200.
38 Ernest Conradie, "Ecumenical Perspectives on Pentecostal Pneumatology," *Missionalia* 43, no. 1 (2015): 63–81.
39 Dube, "Desperation," 25–34.
40 Allan Anderson, *Moya: The Holy Spirit in an African Context* (Pretoria: University of South Africa, 1991).
41 Paul Freston, "Pentecostalism in Brazil: A Brief History," *Religion* 25, no. 1 (1995): 119–33.
42 Kaunda, "The Making of Pentecostal Zambia."
43 Bengt G. Sundkler, *Bantu Prophets in South Africa* (London: International African Institute, 1961).

44 Marthiunus L. Daneel, "The Growth and Significance of Shona Independent Churches," in *Christianity South of the Zambezi*, ed. M. F. C. Bourdillon (Gweru: Mambo, 1977), 177–92; M. L. Daneel, *Quest for Belonging: Introduction to a Study of African Independent Churches* (Gweru: Mambo, 1987).

45 Kaunda, "The Making of Pentecostal Zambia," 19.

46 Zimunya and Gwara, "Pentecostalism," 193.

47 Kwabena Asamoah-Gyadu, "'Unction to Function': Reinventing the Oil of Influence in African Pentecostalism," *Journal of Pentecostal Theology* 13, no. 2 (2005a): 231–56; J. K. Asamoah-Gyadu, *Pentecostalism and the Transformation of the African Christian Landscape* (Leiden: Brill, 2005), 100–1.

48 Tabona Shoko and Agness Chiwara, "The Prophetic Figure in Zimbabwean Religions A Comparative Analysis of Prophet Makandiwa of the United Family International Church (UFIC) and the N'anga in African Traditional Religion," in *Prophets, Profits and the Bible in Zimbabwe*, eds. J. Kügler, M. R. Gunda, L. Togarasei, and E. S. Onomo (Bamberg: University of Bamberg Press, 2013), 217–230.

49 Canisius Mwandayi, "Traversing the Thin Line Between 'Chibhoyi' (Indigenous Spirituality) and Miracle Working: A Case Study of Miracle Working in the Impact for Christ Ministries in Gweru," in *Prophets, Profits and the Bible in Zimbabwe*, eds. J. Kügler, M. R. Gunda, L. Togarasei, and E. S. Onomo (Bamberg: University of Bamberg Press, 2013), 231–44.

50 Quayesi-Amakye, "Ghana's New Prophetism," 2.

51 Collium Banda, "Complementing Christ? A Soteriological Evaluation of the Anointed Objects of the African Pentecostal Prophets," *Conspectus: The Journal of the South African Theological Seminary* [online] (2018): 55–69, 59, accessed April 2, 2020, www.sats.edu.za/banda-complementing-christ.

52 Quayesi-Amakye, "Ghana's New Prophetism," 2.

53 Shepherd Bushiri service held on day 20 of lockdown, accessed April 18, 2020, www.facebook.com/shepherdbushiriministries/videos/1428514677 309880/. Shepherd Bushiri service held on day 19 of lockdown, accessed April 18, 2020, www.facebook.com/shepherdbushiriministries/videos/1444711375711590/.

54 Lesego Daniel service held on day 19 of lockdown, www.facebook.com/rabboniministries/videos/692442304859059/ Lesego Daniel service held on day 21 of lockdown, accessed April 18, 2020, www.facebook.com/rabboniministries/videos/860595351091417/.

55 Nana Poku KPMI service held on day 8 of lockdown, accessed April 18, 2020, www.facebook.com/ProphetNanaPokuOfficial/app/212104595551052/. Nana Poku KPMI service held on day 5 of lockdown, accessed April 18, 2020, www.facebook.com/ProphetNanaPokuOfficial/app/212104595551052/.

56 Vijaykumar Harbishettar and Suresh Bada Math, "Violence Against Women in India: Comprehensive Care for Survivors," *Indian Journal of Medical Research* 40, no. 2 (2014): 157–59.

57 Ian Parker, *Discourse Dynamics: Critical Analysis for Social and Individual Psychology* (London: Taylor & Frances/Routledge, 1992).

58 Norman Fairclough and Ruth Wodak, "Critical Discourse Analysis," in *Discourse Studies: A Multidisciplinary Introduction*, ed. T. A. Van Dijk (Newcastle upon Tyne: Sage, 1997), 258.

59 Michael Alexander Kirkwood Halliday, *Language as Social Semiotic* (London: Edward Arnold, 1978).

60 Vinson Synan, *The Holiness-Pentecostal Tradition: Charismatic Movements in the Twentieth Century* (Grand Rapids, MI: Eerdmans, 1997).

61 Tim Hartman, "The Promise of an Actualistic Pneumatology: Beginning with the Holy Spirit in African Pentecostalism and Karl Barth Modern Theology," *Modern Theology* 33, no. 3 (2017): 333–47, 338.

62 Poku, day 5 of lockdown.

63 Kaunda, "The Making of Pentecostal Zambia," 18; Birgit Meyer, ' "Make a Complete Break with the Past': Memory and Post-Colonial Modernity in Ghanaian Pentecostal Discourse," *Journal of Religion in Africa* 28, no. 1 (1998): 316–49.

64 Kärkkäinen, "Pneumatologies in Systematic Theology," 224.

65 Steven M. Studebaker, "Pentecostal Soteriology and Pneumatology," *Journal of Pentecostal Theology* 11, no. 2 (2003): 248–70, 248.

66 Ibid., 248.

67 Poku, day 8 of lockdown.

68 Ibid.

69 Masiiwa R. Gunda and Francis Machingura, "The 'Man of God' Understanding Biblical Influence on Contemporary Mega-Church Prophets in Zimbabwe," in *Prophets, Profits and the Bible in Zimbabwe*, eds. Ezra Chitando, Masiiwa Ragies Gunda, and Joachim Kügler (Bamberg: University of Bamberg Press, 2013), 15–27, 26.

70 Daniel, day 21 of lockdown.

71 Ibid.

72 Bushiri, day 20 of lockdown.

73 Poku, day 8 of lockdown.

74 Ibid.

75 Ibid.

76 Collium Banda, "Managing an Elusive Force? The Holy Spirit and the Anointed Articles of Pentecostal Prophets in Traditional Religious Africa," *Verbum et Ecclesia* [online] 40, no. 1 (2019): 76, accessed April 2, 2020, https://doi.org/10.4102/ve.v40i1.2025.

77 Bushiri, day 20 of lockdown.

78 Daniel, day 19 of lockdown.

79 Poku, day 5 of lockdown.

80 Ibid.

81 Banda, "Complementing Christ?" 57.

82 Asamoah-Gyadu, "Unction to Function."

83 Bushiri, day 20 of lockdown.

84 Conradie, "Ecumenical," 76.

85 Kwabena Asamoah-Gyadu, *Contemporary Pentecostal Christianity: Interpretations from an African Context* (Oxford: Regnum Books, 2013), 96.

86 Poku, day 8 of lockdown.

87 Ibid.

88 Asamoah-Gyadu, *Contemporary Pentecostal Christianity*, 100, 234.

89 Kaunda, "The Making of Pentecostal Zambia."

90 Bushiri, day 20 of lockdown.

91 Daniel, day 21 of lockdown.

92 Banda, "Complementing Christ?" 62–63.

93 Kaunda, "The Making of Pentecostal Zambia," 15.

94 Linda Van der Kamp, *Conversion: Brazilian Pentecostalism and Urban Women in Mozambique* (Suffolk, NY: Boydell & Brewer, 2016).

95 Illana Van Wyk, *The Universal Church and the Kingdom of God in South Africa* (Johannesburg: Wits University Press, 2015).

96 Banda, "Complementing Christ?" 57.

97 Asamoah-Gyadu, *Contemporary Pentecostal Christianity*, 109, 116; Kaunda, "The Making of Pentecostal Zambia"; Anderson, *Moya*, 68.

98 Conradie, "Ecumenical Perspectives on Pentecostal Pneumatology," 78.
99 Ibid.
100 Daniel, day 21 of lockdown.
101 Ibid.
102 Ibid.
103 Bushiri, day 20 of lockdown.
104 Ibid.
105 Poku, day 8 of lockdown.
106 Ibid.
107 Andrzej Kobylinski, "The Global Pentecostalization of Christianity and Its Ethical Consequences," [Online] (2016): 106, accessed April 2, 2020, www.research-gate.net/publication/310796722_The_Global_Pentecostalization_of_Christi anity_ and_Its_Ethical_Consequences.
108 Conradie, "Ecumenical Perspectives on Pentecostal Pneumatology," 76.
109 Bushiri, day 20 of lockdown.
110 Ibid.
111 Ibid.
112 Daniel, day 19 of lockdown.
113 Poku, day 8 of lockdown.
114 Ibid.
115 Bushiri, day 20 of lockdown.
116 Ibid.
117 Ibid.
118 Ibid.
119 Daniel, day 19 of lockdown.
120 Poku, day 5 of lockdown.
121 Daniel, day 21 of lockdown.
122 Daniel, day 19 of lockdown.
123 Bushiri, day 20 of lockdown.
124 Ibid.
125 Poku, day 8 of lockdown.
126 Daniel, day 19 of lockdown.

References

Amanze, James, N. "The Role of Prophecy in the Growth and Expansion of the Synagogue Church of All Nations." *Scriptura* 112, no. 1 (2013): 1–14. Accessed April 2, 2020. http://scriptura.journals.ac.za.

Anderson, Allan. *Moya: The Holy Spirit in an African context*. Pretoria: University of South Africa, 1991.

Asamoah-Gyadu, J. Kwabena. "'Unction to Function': Reinventing the Oil of Influence in African Pentecostalism." *Journal of Pentecostal Theology* 13, no. 2 (2005a): 231–56.

———. *Pentecostalism and the Transformation of the African Christian Landscape*. Leiden: Brill, 2005b.

———. *Contemporary Pentecostal Christianity: Interpretations from an African Context*. Oxford: Regnum Books, 2013.

Banda, Collium. "Complementing Christ? A Soteriological Evaluation of the Anointed Objects of the African Pentecostal Prophets." *Conspectus: The Journal of the South African Theological Seminary* [online] (2018): 55–69. Accessed April 2, 2020. www.sats.edu.za/banda-complementing-christ.

————. "Managing an Elusive Force? The Holy Spirit and the Anointed Articles of Pentecostal Prophets in Traditional Religious Africa." *Verbum et Ecclesia* [online] 40, no. 1 (2019). Accessed April 2, 2020. https://doi.org/10.4102/ve.v40i1.2025.

Brueggemann, Walter. *The Prophetic Imagination.* Johannesburg: Fortress Press, 1978.

Clifton, Shane. "The Spirit and Doctrinal Development: A Functional Analysis of the Traditional Pentecostal Doctrine of the Baptism in the Holy Spirit." *Pneuma* 29, no. 1 (2007): 5–23.

Conradie, Ernst M. "Ecumenical Perspectives on Pentecostal Pneumatology." *Missionalia* 43, no. 1 (2015): 63–81.

Daneel, Martinus. "The Growth and Significance of Shona Independent Churches." In *Christianity South of the Zambezi*, edited by M. F. C. Bourdillon, vol. 2, 177–92. Gweru: Mambo, 1977.

————. *Quest for Belonging: Introduction to a Study of African Independent Churches.* Gweru: Mambo, 1987.

Dube, Elijah. "Desperation in an Attempt to Curb Modern-Day Prophets: Pentecostalisation and the Church in South Africa and Zimbabwe." *Conspectus* 27, no. 1 (2018): 25–34.

Fairclough, Norman, and Ruth Wodak. "Critical Discourse Analysis." In *Discourse Studies: A Multidisciplinary Introduction*, edited by T. A. Van Dijk, vol. 2. Newcastle upon Tyne: Sage, 1997.

Frahm-Arp, Maria. "Pentecostalism, Politics and Prosperity in South Africa." *Religions* 9, no. 10 (2018): 289–317.

————. '"Can't They See They Are Being Manipulated?': Miracle-Prophets and Secular South African Radio." In *Radio, Public Life and Citizen Deliberation in South Africa*, edited by S. Chiumbu. Routledge, forthcoming.

Freston, Paul. "Pentecostalism in Brazil: A Brief History." *Religion* 25, no. 1 (1995): 119–33.

Fohrer, Georg. *History of Israelite Religion.* London: SPCK, 1972.

Gunda, Masiiwa Ragies, and Francis Machingura. "The 'Man of God': Understanding Biblical Influence on Contemporary Mega-Church Prophets in Zimbabwe." In *Prophets, Profits and the Bible in Zimbabwe*, edited by Ezra Chitando, Masiiwa Ragies Gunda, and Joachim Kügler, 15–27. Bamberg: University of Bamberg Press, 2013.

Halliday, Michael Alexander Kirkwood. *Language as Social Semiotic.* London: Edward Arnold, 1978.

Harbishettar, Vijaykumar, and Suresh Bada Math. "Violence Against Women in India: Comprehensive Care for Survivors." *Indian Journal of Medical Research* 40, no. 2 (2014): 157–59.

Hartman, Tim. "The Promise of an Actualistic Pneumatology: Beginning with the Holy Spirit in African Pentecostalism and Karl Barth Modern Theology." *Modern Theology* 33, no. 3 (2017): 333–47.

Jugaru, Eugen. "Two Distinct Perspectives on Pneumatology: Similarities and Differences Between the Romanian Pentecostal and Evangelical Theology." *Ecumenical Review Sibiu* 7, no. 2 (2015): 243–55.

Kalu, Ogbu. *African Pentecostalism: An Introduction.* Oxford: Oxford University Press, 2008.

Kärkkäinen, Veli-Matti. "Pneumatologies in Systematic Theology." In *Studying Global Pentecostalism: Theories and Methods*, edited by A. Anderson, M.

Bergunder, A. Droogers, and C. van der Laan, 223–44. Oakland, CA: University of California Press, 2010.

Kaunda, Chammah. "The Making of Pentecostal Zambia: A Brief History of Pneumatic Spirituality." *Oral History Journal of South Africa* 4, no. 1 (2016): 15–45.

Kayange, Grivas M. "Rediscovering Individual-Based Values in Ubuntu Virtue Ethics: Transforming Corporate Entities in Post-Colonial Africa." In *An African Path to a Global Future*, edited by Rianna Oelofsen and Kọ́lá Abímbọ́la. Washington, DC: Council for Research in Values and Philosophy, 2018.

Kgatle, Mookgo S. "The Unusual Practices Within Some Neo-Pentecostal Churches in South Africa: Reflections and Recommendations." *HTS Teologiese Studies / Theological Studies* 73, no. 3 (2017): 46–56.

———. *The Fourth Pentecostal Wave in South Africa: A Critical Engagement.* Abingdon: Routledge, 2019.

———. "Reimagining the Practice of Pentecostal Prophecy in Southern Africa: A Critical Engagement." *HTS Teologiese Studies / Theological Studies* 75, no. 4 (2019): 51–83. https://doi.org/10.4102/hts.v75i4.5183.

Kobylinski, Andrzej. "The Global Pentecostalization of Christianity and Its Ethical Consequences" [Online], 2016. Accessed April 2, 2020. www.researchgate.net/publication/ 310796722_The_Global_Pentecostalization_of_Christianity_and_ Its_Ethical_Consequences.

Lindbeck, George. *The Nature of Doctrine: Religion and Theology in a Postliberal Age.* Louisville, KY: Westminster Press, 1984.

Lonergan, Bernard. *Method in Theology.* London: Darton, Longman & Todd, 1972.

Mangena, Fainos, and Samson Mhizha. "The Rise of White Collar Prophecy in Zimbabwe: A Psycho-Ethical Statement." In *Prophets, Profits and the Bible in Zimbabwe*, edited by Ezra Chitando, Masiiwa Ragies Gunda, and Joachim Kügler, 133–53. Bamberg: University of Bamberg Press, 2013.

Manyeruke, Charity, and Shakespear Hamauswa. "Prophets and Politics in Zimbabwe." In *Prophets, Profits and the Bible in Zimbabwe*, edited by Ezra Chitando, Masiiwa Ragies Gunda, and Joachim Kügler, 281–97. Bamberg: University of Bamberg Press, 2013.

Mbembe, Achile. "Religion, Politics and Theology: A Conversation with Achile Mbembe." *Boundary* 34, no. 2 (2007): 149–70.

Mbiti, John S. *African Religions and Philosophy.* 2nd ed. London: Heinemann, 1969.

Meyer, Birgit. ' "Make a Complete Break with the Past': Memory and Post-Colonial Modernity in Ghanaian Pentecostal Discourse." *Journal of Religion in Africa* 28, no. 1 (1998): 316–49.

Mwandayi, Canisius. "Traversing the Thin Line Between 'Chibhoyi' (indigenous spirituality) and Miracle-Working: A Case Study of Miracle-Working in the Impact for Christ Ministries in Gweru." In *Prophets, Profits and the Bible in Zimbabwe*, edited by Ezra Chitando, Masiiwa Ragies Gunda, and Joachim Kügler, 231–44. Bamberg: University of Bamberg Press, 2013.

Ngong, David. "African Pentecostal Pneumatology." In *Pentecostal Theology in Africa*, edited by C. R. Clark. Eugene, OR: Pickwick Publications, 2014.

Parker, Ian. *Discourse Dynamics: Critical Analysis for Social and Individual Psychology.* London: Taylor & Frances/Routledge, 1992.

Pinnock, Clark. "Church in the Power of the Holy Spirit: The Promise of Pentecostal Ecclesiology." *Journal of Pentecostal Theology* 14, no. 2 (2006): 147–65.

Quayesi-Amakye, Joseph. "Ghana's New Prophetism: Antecedents and Some Characteristic Features." *Australasian Pentecostal Studies* [online] 15 (2015). Accessed April 2, 2020. http://aps-journal.com/aps/index.php/APS/ article/view/125/122.

Ramsey, Michael. "The Authority of the Bible." In *Peake's Commentary on the Bible*, edited by M. Black and H. H. Rowley. Middlesex: Thomas Nelson & Sons, 1977.

Sears, Joshua M. "False Prophets in Ancient Israelite Religion." *Studia Antiqua* 7, no. 1 (2009): 97–106.

Shoko, Tabona, and Agness Chiwara. "The Prophetic Figure in Zimbabwean Religions: A Comparative Analysis of Prophet Makandiwa of the United Family International Church (UFIC) and the N'anga in African Traditional Religion." In *Prophets, Profits and the Bible in Zimbabwe*, edited by Ezra Chitando, Masiiwa Ragies Gunda, and Joachim Kügler, 217–30. Bamberg: University of Bamberg Press, 2013.

Studebaker, Steven M. "Pentecostal Soteriology and Pneumatology." *Journal of Pentecostal Theology* 11, no. 2 (2003): 248–70.

Sundkler, Bengt G. *Bantu Prophets in South Africa*. 2nd ed. London: International African Institute, 1961.

Synan, Vinson. *The Holiness-Pentecostal Tradition: Charismatic Movements in the Twentieth Century*. Grand Rapids, MI: Eerdmans, 1997.

Togarasei, Lovemore. "The Pentecostal Gospel of Prosperity in African Contexts of Poverty: An Appraisal." *Exchange* 40, no. 1 (2011): 336–50.

Van der Kamp, Linda. *Violent Conversion: Brazilian Pentecostalism and Urban Women in Mozambique*. Suffolk, NY: Boydell & Brewer, 2016.

Van Wyk, Illana. *The Universal Church and the Kingdom of God in South Africa*. Johannesburg: Wits University Press, 2015.

Vanhoozer, Kevin J. *The Drama of Doctrine: A Canonical Linguistic Approach to Christian Theology*. Louisville, KY: Westminster John Knox, 2005.

Wacker, Grant. "Early Pentecostals and the Study of Popular Religious Movements in Modern America." In *The Work of the Spirit: Pneumatology and Pentecostalism*, edited by M. Welker, 126–46. Grand Rapids, MI: Eerdmans, 2006.

Whybray, Roger Norman. "Prophets." In *The Oxford Companion to the Bible*, edited by B. M. Metzger and M. D. Coogan, 621. Oxford: Oxford University Press, 1993.

Zimunya, Clive Tendai, and Joyline Gwara. "Pentecostalism, Prophets and the Distressing Zimbabwean Milieu." In *Prophets, Profits and the Bible in Zimbabwe*, edited by Ezra Chitando, Masiiwa Ragies Gunda, and Joachim Kügler, 187–201. Bamberg: University of Bamberg Press, 2013.

9 The poor's weapon against inequality?

A critique of the public role of neo-Pentecostalism in unequal South Africa

Collium Banda

9.1 Introduction

The main focus of this chapter is the role played by the controversial South African neo-Pentecostal (SANP) churches in the public realm. Neo-Pentecostalism, also known as the new charismatic movement, is distinct from classical Pentecostalism due to its emphasis on material prosperity and health as a right for all God's children in this present age. The older classical movement lays a stronger emphasis on holiness and otherworldly spirituality. While classical Pentecostalism tends to be denominational, neo-Pentecostalism is a movement of prophet-pastors and prophet-apostles all claiming a unique anointing from God. Kgatle describes it as a movement that revolves around personalities.[1] There are various strands among SANP churches, and this chapter concentrates on the ones that have attracted controversy by their unusual and highly controversial activities detailed below. The widespread outcry over these controversial activities caused the Commission for the Promotion and Protection of the Rights of Cultural, Religious and Linguistic Communities (the CRL Rights Commission) to institute two investigative studies on the state of religion in South Africa. One study was conducted by the CRL Rights Commission itself and resulted in a report titled, *Report on the Hearings on the Commercialisation of Religion and Abuse of People's Beliefs Systems.*[2] The other study was commissioned by the CRL Rights Commission and conducted by the Bureau of Market Research in the College of Economic and Management Sciences of the University of South Africa and led to a report entitled *An Investigative Study of the Commercialisation of Religion in the Republic of South Africa 2016: Gauteng Pilot Study.*[3] Both reports made damning findings against several of these religious groups in South Africa. Most of the aspects cited as points of grave concern and warranting government intervention implicated the controversial SANP churches. However, despite being associated with grievous religious activities the SANP churches still remain strong.

This leads to the question: what is the essence of the controversial strand of neo-Pentecostalism in South Africa that makes it continue to thrive despite opposition from state authorities and concerned citizens? Since these churches function as places of hope for many poor South Africans, what should these churches do to play a really meaningful role among poor people? To answer these research questions, the theoretical framework of religion as a means to human flourishing will be described. This will be followed by an analysis of how the controversial religious activities are key into people's longing for human flourishing. The South African context of socioeconomic inequality will be analysed to show how it causes the poor to turn to controversial religious practices for the power to deal with the context of inequality. This is followed by discussing the role played by neo-Pentecostalism in empowering the poor to confront inequality in South Africa. Aspects of neo-Pentecostalism that need improvement to enable a more meaningful engagement with the public realm will be examined. In conclusion a proposal will be made on what neo-Pentecostalism should do to empower poor South Africans to address their lack of human flourishing in a meaningful way. The contribution of this chapter lies in highlighting the significant role of these churches in the lives of many poor South Africans who rely on them for support in engaging their socioeconomic challenges.

9.2 Religion as a means to human flourishing

Human flourishing is expressed by the idea of human wellbeing in a holistic sense that includes material, social, spiritual and other aspects of human existence. The "public realm" is used in this chapter to refer to the social, economic and political realm where physical existence takes place. Smit understands "public" as "designating life in general, everyday life in reality with all and everybody".[4] "The public realm" encompasses the "totality of life with others in the world, in a variety of forms of social institutions and relations".[5] Therefore, the public realm is the sphere in which human beings live their social, political and economic life. These are aspects that have a fundamental effect on human flourishing or a lack thereof. This chapter attempts to discern the function of neo-Pentecostalism in promoting human flourishing in the South African public realm.

The idea of human flourishing that guides this chapter emanates from the African notion of *ubuntu* as dignified human existence; a full life that upholds authentic humanness. As Okorocha points out, "a life worth living [is] the *summum bonum* of Igbo religiousness".[6] This seems to be shared by other African communities, as Mbiti says, to traditional Africans "religion permeates all the departments of life"[7] for the "acts of worship and turning to God are pragmatic and utilitarian rather spiritual or mystical".[8] The idea of *ubuntu* as human flourishing emanates from the anthropocentric nature of African traditional religiosity. The African religious quest for a "viable life, full life, a life which is worth living" is because "[l]ife is important, life is supreme for African peoples".[9] Thus, religion functions as a means to human flourishing. Similarly, Banda in his article "Ubuntu as human flourishing"[10] argues against the common tendency of imagining *ubuntu* only in terms of virtuous personhood,[11] communal relationality[12] and human dignity[13] without also attaching the element of human flourishing in the sense of the socioeconomic wellbeing of individuals. The underlying idea is that "at an individual personal level, the African quest for *ubuntu* is often a quest for dignified human existence".[14] It is to flourish as a human being and live a life that leads one to be recognised as *umuntu* (Zulu for "a person") and not be reduced to a state of *into* (Zulu for "a thing").

The function of religion as a means to human flourishing in Africa is an important framework for understanding why, despite many widely reported cases of abuse in some SANP churches, many poor South Africans continue to flock to these churches. Contemporary South Africa is marked by gross socioeconomic inequality that prompts many people to rely on controversial churches for the spiritual strength to overcome barriers to their human flourishing. However, while many poor people rely on neo-Pentecostalism as a means to human flourishing, the CRL Rights Commission has called for the regulation of religion in a way that questions the constructive value of neo-Pentecostalism in the lives of people.

Indeed, to some extent, the Commission's conclusion that some unscrupulous clergy enrich themselves and impoverish many unsuspecting people by commercialising religion and abusing people's belief systems[15] is painfully true. Several scholars have pointed out the problem of commercialising and commodifying religion by neo-Pentecostal church leaders.[16] However, the Commission's analysis of religion in South Africa is defective and incomplete because, among many other things, it limited itself to a "secularist" view of religion.[17] Because of its secularist approach, the Commission did not critically engage the religiosity of people who are members of these controversial churches to establish why they cling to pastors and churches that supposedly and sometimes evidently abuse and impoverish them.

The framework of human flourishing further provides a theological opportunity of critiquing the disturbing practices and methods of the neo-Pentecostal prophets. These controversial prophets need to be challenged to reflect on the nature of a biblically informed prophetic model of enabling the poor to experience human flourishing. Conversely, the framework also provides a basis of challenging the people who submit to the questionable practices of the neo-Pentecostal prophets. They, in turn, need to reflect on what a truly biblically informed prophetic model would look like if it were to help them in their quest to flourish as human beings.

9.3 The controversial religious acts and the search for human flourishing

Several scholars have attempted detailed analysis of the very disturbing activities of the controversial South African neo-Pentecostals.[18] This chapter will limit itself to the theme of a quest for human flourishing that undergirds these controversial activities. As widely reported in the news, the controversial activities included some pastors commanding congregants to eat grass,[19] making congregants eat snakes, using rat meat and dog meat for communion,[20] spraying congregants with a house insect repellent called Doom,[21] making congregants drink engine cleaning fluid,[22] making congregants drink rat poison[23] and driving over two female congregants.[24] These outrageous religious activities received strong condemnation and derision from many people, both within and outside the church. In a joint statement, the Commission for Gender Equality and the CRL Rights Commission condemned these controversial acts by declaring:

> We cannot allow religious institutions practising unsavoury harmful religious practices and continue to make pronouncements that are dangerous to the health and well-being of people, especially pregnant women, in the name of religion.[25]

Resane condemned these practices as harmful activities that "undermine human dignity".[26] To Resane "human life is put at risk" and Christianity is turned into "a high-risk religion"[27] through these activities. As indicated by the widespread condemnation, the controversial activities hindered human flourishing by undermining and violating the human rights and human dignity of the congregants.

Similar controversial practices that raised criticism were seen in the church of Pastor Paseka Motsoeneng, popularly known as Pastor Mboro,[28] who seems to specialise in women's reproductive issues. Kgatle therefore describes him as a "divine gynaecologist".[29] Motsoeneng's healing methods reportedly include touching women's private parts and stepping on their stomachs to drive out demons from them.[30] However, in interviews with a journalist and a radio talk show host[31] Motsoeneng denied touching women in a sexually inappropriate manner or undressing them.[32] He was however quoted adding that he only touched the private parts of women who asked him to do so, saying "at times they would ask me to touch their 'biscuits' [vagina] because they believed when I touched them there they would be healed".[33] Motsoeneng has also appeared on video instructing women congregants to wave their underwear in the air in church so that he could anoint the underwear by speaking into it the power of God, to drive away evil spirits that sexually molest people during their sleep and to heal sexually ill-functionality among married people.[34] Motsoeneng's ministry shows the intense daily struggles for human flourishing in this area by many ordinary South African women.

Judging by Pastor Motsoeneng's ministry, in the patriarchal South African context where many ordinary women are dependent on men for survival, a quest for human flourishing for many women would include fertility because motherhood is a status of honour in traditional African cultures. It could also include a quest for a stable marriage with a supportive husband in a context where many marriages are often abusive. It may include a quest to be sexually pleasing to one's husband to prevent him from chasing after other women, resulting in loss of financial support in a context where many women rely on their husbands because of limited job opportunities. The lack of human flourishing of many women and their children is often caused by patriarchal culture, gender inequality and poor education, which often translates into limited economic activity. Consequently, in their quest for human flourishing and that of their children, many ordinary women will accept the indignity of even having a Pastor Motsoeneng touching their genitals or stepping on their stomachs if it will result in much needed blessings. Many vulnerable women will oblige when the pastor instructs them to wave their underwear in the air in order for them to be blessed by him; they will basically do everything as long as their human dignity can be restored and they can be led to a state of human flourishing. This shows that the work done by controversial SANP pastors such as Motsoeneng at least allows women to engage not just their spiritual needs but also their personal struggles that have public relevance, even though the ways in which this happen are very disturbing.

There are also other reported cases that are disturbing, mostly because of their criminal nature while claiming to lead people to a state of human flourishing. This includes cases of sexual abuse and exploitation by church leaders. A notable example is that of the Nigerian-born pastor, Timothy Omotoso, leader of the Jesus Dominion International Church, who, with two female accomplices, were at the time of writing undergoing a protracted trial on charges of 63 accounts of rape and human trafficking. Although Omotoso's rape trial is yet to be concluded and no convictions have been made yet, the whole scenario reeks of someone misusing their pastoral authority to sexually abuse vulnerable girls by promising blessings to those who consent and curses to those who refuse.

The same pattern presents itself in the infamous case of the Mancoba Seven Angels Ministry, in the small village of Ngcobo in the Eastern Cape. Under the leadership of seven brothers who considered themselves angels sent from heaven, the group established a compound where most of their followers were kept after having surrendered all their possessions such as pension pay-outs, cars, salaries and proceeds from the sale of goods and properties to the ministry. They also kept women and girls as young as 12 as sex slaves.[35] This ungodly and very disturbing scenario has all the hallmarks of people that had been promised an elusive utopia that unfortunately ended in a total disaster. Sadly, the ordinary members, especially those who gave up their possessions and liberty to reside in the compound, were in search of something divine that would make their lives flourish and turn them into dignified, blessed individuals with a full life. Alas, what awaited them were disillusionment, disaster and probably more human brokenness than before. Rightly so, this episode left the CRL Rights Commission fuming and intensifying their call for the regulation of religion in South Africa. Despite these serious crimes, neo-Pentecostal leaders in South Africa remain popular and continue to attract large crowds of followers, as many people continue to rely on them in their search for spiritual and human flourishing.

These controversial activities by some SANP churches are undergirded by a search for human flourishing because the people attracted to these activities are often in needy situations. There seems to be a sincere belief by the SANP church leaders and their followers that despite their controversial nature, these religious activities function as a means of equipping and empowering needy people to confront the various issues that prevent them from flourishing as human beings. What is significant in all of this, however, is that the prophets seem to be attuned to their followers' basic human needs such as sexual reproductive issues and appear to offer them some sort of spiritual solution for their problems, albeit controversial. As such they are actually ideally placed to help their followers confront their socioeconomic and political challenges.

9.4 Socioeconomic inequality as the context of controversial religious practices in South Africa

To really understand why many poor South Africans rely on such controversial prophets one needs to fully grasp the structural nature of socioeconomic inequality in the country which hinders the human flourishing of many poor people.

9.4.1 The state of socioeconomic inequality in South Africa

Socioeconomic inequality in South Africa is a serious impediment to the human flourishing of many black South African people. This socioeconomic inequality also promotes intergenerational poverty in many black communities. Poverty definitely plays a big role in black South Africans' dependence on controversial neo-Pentecostal churches. One must guard against reductionism, however, because there are many other contributing factors to the African reliance on controversial prophets, such as the resonance of the African neo-Pentecostal worldview and the African traditional religious worldview. But still, the problem of poverty faced by many ordinary black South Africans contributes significantly to their dependence on controversial neo-Pentecostal churches.

In its criticism of the controversial pastors that led to its recommendation for the regulation of religion in South Africa, the CRL Rights Commission noted that the pastors concerned were abusing poor and vulnerable people by demanding payment before praying for them.[36] In fact, one of the stated objectives of the Commission's investigation of the commercialisation and abuse of religion was to "understand the deep societal thinking that makes some members of our society vulnerable and gullible on views expressed and actions during religious ceremonies".[37] In other words, the Commission wanted to understand, among other things, why people were willing to pay substantial amounts of money to the pastors and prophets for prayers to become rich. Unfortunately, except for scanty passing references to poverty and vulnerable people, the Commission's 2017 report does not provide a detailed analysis of the state of poverty that drives poor people to turn to prophets and pastors who make them partake in despicable rituals in order to become blessed. The lack of understanding of the relationship between poverty and dependence on prophets in South Africa is also missing in the other investigative study which the CRL Rights Commission commisioned, *An Investigative Study of the Commercialisation of Religion in the Republic of South Africa 2016: Gauteng Pilot Study.*[38] This study attempts to show that there is widespread commercialisation of religion in South Africa that exploits poor and vulnerable people to give their money to religious institutions in exchange for blessings of riches. It can be argued that the study's main focus is to highlight the need for financial accountability structures within religious institutions that receive money from the public. The report concludes that religion is commercialised in South Africa yet does not provide a thorough analysis of the reality of poverty in South Africa that drives the poor to give money to religious institutions as a means to overcoming their poverty.[39] It makes it difficult to see how the commercialisation of religion and the abuse of the poor can be stopped if the poverty that undergirds the commercialisation of religion is not adequately addressed or acknowledged.

Despite having a progressive national constitution that guarantees and protects the human equality of all races, contemporary post-apartheid South Africa continues to bear the "infamous history of high inequality with an overbearing racial stamp".[40] Economic inequality continues to dominate the post-apartheid landscape,[41] leaving democratic South Africa with "one of the world's highest levels of inequality".[42] The high inequality in South Africa is often expressed by using terms such as "white monopoly capital" and its intergenerational nature by terms such as "white privilege". After the fall of apartheid, the new democratic government implemented various social and economic development policies to improve the economic wellbeing of the previously marginalised and impoverished black population. The economic development policies adopted by the post-1994 government included the Reconstruction and Development Plan (RDP), the Growth Employment and Reconstruction strategy (GEAR), Accelerated Shared Growth Initiative for South Africa (ASGISA), and the National Development Plan (NDP). Through these developmental policies, the government's efforts to reduce inequality focused on higher social spending, targeted government transfers, and affirmative action to diversify wealth ownership and promote entrepreneurship among previously marginalised people.[43]

However, the government's efforts towards poverty reduction and bridging the huge chasm between the rich and the poor have not yielded the desired results. The World Bank estimated that the $1.90 per day poverty rate in South Africa increased from 16.8 percent to 18.8 percent between 2011 and

2015.[44] Some key factors in this increase of poverty levels included structural challenges and weak growth since the global financial crisis of 2008, and labour market developments that demand skills that the country's poor currently lack.[45] The legacy of exclusion and the unequal nature of economic growth, which is not pro-poor and does not generate sufficient jobs, perpetuate high inequality.[46] The IMF estimated that the top 20 percent of the population holds over 68 percent of income (compared to a median of 47 percent for similar emerging markets). Similarly, the bottom 40 percent of the population holds 7 percent of income (compared to 16 percent for other emerging markets).[47] Over the past decade the economic growth has been subdued, jeopardising government efforts to promote an inclusive economy.[48] The stagnated economic growth means that not enough jobs have been created to absorb the unemployed and the new school-leavers and graduates entering the labour market. Unemployment remains a serious problem in South Africa as it was estimated at 27.6 percent in the first quarter of 2019; among the youth it was much higher, around 55.2 percent.[49] The unemployment figure in 2020 has just increased further, largely due to the devastating effect of the COVID-19 pandemic. Furthermore, the intergenerational socioeconomic mobility remains low meaning that inequalities are passed down from generation to generation with little change in inequality over time.[50]

Overall, the economic landscape of post-apartheid South Africa has not changed much from the former apartheid period as a large portion of the economy still remains in white hands. Economic hubs such as finance, minerals and land continue to disproportionately remain under white control, leaving the majority black population largely landless and often in the role of poorly skilled cheap labourers. However, while inequality in post-apartheid South Africa is increasing and large sections of the economy remain in white hands, a black elite has emerged in the upper end of income distribution which has created within-race inequality.[51] This means that in the small portion of the economy that is controlled by blacks there is a huge gap between rich and poor blacks. However, it is interesting to note that the sharp increase in the growth of the black economic elite may be caused by black peoples' ascendancy to senior management roles previously occupied by whites, not so much because of their ownership of new businesses. Therefore, ultimately, inequality still remains racially oriented even in post-apartheid South Africa. A visual representation of the socioeconomic inequality in South Africa can be seen in the side-by-side existence of Sandton, described as the richest square mile in Africa, with Alexandra, a very poor high-density township with many shack dwellers. This pattern of an affluent suburb next to an impoverished township can be seen in many cities and towns across South Africa.

A thorough grasp of the structural nature of socioeconomic inequality in South Africa is fundamental in understanding why many black people rely on divine or spiritual intervention to try and overcome their socioeconomic burdens. A study of the commercialisation of religion and abuse of people's belief systems in South Africa that does not pay serious attention to the structural socioeconomic inequality will only anathematise religion, and not find meaningful solutions to the problems faced by the poor who turn to it for their survival. It is not just that the poor are poor; the poor find themselves structurally powerless to overcome their poverty. This is often expressed through various protests – sometimes even violent and destructive protests – because aggression has proved to be the only language of the poor that the rich rulers are able to hear and sometimes even respond to.

9.4.2 Socioeconomic inequality and the reliance on controversial neo-Pentecostal prophets

Socioeconomic inequality has played a significant role in promoting reliance on controversial neo-Pentecostal prophets. A critical problem in this inequality is the lack of access to decent living conditions by the poor in a country facing serious service delivery problems. The problem of socioeconomic inequality in South Africa was aptly described by Tinyiko Maluleke after the death of 84 South Africans and 31 other people, on September 12, 2014, when a guesthouse collapsed on them at Temitope Balogun (T.B.) Joshua's Synagogue Church of All Nations in Lagos, Nigeria.[52] As Maluleke expressed it:

> Whereas some rich people fly to London for the therapy of shopping, Joshua's followers seek a similar thrill in Lagos. With fewer than 10-million (out of 51-million) South Africans on medical aid, it means that more than 80% of South Africans have no medical insurance whatsoever. Add to this scenario an unemployment rate of more than 25%, the 3.5-million young South Africans not at school, work or being trained in any skill, as well as a failing public service and education system.[53]

This scenario described by Maluleke in 2014 has not changed much up to today (June 2020). The situation has in fact been sliding in a negative direction as company closures and unemployment levels have risen significantly during the COVID-19 pandemic.

Many poor South Africans live in a context of a "mix of poverty, the fear of slipping deeper or back into hardship, ignorance born out of little or no education, nihilistic meaninglessness, desperation, the survival instinct, collapsed social institutions, defunct public systems and services, and rampant corruption".[54] While the rich have access to various options of excellent medical care, "many poor people watch whole families die out, one by one, from entirely preventable and treatable diseases".[55] While rich childless couples can easily access fertility specialists and adoption, poor couples have to bear the brunt of infertility with limited or no choices at all. Corruption expressed by, for example, a demand for a bribe to obtain an identity document, a house or a social grant, selective and poor service delivery, and the impossibly high cost of legal and other services that could potentially bring about human security and human flourishing are all signs of the prevailing socioeconomic inequality. It is this state of affairs that causes poor people to turn to questionable prophets to work miracles in their desperate lives.

Those who rely on controversial prophets may be viewed as "gullible and vulnerable"[56] or as lazy people seeking an easy and quick-fix way to become rich. There is indeed some truth in views such as this. However, to only condemn the poor as lazy, unjustly fails to realise and acknowledge that many black South Africans seeking the services of prophets are hungry for "a country in which needs are met, effort is rewarded and merit duly recognised".[57] They have tried to compete, but found the ground grossly uneven. When carefully examined, many poor and powerless South Africans turn to unusual neo-Pentecostal practices in search of God's power to break the yoke of inequality they experience in their daily lives. They turn to the prophets because socioeconomic structural inequality leaves them impoverished and powerless to flourish as human beings.

9.5 Neo-Pentecostalism in empowering the poor to confront inequality in South Africa

In the South African context of socioeconomic inequality SANP churches function as sources for tools for confronting inequality in pursuit of human flourishing.

9.5.1 A religion that promotes a vision for human flourishing

Neo-Pentecostalism provides the poor with a vision for a better life. Many poor South Africans are attracted to neo-Pentecostal prophets because they provide a *vision* for human flourishing. The resilience of the controversial SANP churches lies in their power to spell out what a good life worthy of living ought to look like. Likewise, they spell out what a life not worth living looks like; such a life should be rejected and discarded and a better one sought. An example is provided by one of Zimbabwe's leading controversial neo-Pentecostal prophets, Walter Magaya, stating:

> The worst person today is the Pastor or Apostle who is still teaching congregants that we shall rejoice in heaven and we must be ready to suffer here on earth. That's heresy, you are busy preaching doom in those churches right on the altar by the pulpit [sic.].[58]

This means that poverty and suffering must be rejected. Magaya's ministry is called Prophetic, Healing and Deliverance (PHD) Ministry. This sets him up as someone anointed with God's power to administer healing from diseases and deliverance from things preventing people to flourish as human beings.

A South African example of a controversial prophet who promotes a vision of human flourishing is the flamboyant King Dr. Hamilton Qhoshangokwakhe Nala, leader of Nala Mandate International. Nala is known for his flashy lifestyle and has claimed to have miraculous powers to heal incurable diseases such as HIV/AIDS. The motto of Nala Mandate International is "word of plenty and more than enough".[59] According to his ministry's website, Bishop Nala "believes in plentianity a life of more than enough".[60] He is described as "the plentiologist" because of his world of plenty philosophy, "plentiology" (which is a study of plenty). According to their website, "this philosophy has changed thousands of people for the better".[61] In Zulu the word *nala* means plenty or a plentiful harvest. The essence of all aspects of Nala's ministry is a vision that authentic human existence is a life of "plenty and more than enough". His belief in what he calls "plentianity", his reference to himself as a "plentiologist" and his teaching of "plentiology" provide poor people with a vision of human flourishing. His ministry connects the poor with plenty. It is worth noting that the controversial SANP churches' prophets and pastors do not just preach about a good life, through their flamboyance they display what they mean by a good life. Their preaching about a good life seems authentic because it is confirmed by their lifestyle, albeit promoting materialism and consumerism that contradicts the simple life displayed and preached by Christ (e.g. Luke 9:58).

Furthermore, some controversial SANP prophets such as Pastor Motsoeneng present a holistic vision of human flourishing, including sexuality. Pastor Motsoeneng's earlier noted interest in sexual reproductive issues indicates an underlying belief that people must enjoy life in its fullness – including the dimension of sexuality. He explained in a radio interview that there were evil spirits called spiritual husbands (and spiritual wives) that visited people during their sleep to sexually torment or rape them, causing damage to their sexual reproductive health.[62] He stated:

> So instead of laying my hands, we call that transferation of the anointing. I speak the word, you must know that God created everything through the word, I speak the word to those underwears and the power of God, and all that. The power of God will get in there, and when they wear it, God does something.[63]

In this regard Pastor Motsoeneng appeared in a video asking his congregants during a church service to place their hands over their private parts while he prayed for them.[64] This controversial sexualised religious act performed in front of children, respected relatives and within a mixed gathering of men and women is disturbing because of its immoral tastelessness. The waving of underwear and touching sexual organs during a worship service violet the sacredness of the worship service. However, because of their deep desperateness, many people are will to be debased and be sexually violated in order to find relief. In another video, Motsoeneng is seen praying for a married couple struggling with sexual issues, opening a condom and blessing it for this couple.[65] In the video the wife prays, telling Satan to leave her husband and declares that they will have satisfying sexual intercourse.[66] Even though this controversial act may be dismissed as immoral, Pastor Motsoeneng does demonstrate a concern that the couple's marriage reaches its full potential. He explains in the video that marriage (including sex) is a gift from God to be enjoyed. In this case the positive aspect of his religious view is its comprehensive vision of human flourishing, something which is often missing in more conservative churches. In this instance, Pastor Motsoeneng portrays himself as someone who openly addresses people's basic problems to try and ensure that they fully thrive in their personal life. The power of controversial SANP prophets and pastors such as Pastor Motsoeneng is that from their church pulpits they openly deal with sensitive issues that prophets and pastors in conservative churches may find unimportant or not suitable material to be addressed openly in the church's pulpit. Albeit it through controversial and sometimes very disturbing acts, they do practice a religion that takes into account the need for human flourishing.

9.5.2 A religion of the marginalised

The resilience of the controversial SANP churches lies in their being a religion for the marginalised. The many people who participate in seemingly gross and degrading practices such as eating grass do so because the precarious state of their health, their economic situation and spiritual problems have pushed them to the boundaries of life. In participating in these controversial acts they hope to be rescued from the margins and thrust into the centre of life.

There is a strong resonance between the ethos of neo-Pentecostalism and the African Independent Churches (AICs). As early as 1925, some officials of the white government acknowledged that some AICs arose out of "extreme social distress like detribalisation, urbanisation, culture clashes, natural disasters and socio-racial conflicts".[67] The important role played by the AICs in the lives of marginalised black people is highlighted by Masondo who points out that in the apartheid era, "grown-up men were treated as overgrown children by their white employers. It was only within the context of the church where they rose to prominence and respectability".[68] This observation is corroborated by Sundkler who says, "to the African masses in Reserve or City, their Churches appeared as definitely Christian organizations, adapted to their own real needs . . . and as bridges to a new and richer experience of life".[69] He adds that "in the city, with its rapidly industrialized civilisation, they functioned as 'adaptive structures'".[70] In other words, the AICs epitomised "the African struggle for self-identification and self-realisation".[71]

The question may be asked, to what extent does the same principle apply in the emergence and growth of the controversial SANP churches? The answer may be found in the fact that in South Africa many of the neo-Pentecostal African churches "are not *fundamentally* different from the Holy Spirit movements and 'Spirit' churches that preceded them in the African Initiated Churches (AICs), but are a continuation of them in a quite different situation".[72] However, some tensions exist between the two movements, for example, neo-Pentecostals often demonise the AICs by saying they use the power of demons and evil spirits.[73] Furthermore, unlike many traditional AICs that are led by elderly men, the new churches are modern, and in certain ways function as pacesetters of modern culture. Church leaders like Motsoeneng and Nala, by their flashy lifestyle(s), function as symbols of modern culture that stress sensuality and consumerism. The common element in both, however, is that they respond to African existential needs that emerge from "the inequalities of power and class accentuated by the apartheid system".[74] As already noted, contemporary socioeconomic life in South Africa continues to reflect the legacy of apartheid. The controversial churches are attractive to the poor and powerless because they promise to provide the needed divine power allowing them to break out of the socioeconomic margins and thrust them into the centre. It is important to realise that "in a context riddled with high economic inequality and powerlessness, religion is a powerful tool for the poor and powerless".[75]

9.5.3 A religion of engaging the public realm

As a religion that promotes a vision for human flourishing among the poor and also fights the economic marginalisation of the poor and powerless, the controversial SANP churches effectively function as a religion of engaging the public realm. Neo-Pentecostals are often heavily criticised for their lack of engagement with structural societal issues and only emphasising prayer and the spiritual dimensions of suffering. However, in many ways the SANP churches show awareness of the social and political structural dimensions underlying poverty, although they do see poor people's marginalisation from a spiritual perspective. For instance, Pastor Motsoeneng reportedly appeared in a video, encouraging the poor to open their hearts and let him pray for them.[76] Pastor Motsoeneng reportedly stated:

> They can no longer live in their leaking houses. They cannot live in their leaking shacks. Some are homeless. Some do not have land. Some have tried everything they can but there is no progress in their lives. Now we need to take God in his word and decide to move forward.[77]

Pastor Motsoeneng reportedly instructed the poor to say the following prayer:

> Start with these words: "Dear God, in the name of Jesus, bless my home. I need land. I need a house. I need a blessing Lord, I agree with ntate [father/Mr] Mboro for the change of my life and home. Lord, I declare the blessings onto my loved ones". Let us work together and break the cycle of poverty. Be blessed, God bless you.[78]

Pastor Motsoeneng's words show an awareness of what poverty is – poor housing, homelessness, landlessness and lack of economic success. The fact that poverty involves physical elements shows that it can be solved by physical solutions. Pastor Motsoeneng therefore asked God to provide these things. As someone who lives in a township and has encountered the real struggles of poor and marginalised people, Pastor Motsoeneng must be aware of the corruption, poor service delivery and poor planning that characterise many municipalities on local government level in South Africa. Yet, as we can see in the above quote, instead of calling for corrupt local councillors to be suspended or calling on the government to provide houses for the poor, he prays to God instead. This reflects a spiritualised view of poverty and a belief that only divine action can change the status quo. In this, the public realm is not engaged directly, but through the spiritual realm.

Neo-Pentecostalism engages the public realm by emphasising a

> personal encounter with God through the power of the Spirit, healing from sickness and deliverance from evil in all its manifestations, whether spiritual, social or structural – although most of these churches do not major on the social and structural manifestations of evil.[79]

However, this non-engagement with structural issues must be seen from a neo-Pentecostal point of view which claims that behind the physical manifestations of evil there are demonic spirits doing the work of Satan. According to this view, poverty and suffering are ultimately spiritual issues and the solution to dealing with evil powers that marginalise the poor and powerless does not lie in dealing with the physical realities, but rather with the evil spiritual forces behind the evil acts. In other words, instead of deploying forces to fight micro issues such as a lack of housing or corrupt political leaders, neo-Pentecostals engage the macro issue of evil spiritual powers that cause authorities to act unfairly and corrupt. They take as their point of departure the biblical notion that "the battle is not yours but God's" (2 Chronicles 20:15); also that the battle is not against flesh and blood, but against spiritual powers (Ephesians 6:12). Consequently, by aspects of prayer, fasting, casting out evil spirits, praying against strongholds and evil principalities that take charge of geographical territories, neo-Pentecostals see themselves as fighting a spiritual battle against their societal marginalisation. Neo-Pentecostalism functions as a faith that calls the poor to come out of their poverty and empowers them to engage their unfavourable socioeconomic circumstances and the political impediments preventing them from flourishing as human beings.

9.6 Aspects needing improvement in the SANP churches' engagement with the public realm

Although the controversial SANP churches can be described as equipping and empowering the poor to engage spiritually with public issues of deprivation, there are areas of serious concern.

9.6.1 A theology of human flourishing lacking knowledge of the public realm

A notable weakness among controversial SANP churches is that their theology of human flourishing lacks critical engagement with the structural components of public issues. This means that the SANP churches subscribe to a quest for poverty eradication that does not engage in trying to understand the structural issues of socioeconomic life. These churches' view of human flourishing is one-sidedly spiritual and doesn't directly engage the structural issues underlying poverty and ill-health in poor communities. As Methula argues, at the root of social problems such as crime, substance abuse, alcoholism and juvenile delinquency "lies the fundamental structural crisis of economic injustice and elite policies that only serve those with economic might, political power and social privileges".[80] Poverty is indeed a spiritual issue, yet it expresses itself in socioeconomic and political structural ways that make the physical human body suffer real pain. A critical issue is that SANP churches promote an inward view of human flourishing without also emphasising the importance of public structures that can ensure the equality of all people. There is a need to realise that human flourishing does not only come from trusting God to meet one's needs; it also results from just and equitable socioeconomic and political structures.

Moreover, the SANP churches often give simplistic and overly spiritual solutions as if lacking food, clothing and necessary skills are only spiritual realities. The over-spiritualised and simplistic solutions they prescribe for poor people often further disempower them and leave them unable to engage meaningfully with their poverty. The SANP churches should be challenged to develop an understanding of how social, economic and political systems function. Considering that some SANP pastors such as Motsoeneng live in townships that generally suffer selective and poor service delivery, it is important for them to empower their congregants with, for example, the knowledge and skills to challenge local councillors to fulfil their electoral mandate of developing local communities. Furthermore, South African townships and informal settlements are often affected by violent protests that almost always lead to the destruction of much needed public property. A thorough understanding of the way public systems work will enable these pastors to guide their followers to direct their anger and frustration at the right places. An understanding of the public realm can enable these prophets to teach their communities that instead of burning schools and libraries to air their grievances, they should dialogue with their local government leaders, hold them accountable and encourage them to develop their communities. A theology of human flourishing informed by sound knowledge of the public realm can help SANP prophets and pastors to influence their congregants to vote for good councillors who will develop their communities. In South Africa where there is gross inequality, a knowledge of the public realm can assist in addressing the structures that promote and maintain this inequality. To meaningfully empower South Africa's poor masses, SANP churches need to prioritise social justice. They need to realise that the "struggle for economic well-being of the poor is essentially a struggle for economic justice and therefore not just a spiritual problem".[81]

9.6.2 The promotion of greed underpinned by primitivistic superstition that undermines human agency

The SANP message of material prosperity is useful in challenging poor South Africans to reject poverty and to rise up and address it. However, SANP churches tend to promote greed that is underpinned by primitivistic superstition that sees the world in pre-scientific terms as under the control of spirits which means that success is determined by gaining control of the spiritual realm. The problem is that this view of reality ultimately weakens human agency and human responsibility because failure is blamed on evil spiritual powers or the failure to gain control of the spiritual realm and making it work for oneself.

As affirmed by Mashau and Kgatle, "[the] prosperity gospel has given birth to the culture of greed and consumption".[82] The controversial SANP churches subscribe to a prosperity gospel framework that "emphasises the spiritual value of earthly or material blessings".[83] The element of greed and materialism is promoted by making "money [and material wealth] . . . a prominent symbol of God's blessing".[84] The uncritical quest to maintain spiritual control over money and other material things fosters superstition by believing that doing certain actions as commanded by the pastor, even disturbing actions such as eating grass, can usher one into a state of blessedness that translates into abundant material wealth. The notion of superstition thrives on the belief that the key to material success lies in pleasing the prophets which leads to giving them large sums of money. Ordinarily, superstition leads to the sacralisation of the body of the prophet which promotes the idea that by touching the prophet, giving to the prophet and obeying the prophet, one is obeying God. This undermines human agency and human responsibility, for poverty and poor health are attributed to neglecting one's spiritual obligations. The priority of work, planning, undergoing a timely medical check-up and taking one's medication gets superseded by religious observances, while saving and investing one's money are being replaced by giving to the "man of God".

From a human agency perspective, the superstitious spiritualisation of wealth leaves the poor reliant on the spiritual intervention of these prophets in a way that cripples their own active engagement. Reliance on the prophets operates in a way that makes it difficult for the poor to see how they unknowingly contribute to their own poverty. In this scheme, escaping from poverty is reduced to giving to the "man of God", planting a spiritual seed by giving money to the prophet, and paying the prophet to say a special blessing over one.

All these practices undermine the need for personal responsibility. The huge reliance on controversial prophets in South Africa simply means that many poor people hope their poverty will end without them having to engage directly in the socioeconomic realm. For instead of the poor actively participating in the economy by seeking to understand how it works and looking for ways in which they can participate and help it to improve, they withdraw and rather invest their efforts in spiritual interventions. Furthermore, instead of saving their social grants or investing them in something that can bring them better financial returns, they give it to the prophets hoping that one day they will somehow receive money back, miraculously multiplied.

Furthermore, the poor who rely on the SANP prophets are caught in a vicious cycle where they continually give away their livelihood to the prophets and remain in poverty while the prophets continually amass wealth. The emphasis on the faith of the poor means that the prophets can never be held accountable for the failure of the poor to move out of poverty because the poor will simply be blamed for their lack of faith. Disgruntled with one prophet, the poor move on to another prophet to begin the same process of giving away their livelihood. This means within SANP churches there is a vicious cycle of rich prophets and poor congregants.

It is therefore necessary for SANP churches to promote a responsible attitude towards socioeconomic issues that involves restraint, responsibility and human agency. The SANP churches fail to be the salt and light in the world because it upholds capitalist materialism and encourages a consumeristic quest for amassing more wealth. The superstitious tendencies must be addressed by preaching a holistic perspective towards poverty. While spiritual causes to poverty should not be underemphasised, human responsibility must also not be undermined.

9.6.3 Promoting human flourishing without practicing justice and righteousness: a serious weakness

Something which is seriously lacking with the conceptualisation of human flourishing among the controversial prophets is the issue of personal justice and righteousness. Whereas the above section concentrated on justice in public structures, this point concentrates on justice and righteousness (or a lack thereof) in the conduct of the churches. Some SANP churches who busy themselves with promoting the human flourishing of the poor do not themselves practice justice and righteousness when dealing with the poor. Among some SANP churches injustice manifests itself in that some prophets preach the human flourishing of the poor, but dispossess the same poor people by taking away even their social grants given by the government to cushion them against poverty. The mere fact that the CRL Rights Commission had to have two investigations into churches and their commercialisation of religion and abuse of people's beliefs systems indicts the churches for a lack of justice and righteousness. For example, after detailing concerns about pastors using religion for self-enrichment, the study commissioned by the CRL Rights Commission stated, "The problem is currently big enough to require government to step in".[85] The feeling by the ordinary community and even non-Christian critics that there is no justice and righteousness in the church indicates a serious loss of credibility. That people will go to the extent of calling on a secular government to regulate the church speaks volumes about the discredited nature of some churches. It is a serious indictment that there is a strong public perception that some churches in South Africa are becoming places of exploiting the poor instead of places of charity for the poor. In addition to discrediting religion, when churches fail to uphold justice they aid and give approval to secular institutions that take advantage of the weak members of society.

Some SANP pastors such as Pastor Motsoeneng have been reported in the media giving away houses to the poor and also fixing poor peoples' houses.[86] Pastor Motsoeneng was quoted in the news declaring that he had built 22 houses, with a 23rd one about to be completed; all were donated to the poor.[87] He reportedly stated that he had rebuilt hostels, schools and handed out bursaries.[88] However, on the whole, it remains "unfortunate that many Pentecostal prophets are not known for being concerned with social injustice".[89] Even in cases where they get engaged in charity work, their charity efforts do not often function in a prophetic manner that challenges oppressive structures impoverishing the poor.[90] Because at present in the prosperity gospel only pastors benefit and no one else, there is a need to reverse this culture of greed and injustice so that the income in the churches will benefit everyone, including the poor.[91]

9.7. Towards a religion that empowers the poor to fulfil their need for human flourishing

In the light of the above discussion, what should a meaningful religion entail if it were to empower the poor to fulfil their quest for human flourishing?

9.7.1 *A genuine concern about poverty*

For SANP churches to practice a religion that empowers the poor to realise human flourishing, there must be a genuine concern about the reality of poverty. By approaching poverty with an uncritically spiritualised approach, SANP churches show a lack of genuine concern about poverty. A genuine concern about poverty will show that it is a complex and complicated reality that needs more than just prayer and exorcism to eradicate; SANP prophets will need to engage technical experts who are more informed about the human, social, psychological, economic and political dimensions of poverty. SANP churches are challenged to deepen and broaden their understanding of the reality of poverty to be able to provide their poor congregants with meaningful ways of responding to their life situation.

9.7.2 *A genuine concern for the human dignity of the poor*

As highlighted in the above discussion, SANP churches stand accused of using their spiritual authority to trample on the human dignity of the poor. Some of the methods used by SANP prophets and pastors to heal people are not just unorthodox, but also demeaning and dehumanising. The controversial acts discussed above usually do not show a concern for the human dignity of the poor. Jesus never made a public spectacle or humiliated the people that sought him for healing. He treated them with respect and dignity. When prophets and pastors dispossess the poor of their social grants given to them by the government to cushion them against poverty, it shows a huge lack of compassion and respect for the poor.

Respecting the human dignity of the poor will challenge pastors and prophets to take the reality of poverty seriously, and implement poverty eradication programmes that are well thought through. A genuine concern for the human dignity of the poor should radically challenge the pastors and prophets in how they handle and use people's hard-earned money that they give to the church.

9.7.3 *A genuine concern about justice*

As discussed above, poverty is also a structural issue. It is beyond dispute that sometimes poor people cause their own poverty in a variety of ways such as ignorance, poor planning and laziness. Yet, one can possess all the knowledge about setting up a business, have a good plan and be industrious, but if the socioeconomic and political structures are oppressive, all the good ideas, careful planning and hard work may yield nothing. SANP churches must therefore develop a deep understanding of justice and just socioeconomic structures. SANP prophets and pastors need to be challenged to develop a concern for social justice, structural transformation and overcoming the evils of capitalism[92] that allow a handful of people to control most of the economy while the majority have nothing. They should start by upholding justice and righteousness in their own personal lives and ministries.

9.7.4 The fear of God and respect for the laws of the country

The scandalous activities by the controversial SANP pastors and prophets reflect a serious lack of the fear of God, as well as very little respect for the laws of the country. The fear of God and respect for the laws of the land will definitely put an end to these prophets' exploitation of the poor for their own self-enrichment. It will also curtail criminal acts like tax evasion and cause these prophets and pastors to empower the poor instead of using them as a means for personal enrichment. The fear of God is necessary to challenge the commercialisation of religion and the abuse of people's faith in God. It will challenge the commodification of the poor. The fear of God will cause the prophets to stop using God's name to rob the poor and powerless but instead empower them with the means of addressing their poverty.

9.8 Conclusion

The above discussion shows that many poor people in South Africa turn to the SANP churches to enable them to overcome their poverty and somehow find the human flourishing they so desperately need. However, the spiritualised interventions provided by some SANP churches leave the poor powerlessly unengaged in the main socioeconomic life in South Africa. Some poor people give away their livelihood to the prophets and in so doing entrench themselves deeper into poverty. A prominent concern raised by the CRL Rights Commission and other critics is that these controversial churches take advantage of poor and desperate South Africans by giving them false hope, abusing their human rights and dignity as well as infringing on their constitutional rights.

However, the main argument of this chapter is that the poor and powerless are attracted to these controversial SANP churches because they claim to empower them with the spiritual resources to overcome the inequality and poverty that prevent their human flourishing. The evidence presented by the CRL Rights Commission in its investigative reports[93] on the commercialisation of religion and abuse of people's beliefs systems call for SANP churches to seriously reflect on how they deal with the lives and hopes of poor South Africans who look up to them to overcome their deep lack of human flourishing.

Historically, governments have regulated the church to silence its voice proclaiming God's righteousness and justice, in other words, they have tried to stop the church from being salt and light. Today, however, it is indeed sad and disappointing that calls for the regulation of the church in South Africa have arisen largely because a big sector of the church has actually lost its ability to be salt and light.

Notes

1 Mookgo S. Kgatle, "The Unusual Practices within Some Neo-Pentecostal Churches in South Africa: Reflections and Recommendations," *HTS Teologiese Studies / Theological Studies* 73, no. 3 (2017): a4656, https://doi.org/10.4102/hts.v73i3.4656, 2.

2 CRL Rights Commission, *Report on the Hearings on the Commercialisation of Religion and Abuse of People's Beliefs Systems* (Pretoria: CRL Rights Commission, 2017).

3 Paul K. Kibuuka, Carel J. van Aardt, and Deon H. Tustin, *An Investigative Study of the Commercialisation of Religion in the Republic of South Africa, 2016: Gauteng Pilot Study* (Pretoria: CRL Rights Commission/UNISA, 2016).

4 Dirkie Smit, "What Does 'Public' Mean? Questions with a View to Public Theology," in *Christian in Public: Aims, Methodologies and Issues in Public Theology*, ed. Len Hansen, vol. 33, 11–46, 34, Beyers Naudé Centre Series on Public Theology (Stellenbosch: African Sun Media, 2007).

5 Ibid., 34.

6 Cyril C Okorocha, "The Meaning of Salvation: An African Perspective," in *Emerging Voices in Global Christian Theology*, ed. Walter A. Dyrness (Grand Rapids, MI: Zondervan Publishing House, 1994), 59–92, 60.

7 John S. Mbiti, *African Religions and Philosophy* (London: Heinemann, 1969), 2.

8 Ibid., 5.

9 Okorocha, "The Meaning of Salvation," 73.

10 Collium Banda, "Ubuntu as Human Flourishing? An African Traditional Religious Analysis of Ubuntu and Its Challenge to Christian Anthropology," *Stellenbosch Theological Journal* 5, no. 3 (2019): 203–28. http://dx.doi.org/10.17570/stj.2019.v5n3.a10.

11 Thaddeus Metz, "Ubuntu as a Moral Theory and Human Rights in South Africa," *African Human Rights Law Journal* 11, no. 2 (2011): 537; Desmond Tutu, *No Future Without Forgiveness* (New York: Random House, 2009), 34.

12 Christine Gichure, "Human Nature/Identity: The Ubuntu World View and Beyond," 2015, 127, https://su-plus.strathmore.edu/bitstream/handle/11071/3758/Human%20nature.pdf?sequence=1&isAllowed=y; Moeketsi Letseka, "In Defence of Ubuntu," *Studies in Philosophy and Education* 31, no. 1 (2012): 48, https://doi.org/10.1007/s11217-011-9267-2.

13 Tutu, *No Future Without Forgiveness*, 35.

14 Banda, "Ubuntu as Human Flourishing?" 216.

15 CRL Rights Commission, 31–33.

16 Ezra Chitando, Masiiwa Gunda and Joachim Kügler, *Prophets, Profits and the Bible in Zimbabwe: Festschrift for Aynos Masotcha Moyo* (Bamberg: University of Bamberg, 2013); Ruth Marshall, *Political Spiritualities: The Pentecostal Revolution in Nigeria* (Chicago, IL: University of Chicago, 2009), 182.

17 Mbuyiseni Ndlozi, "The Trial: The Church on the Cross," *Daily Maverick*, September 21, 2018, http://firstthing.dailymaverick.co.za/article?id=73319#.W8zHUEszZpl.

18 Bekithemba Dube, "Conundrum of Religious Mafia and Legislation in South Africa: When Does Religion Become a National Threat? Reference to the Seven Angels Ministry," *Verbum et Ecclesia* 40, no. 1 (2019): 8, https://doi.org/10.4102/ve.v40i1.1864; Kgatle, "The Unusual Practices"; Tinyiko S. Maluleke, "The Prophet Syndrome: Let Them Eat Grass," *Mail & Guardian*, October 23, 2014, https://mg.co.za/article/ 2014–10–23-the-prophet-syndrome-let-them-eat-grass/; Kelebogile T. Resane, "'And They Shall Make You Eat Grass Like Oxen' (Daniel 4:24): Reflections on Recent Practices in Some New

Charismatic Churches," *Pharos Journal of Theology* 98 (2017): 1–17, www.pharosjot.com/uploads/7/1/6/3/7163688/article_10__vol_98_2017.pdf.

19 Shenaaz Jamal, "In Pictures: From Doom to Rattex – 5 Pastors Turning Communion Wine into Noxious Substances," *TimesLIVE*, February 7, 2017, www.timeslive.co.za/news/south-africa/2017-02-07-in-pictures-from-doom-to-rattex–5-pastors-turning-communion-wine-into-noxious-substances/.

20 Iavan Pijoos, "Polokwane 'Pastor' Boasts of Feeding Congregants 'Dog Meat,' " *SowetanLIVE*, May 22, 2019, www.sowetanlive.co.za/news/south-africa/2019-05-22-polokwane-pastor-boasts-of-feeding-congregants-dog-meat/.

21 Jamal, "In Pictures."

22 Ibid.

23 Ibid.

24 Ahmed Areff, "Snake Pastor 'Shows Power' by Driving Over 2 Congregants," *News24*, June 8, 2016, www.news24.com/SouthAfrica/News/snake-pastor-shows-power-by-driving-over-2-congregants-20160608.

25 "Groups Condemn Harmful Religious Practices," *News24*, October 2, 2014, www.news24.com/SouthAfrica/News/Groups-condemn-harmful-religious-practices-20141002.

26 Resane, "And They Shall Make You Eat Grass Like Oxen," 6.

27 Ibid.

28 In this chapter, expect for unavoidable reference purposes, I refer to Pastor Mboro by his real name, Motsoeneng, because in my native Zimbabwean context "Mboro" means penis in the Shona language. Because the word is treated with respect, I have opted to exercise the African principle of *ukuhlonipha* (avoidance or taboo).

29 Kgatle, "The Unusual Practices," 5.

30 "Pastor Mboro – When a Prophet Takes the Biscuit," *TimesLIVE*, April 14, 2016, www.timeslive.co.za/news/south-africa/2016-04-14-pastor-mboro–when-a-prophet-takes-the-biscuit/.

31 Prophet Mboro speaks of healing through blessing underwear, *Jacaranda FM*, 2016, www.youtube.com/watch?v=49iwlzg1vKg; Ntombizodwa Makhoba, "At home with Pastor Mboro," *News24*, December 21, 2014, www.news24.com/Drum/Archive/at-home-with-pastor-mboro-20170728.

32 Motsoeneng reportedly told *Drum* reporter Ntombizodwa Makhoba, "Why would I touch those biscuits [vaginas]? Most of them are foul-smelling." He reportedly stated that he respects women, instead of touching them with his hand, he puts his foot on the area between their stomachs and "biscuits" when they lay on the floor – but only touched a woman's "biscuit" when she asked him to touch her because she wanted to be healed. Motsoeneng reportedly further stated, I don't undress women in my church. I've never done it and I will never do it. As a Mosotho man I respect private parts – that's why I've come up with names like biscuit and vuvuzela [penis]. Even men come to me asking for prayers when they have vuvuzela problems and I also pray for them.

33 Ibid.

34 *News24*, "Holy Underpants! Prophet Mboro Explains Blessing Panties," www.news24.com/Video/SouthAfrica/News/holy-underpants-prophet-mboro-explains-blessing-panties-20160419.

35 Nosipiwo Manona, "How Ngcobo Cult Kept Its Sex Slaves," *News24*, March 11, 2018, www.news24.com/SouthAfrica/News/how-ngcobo-cult-kept-its-sex-slaves-20180311-3.

36 CRL Rights Commission, 18, 28.

37 Ibid., 5.

38 Kibuuka et al., "An Investigative Study."
39 The study commissioned by the CRL Rights Commission doesn't analyse the biblical or theological basis of why people give money to churches and creates an impression that giving money to churches is a new phenomenon that must be immediately nipped in the bud. The study comes to the same conclusion as the *Report on the Hearings on the Commercialisation of Religion and Abuse of People's Beliefs Systems* that the government must pass a law to regularise religious institutions in South Africa.
40 Murray Leibbrandt et al., "Trends in South African Income Distribution and Poverty Since the Fall of Apartheid," May 28, 2010, 12, https://doi.org/10.1787/5kmms0t7p1ms-en; Ingrid Woolard, "Economists Think South Africa's Persistent Inequality Should Be Tackled with a Wealth Tax," *Quartz Africa*, May 2, 2019, https://qz.com/africa/1610723/south-africas-inequality-can-be-fixed-with-a-wealth-tax/.
41 Leibbrandt et al., Ibid.; Woolard, Ibid.
42 Dorrit Posel and Michael Rogan, "Inequality, Social Comparisons and Income Aspirations: Dividends from a Highly Unequal Country," *Journal of Human Development and Capabilities* 20, no. 1 (2019): 95, https://doi.org/10.1080/19452829.2018.1547272.
43 IMF, "Six Charts Explain South Africa's Inequality," January 30, 2020, www.imf.org/en/News/Articles/2020/01/29/na012820six-charts-on-south-africas-persistent-and-multi-faceted-inequality.
44 World Bank, "Overview," Text/HTML, World Bank, October 10, 2019, www.worldbank.org/en/country/southafrica/overview.
45 Ibid.
46 Ibid.
47 IMF, "Six charts."
48 Ibid.
49 World Bank, "Overview."
50 Ibid.
51 Posel and Rogan, "Inequality," 95.
52 Maluleke, "The Prophet Syndrome."
53 Ibid.
54 Ibid.
55 Ibid.
56 CRL Rights Commission, 5.
57 Maluleke, "The Prophet Syndrome."
58 Walter Magaya, "Thy Kingdom Come," October 5, 2015, http://magaya.hurukuros.com/2015/05/prophet-w-magaya-teaching-on-thy.html.
59 Nala Mandate International, "Nala Mandate International," n.d., www.nalamandate.com/about.html.
60 Ibid.
61 Ibid.
62 *Jacaranda FM*, "Prophet Mboro Speaks."
63 Ibid.
64 *News24*, "Holy Underpants!"
65 Ngwako Malatji, "Mboro Resurrects Manhood – Couple Have Sex in Front of TV Crew after Prayers," *SowetanLIVE*, November 6, 2017, www.sowetanlive.co.za/sundayworld/news/2017-11-05-mboro-resurrects-manhood-couple-have-sex-in-front-of-tv-crew-after-prayers/; Youtube, "Mboro's 4–5 Drive! – YouTube," November 13, 2017, www.youtube.com/watch?v=Zou7PEuxLn0.
66 Malatji, Ibid.; Youtube, Ibid.

67 Joan A. Millard, "A Study of the Perceived Causes of Schism in Some Ethiopian-Type Churches in the Cape and Transvaal, 1884–1925," (DTh thesis, 1995), 124, http://uir.unisa.ac.za/handle/10500/17459.

68 Sibusiso T. Masondo, "The African Indigenous Churches' Spiritual Resources for Democracy and Social Cohesion," *Verbum et Ecclesia* 35, no. 3 (2014), Art. #1341, 2, http://dx.doi.org/10.4102/ ve.v35i3.134.

69 Bengt G.M Sundkler, *Bantu Prophets in South Africa* (London: International African Institute, 1961), 302.

70 Ibid.

71 Masondo, "The African Indigenous Churches," 2.

72 Allan Anderson, "New African Initiated Pentecostalism and Charismatics in South Africa," *Journal of Religion in Africa* 35, no. 1 (2005): 68.

73 Ibid., 69; Cephas N. Omenyo, "African Pentecostalism," in *The Cambridge Companion to Pentecostalism*, ed. Cecil M. Robeck, Jr and Amos Yong (New York: Cambridge University Press, 2014), 138.

74 Anderson, "New African Initiated Pentecostalism," 68.

75 Collium Banda, "Redefining Religion? A Critical Christian Reflection on CRL Rights Commission's Proposal to Regulate Religion in South Africa," *Verbum et Ecclesia* 40, no. 1 (2019): a1948, 10, https://doi. org/10.4102/ve.v40i1.1948.

76 Kyle Zeeman, "Pastor Mboro Believes He Can Help You Get the Land Back," *TimesLIVE*, April 18, 2018, www.timeslive.co.za/tshisa-live/tshisa-live/2018-04-18-pastor-mboro-believes-he-can-help-you-get-the-land-back/.

77 Ibid.

78 Ibid.

79 Anderson, "New African Initiated Pentecostalism," 69.

80 Duminase W. Methula, "Engaging in the Struggle for Economic Justice in the Streets of the City of Tshwane," *Missionalia* 42, no. 1–2 (August 2014): 108, https://doi.org/10.7832/42-1-2-50.

81 Collium Banda, "Not Anointing, But Justice? A Critical Reflection on the Anointing of Pentecostal Prophets in a Context of Economic Injustice," *Verbum et Ecclesia* 39, no. 1 (2018): a1870, https://doi.org/10.4102/ ve.v39i1.1870.

82 Thinandavha D. Mashau and Mookgo S. Kgatle, "Prosperity Gospel and the Culture of Greed in Post-Colonial Africa: Constructing an Alternative African Christian Theology of Ubuntu," *Verbum et Ecclesia* 40, no. 1 (2018): a1901, https://doi.org/ 10.4102/ve.v40i1.1901, 4.

83 Cornelius J. P. Niemandt, "The Prosperity Gospel, the Decolonisation of Theology, and the Abduction of Missionary Imagination," *Missionalia* 45, no, 3 (2017): 203–19, https://doi.org/10.7832/45-3-199, 206.

84 Ibid., 206.

85 Kibuuka et al., "An Investigative Study," 108.

86 Jonisayi Maromo, "Pics: Prophet Mboro Helps Rebuild Houses Destroyed #Alex-Fire," *IOL*, December 10, 2018, www.iol.co.za/news/south-africa/gauteng/pics-prophet-mboro-helps-rebuild-houses-destroyed-alexfire-18444372; Jonisayi Maromo, "Pics: Pastor Mboro Helps to Build New House for Soweto's Gogo Baloyi," *IOL*, January 28, 2019, www.iol.co.za/news/south-africa/gauteng/pics-pastor-mboro-helps-to-build-new-house-for-sowetos-gogo-baloyi-19002821.

87 Katleho Sekhotho, "Pastor Mboro: I Worked Hard for My Money," *EWN*, March 2019, https://ewn.co.za/2019/03/03/pastor-mboro-i-worked-hard-for-my-money.

88 Ibid.

89 Banda, "Not Anointing, But Justice?" 8.

90 Ibid.

91 Mashau and Kgatle, "Prosperity Gospel," 5.

92 Ibid., 7.
93 CRL Rights Commission, "Report on the Hearings"; Kibuuka et al., "An Investigative Study."

References

Anderson, Allan. "New African initiated Pentecostalism and Charismatics in South Africa." *Journal of Religion in Africa* 35, no. 1 (2005): 66–92.

Areff, Ahmed. "Snake Pastor 'Shows Power' by Driving Over 2 Congregants." *News24*, June 8, 2016. www.news24.com/SouthAfrica/News/snake-pastor-shows-power-by-driving-over-2-congregants-20160608.

Banda, Collium. "Not Anointing, But Justice? A Critical Reflection on the Anointing of Pentecostal Prophets in a Context of Economic Injustice." *Verbum et Ecclesia* 39, no. 1 (2018): a1870. https://doi.org/10.4102/ ve.v39i1.1870.

———. "Redefining Religion? A Critical Christian Reflection on CRL Rights Commission's Proposal to Regulate Religion in South Africa." *Verbum et Ecclesia* 40, no. 1 (2019): a1948. https://doi. org/10.4102/ve.v40i1.1948.

———. "Ubuntu as Human Flourishing? An African Traditional Religious Analysis of Ubuntu and Its Challenge to Christian Anthropology." *Stellenbosch Theological Journal* 5, no. 3 (2019): 203–28. http://dx.doi.org/10.17570/stj.2019. v5n3.a10.

Chitando, Ezra, Musiiwa R. Gunda and Joachim Kügler. *Prophets, Profits and the Bible in Zimbabwe: festschrift for Aynos Masotcha Moyo.* Bamberg: University of Bamberg, 2013.

CRL Rights Commission. *Report on the Hearings on the Commercialisation of Religion and Abuse of People's Beliefs Systems* (Pretoria: CRL Rights Commission 2017). www.crlcommission.org.za/docs/Report%20On%20Commecializa tion%20of%20Religion%20and%20Abuse%20of%20People's%20Believe%20 Systems%20final.pdf.

Dube, Bekithemba. "Conundrum of Religious Mafia and Legislation in South Africa: When Does Religion Become a National Threat? Reference to the Seven Angels Ministry." *Verbum et Ecclesia* 40, no. 1 (2019): a1864. https://doi.org/ 10.4102/ ve.v40i1.1864.

Gichure, Christine. "Human Nature/Identity: The Ubuntu World View and Beyond." 2015. https://su plus.strathmore.edu/bitstream/handle/11071/3758/Human%20 nature.pdf?sequence=1&isAllowed=y.

IMF. "Six Charts Explain South Africa's Inequality." January 30, 2020. www.imf.org/en/News/Articles/2020/01/29/na012820six-charts-on-south-africas-persistent-and-multi-faceted-inequality.

Jacaranda, F. M. "Prophet Mboro Speaks of Healing through Blessing Underwear." 2016. www.youtube.com/watch?v=49iwlzg1vKg.

Jamal, Shenaaz. "In Pictures: From Doom to Rattex – 5 Pastors Turning Communion Wine into Noxious Substances." *TimesLIVE*, February 7, 2017. www. timeslive.co.za/news/south-africa/2017-02-07-in-pictures-from-doom-to-rattex – 5-pastors-turning-communion-wine-into-noxious-substances/.

Kgatle, Mookgo S. "The Unusual Practices within Some Neo-Pentecostal Churches in South Africa: Reflections and Recommendations." *HTS Teologiese Studies / Theological Studies* 73, no. 3 (2017): a4656. https://doi.org/10.4102/hts.v73i3.4656.

Kgatle, Mookgo S., and Thabang R. Mofokeng. "Towards a Decolonial Herme-neutic of Experience in African Pentecostal Christianity: A South African Per-spective." *HTS Teologiese Studies / Theological Studies* 75, no. 4 (2019): a5473. https://doi.org/ 10.4102/hts.v75i4.5473.

Kibuuka, Paul K., Carel J. van Aardt, and Deon H. Tustin. *An Investigative Study of the Commercialisation of Religion in the Republic of South Africa: 2016 Gauteng Pilot Study*. Pretoria: CRL Rights Commission/UNISA, 2016.

Leibbrandt, Murray, Ingrid Woolard, Arden Finn, and Jonathan Argent. "Trends in South African Income Distribution and Poverty Since the Fall of Apartheid." May 28, 2010. https://doi.org/10.1787/5kmms0t7p1ms-en.

Letseka, Moeketsi. "In Defence of Ubuntu." *Studies in Philosophy and Education* 31, no. 1 (2012): 47–60. https://doi.org/10.1007/s11217-011-9267-2.

Magaya, Walter. "Thy Kingdom Come." October 5, 2015. http://magaya.huruku ros.com/2015/05/prophet-w-magaya-teaching-on-thy.html.

Makhoba, Ntombizodwa. "At Home with Pastor Mboro." *News24/Drum*, December 21, 2014. www.news24.com/Drum/Archive/at-home-with-pastor-mboro-2017 0728.

Malatji, Ngwako. "Mboro Resurrects Manhood – Couple Have Sex in Front of TV Crew after Prayers." *Sunday World*, November 6, 2017. www.sowetanlive. co.za/sundayworld/news/2017-11-05-mboro-resurrects-manhood-couple-have-sex-in-front-of-tv-crew-after-prayers/.

Maluleke, Tinyiko S. "The Prophet Syndrome: Let Them Eat Grass." *Mail & Guardian*, October 23, 2014. https://mg.co.za/article/2014-10-23-the-prophet-syndrome-let-them-eat-grass/.

———. "On Fraudulent Resurrections and Fake Healings: Why It's a Lucrative Business." *News24*, March 3, 2019. www.news24.com/Columnists/GuestCol-umn/on-fraudulent-resurrections-and-fake-healings-why-its-a-lucrative-busi-ness-20190303.

Manona, Nosipiwo. "How Ngcobo Cult Kept Its Sex Slaves." *News24*, March 11, 2018. www.news24.com/SouthAfrica/News/how-ngcobo-cult-kept-its-sex-slaves-20180311-3.

Maromo, Jonisayi. "Pics: Prophet Mboro Helps Rebuild Houses Destroyed #Alex-Fire." *IOL*, December 10, 2018. www.iol.co.za/news/south-africa/gauteng/pics-prophet-mboro-helps-rebuild-houses-destroyed-alexfire-18444372.

———. "Pics: Pastor Mboro Helps to Build New House for Soweto's Gogo Baloyi." *IOL*, January 28, 2019. www.iol.co.za/news/south-africa/gaut-eng/pics-pastor-mboro-helps-to-build-new-house-for-sowetos-gogo-baloyi-19002821.

Marshall, Ruth. *Political Spiritualities: The Pentecostal Revolution in Nigeria*. Chi-cago, IL: University of Chicago, 2009.

Mashau, Thinandavha D., and Mookgo S. Kgatle. "Prosperity Gospel and the Culture of Greed in Post-Colonial Africa: Constructing an Alternative African Christian Theology of Ubuntu." *Verbum et Ecclesia* 40, no. 1 (2019): 8. https://doi.org/10.4102/ve.v40i1.1901.

Masondo, Sibusiso T. "The African Indigenous Churches: Spiritual Resources for Democracy and Social Cohesion." *Verbum et Ecclesia* 35, no. 3 (2014): 1–8. http://dx.doi.org/10.4102/ ve.v35i3.134.

Mbiti, John. S. *African Religions and Philosophy*. London: Heinemann, 1969.

Mboro's 4–5 drive! YouTube, November 13, 2017. www.youtube.com/watch?v= Zou7PEuxLn0.

Methula, Dumisane W. "Engaging in the Struggle for Economic Justice in the Streets of the City of Tshwane." *Missionalia* 42, no. 1–2 (2014): 107–19. https://doi. org/10.7832/42-1-2-50.

Metz, Thaddeus. "Ubuntu as a Moral Theory and Human Rights in South Africa." *African Human Rights Law Journal* 11, no. 2 (January 1, 2011): 532–59.

Millard, Joann A. "A Study of the Perceived Causes of Schism in Some Ethiopian-Type Churches in the Cape and Transvaal, 1884–1925." 1995. http://uir.unisa. ac.za/handle/10500/17459.

Miya, Ntokozo. "Church Scandals That Left SA Shocked in 2018." *TimesLIVE*, December 27, 2018. www.timeslive.co.za/news/south-africa/2018-12-27-church-scandals-that-left-sa-shooketh-in-2018/.

Nala Mandate International. n.d. www.nalamandate.com/about.html.

Ndlozi, Mbuyiseni. "The Trial: The Church on the Cross." *Daily Maverick*, September 21, 2018. http://firstthing.dailymaverick.co.za/article?id=73319#.W8zHUEszZpl.

News24. "Groups Condemn Harmful Religious Practices." October 2, 2014. www.news24.com/SouthAfrica/News/Groups-condemn-harmful-religious-practices-20141002.

———. "Holy Underpants! Prophet Mboro Explains Blessing Panties." April 19, 2016. www.news24.com/Video/SouthAfrica/News/holy-underpants-prophet-mboro-explains-blessing-panties-20160419.

Niemandt, Cornelius J. P. "The Prosperity Gospel, the Decolonisation of Theology, and the Abduction of Missionary Imagination." *Missionalia* 45, no. 3 (2017): 203–19. https://doi.org/10.7832/45-3-199.

Okorocha, Cyril C. "The Meaning of Salvation: An African Perspective." In *Emerging Voices in Global Christian Theology*, edited by W. A. Dyrness, 59–92. Grand Rapids, MI: Zondervan Publishing House, 1994.

Omenyo, Cephas N. "African Pentecostalism." In *The Cambridge Companion to Pentecostalism*, edited by Cecil M. Robeck Jr. and Amos Yong, 132–51. New York: Cambridge University Press, 2014.

Pijoos, Iavan. "Polokwane 'Pastor' Boasts of Feeding Congregants 'Dog Meat.'" *SowetanLive*, May 22, 2019. www.sowetanlive.co.za/news/south-africa/2019-05-22-polokwane-pastor-boasts-of-feeding-congregants-dog-meat/.

Posel, Dorrit, and Michael Rogan. "Inequality, Social Comparisons and Income Aspirations: Evidence from a Highly Unequal Country." *Journal of Human Development and Capabilities* 20, no. 1 (January 2, 2019): 94–111. https://doi. org/10.1080/19452829.2018.1547272.

Resane, Kelebogile T. "'And They Shall Make You Eat Grass Like Oxen' (Daniel 4: 24): Reflections on Recent Practices in Some New Charismatic Churches." *Pharos Journal of Theology* 98 (2017): 1–17. www.pharosjot.com/ uploads/7/1/6/3/7163688/article_10__vol_98_2017.pdf.

Sekhotho, Katleho. "Pastor Mboro: I Worked Hard for My Money." *EWN*, March 3, 2019. https://ewn.co.za/2019/03/03/pastor-mboro-i-worked-hard-for-my-money.

Smit, Dirkie. "What Does 'Public' Mean? Questions with a View to Public Theology." In *Christian in Public: Aims, Methodologies and Issues in Public Theology*, edited by Len Hansen, 11–46, Beyers Naudé Centre Series on Public Theology. Stellenbosch: African Sun Media, 2007.

SowetanLive. "Controversial Church Leader Shepherd Bushiri Arrested." *Sowetan-Live*, February 1, 2019. www.sowetanlive.co.za/news/south-africa/2019-02-01-controversial-church-leader-shepherd-bushiri-arrested/.

Sundkler, Bengt G. M. *Bantu Prophets in South Africa*. London: International African Institute, 1961.

TimesLive. "Pastor Mboro – When a Prophet Takes the Biscuit." *TimesLive*, April 14, 2016. www.timeslive.co.za/news/south-africa/2016-04-14-pastor-mboro–when-a-prophet-takes-the-biscuit/.

Tutu, Desmond. *No Future without Forgiveness*. New York: Random House, 2009.

Woolard, Ingrid. "Economists Think South Africa's Persistent Inequality Should Be Tackled with a Wealth Tax." *Quartz Africa*, May 2, 2019. https://qz.com/africa/1610723/south-africas-inequality-can-be-fixed-with-a-wealth-tax/.

World Bank. "Overview." October 10, 2019. www.worldbank.org/en/country/southafrica/overview.

Zeeman, Kyle. "Pastor Mboro Believes He Can 'Help You Get the Land Back'." *TimesLIVE*, April 18, 2018. www.timeslive.co.za/tshisa-live/tshisa-live/2018-04-18-pastor-mboro-believes-he-can-help-you-get-the-land-back.

Epilogue

Mookgo S. Kgatle and Allan H. Anderson

This book has studied the abuse of the Spirit in the burgeoning neo-prophetic movement in South Africa from different approaches, including history, biblical studies, migration theory, discernment of spirits, commercialisation of religion, and economics. This is an important collection for several reasons. In the first place, it has identified a form of Pentecostalism that has little in common with other forms that have been studied, even though there are common roots. This neo-prophetic form focusses on prophecies and is popular in South Africa as well as further north, and the book identifies connections with similar movements in Zimbabwe, Nigeria and Ghana. It is important that scholars do not generalize either about "Pentecostalism" as a whole or about the "prosperity gospel", because there are so many different kinds that categorisations – including the ones made in this book – have exceptions and varieties.

The authors of this book have pointed out the scandals and exploitations that sometimes occur in these megachurches, and the approbation that follows from the media and government-appointed commissions. This is characterised as an "abuse of the Spirit", which is when these prophetic leaders claim the authority of the Holy Spirit for actions that are sometimes outrageous or bizarre, when the gullible and unsuspecting are duped into following them and financing their extravagant life-styles, usually with detrimental effects for the followers themselves. Aspects and repercussions of the "abuse of the Spirit" discussed in this book are relevant in other regions across the SubSahara – indeed, it could be argued that this abuse has its origins elsewhere.

The second reason for this book's importance is more positive. The various essays point to the causes for the proliferation of this new type of Pentecostal/Charismatic Christianity. Throughout the world, people have a need for their insecurities, fears, and oppressions to be overcome through a greater power than the powers that threaten them. Those powers are everywhere, hindering every attempt to have a flourishing, fulfilling life, especially where poverty and disease are widespread. When the infilling of the Holy Spirit into the human spirit is a central message, the result is to provide an ability to overcome these evil powers and have peace through the storms of life. This is the message that makes Pentecostalism attractive all over the world. The sense of a pervasive and threatening spirit world is radically altered by the fullness of the Spirit, who comes to displace every other spirit, to bestow power against the evil spirits, and who bears witness to the inner life of Christ who makes a new creation. The power of the Spirit gives a person dignity, meaningfulness, freedom from oppression and everything that demeans and lessens life and purpose, wholeness and success.

The authors of this collection make the following recommendations. Firstly, in order to address the problem of the abuse of the Spirit, these scholars of South African Pentecostalism call for the modern Pentecostal preachers who have "turned commercial" to return to the principles and standards of their Pentecostal forebears. This means returning to the doctrine of holiness, eschatological hope and humility that characterised the Pentecostal preachers of the twentieth century.

Secondly, in order to return to these basic principles, Pentecostal preachers need to have thorough training in theological education and formation that addresses the needs of the believers at the grass roots, in their real life situations.

Thirdly, some neo-prophetic preachers like Alph Lukau and Shepherd Bushiri are migrants who need to develop a better dialogue with local faith communities and government organisations. In other words, these foreign pastors should strive for peace and reconciliation in their host country, South Africa, by being openly transparent and having the humility to learn from others.

Fourthly, Pentecostal preachers as a whole should seriously consider how they deal with the lives and hopes of poor South Africans, who look up to them to overcome their lack of human flourishing. They should reflect on whether they are acting in the best interests of their followers or are merely exploiting them.

Fifthly, the church should teach the poor and vulnerable not to blindly follow the prophets just because they are poor, but should help them to be able to assess the practices of the prophets. Therefore, all believers should develop discernment in order to tell what type of spirit is operating in the prophets and where necessary, to avoid those who abuse people under the guise of the "Holy Spirit".

Finally, there is a need for the reintroduction of religious studies in schools as a hegemonic strategy to counter the so-called "religious mafia", those preachers who use the "Holy Spirit" to exploit their followers.

Moreover, although these neo-prophetic churches deserve criticism for their outrageous acts, however, by addressing African predilections they have provided what both classical Pentecostalism and neo-Pentecostalism have failed to provide in recent years. In providing an alternative to the abuses, both church and government should not only look at the spiritual aspects of the abuse of the Spirit but the economic aspects also. Therefore, both the government and the churches have a role to play in taking care of their fellow citizens, in order to lead the public away from the abuse of the Spirit by those who prey on them.

Index

Printed in Great Britain
by Amazon

40052692R00123